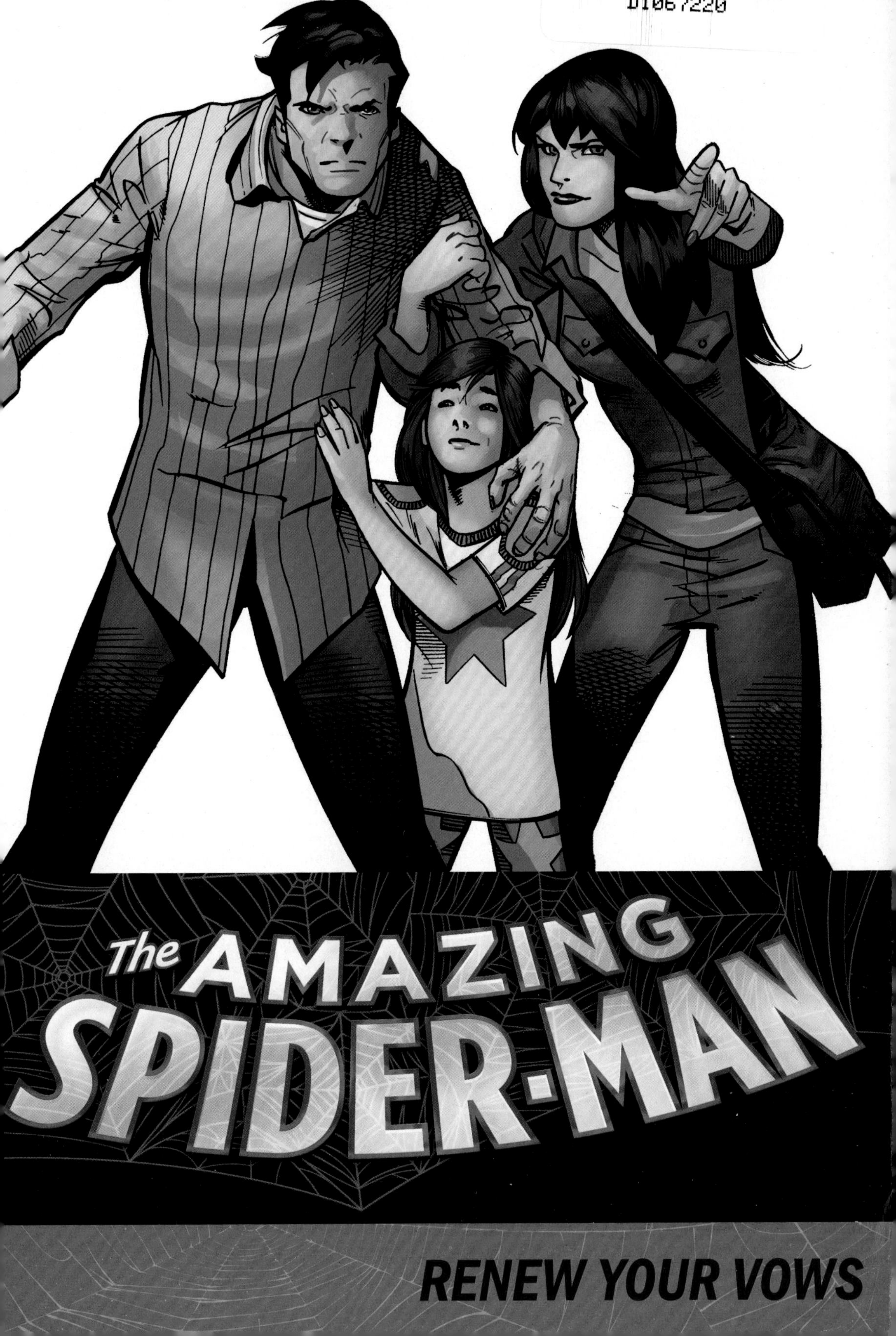

The AMAZING SPIDER-MAN

RENEW YOUR VOWS

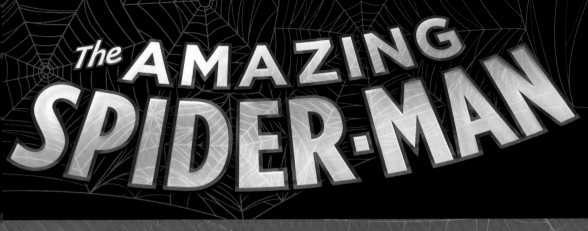

The AMAZING SPIDER-MAN

RENEW YOUR VOWS

WRITER:
DAN SLOTT

ISSUES #1-3
PENCILER:
ADAM KUBERT
INKER:
JOHN DELL
WITH ANDREW HENNESSY & MARK MORALES (#3)

ISSUES #4-5
ART:
ADAM KUBERT &
SCOTT HANNA

COLOR ARTIST:
JUSTIN PONSOR

COVER ART:
ADAM KUBERT WITH JUSTIN PONSOR (#1-3),
MORRY HOLLOWELL (#4)
& **JIM CAMPBELL** (#5)

ASSISTANT EDITOR:
DEVIN LEWIS

EDITOR:
NICK LOWE

"IT'S THE LITTLE THINGS"

WRITER: **DAN SLOTT** ARTIST: **TY TEMPLETON** COLOR ARTIST: **ANDREW CROSSLEY**
LETTERER: **TRAVIS LANHAM** COVER ART: **GIUSEPPE CAMUNCOLI** & **ANTONIO FABELA**
ASSISTANT EDITOR: **DEVIN LEWIS** EDITORS: **NICK LOWE** & **ELLIE PYLE**

SPIDER-MAN CREATED BY STAN LEE & STEVE DITKO

Collection Editor: **Jennifer Grünwald**
Assistant Editor: **Sarah Brunstad**
Associate Managing Editor: **Alex Starbuck**
Editor, Special Projects: **Mark D. Beazley**
Senior Editor, Special Projects: **Jeff Youngquist**
SVP Print, Sales & Marketing: **David Gabriel**

Editor in Chief: **Axel Alonso**
Chief Creative Officer: **Joe Quesada**
Publisher: **Dan Buckley**
Executive Producer: **Alan Fine**

AMAZING SPIDER-MAN: RENEW YOUR VOWS. Contains material originally published in magazine form as AMAZING SPIDER-MAN: RENEW YOUR VOWS #1-5 and SPIDER-VERSE #2. First printing 2015. ISBN# 978-0-7851-9886-4. Published by MARVEL WORLDWIDE, INC., a subsidiary of MARVEL ENTERTAINMENT, LLC. OFFICE OF PUBLICATION: 135 West 50th Street, New York, NY 10020. **Printed in Canada.** ALAN FINE, President, Marvel Entertainment; DAN BUCKLEY, President, TV, Publishing and Brand Management; JOE QUESADA, Chief Creative Officer; TOM BREVOORT, SVP of Publishing; DAVID BOGART, SVP of Operations & Procurement, Publishing; C.B. CEBULSKI, VP of International Development & Brand Management; DAVID GABRIEL, SVP Print, Sales & Marketing; JIM O'KEEFE, VP of Operations & Logistics; DAN CARR, Executive Director of Publishing Technology; SUSAN CRESPI, Editorial Operations Manager; ALEX MORALES, Publishing Operations Manager; STAN LEE, Chairman Emeritus. For information regarding advertising in Marvel Comics or on Marvel.com, please contact Jonathan Rheingold, VP of Custom Solutions & Ad Sales, at jrheingold@marvel.com. For Marvel subscription inquiries, please call 800-217-9158. **Manufactured between 10/23/2015 and 11/30/2015 by SOLISCO PRINTERS, SCOTT, QC, CANADA.**

10 9 8 7 6 5 4 3 2 1

RENEW YOUR VOWS PART 1
"WHY WE CAN'T HAVE NICE THINGS"

SECRET WARS

THE MULTIVERSE WAS DESTROYED!

·

THE HEROES OF EARTH-616 AND EARTH-1610
WERE POWERLESS TO SAVE IT!

·

NOW, ALL THAT REMAINS...IS **BATTLEWORLD**:
A MASSIVE, PATCHWORK PLANET COMPOSED OF THE FRAGMENTS OF
WORLDS THAT NO LONGER EXIST, MAINTAINED BY THE IRON WILL OF ITS
GOD AND MASTER, VICTOR VON DOOM!

·

EACH REGION IS A DOMAIN UNTO ITSELF!

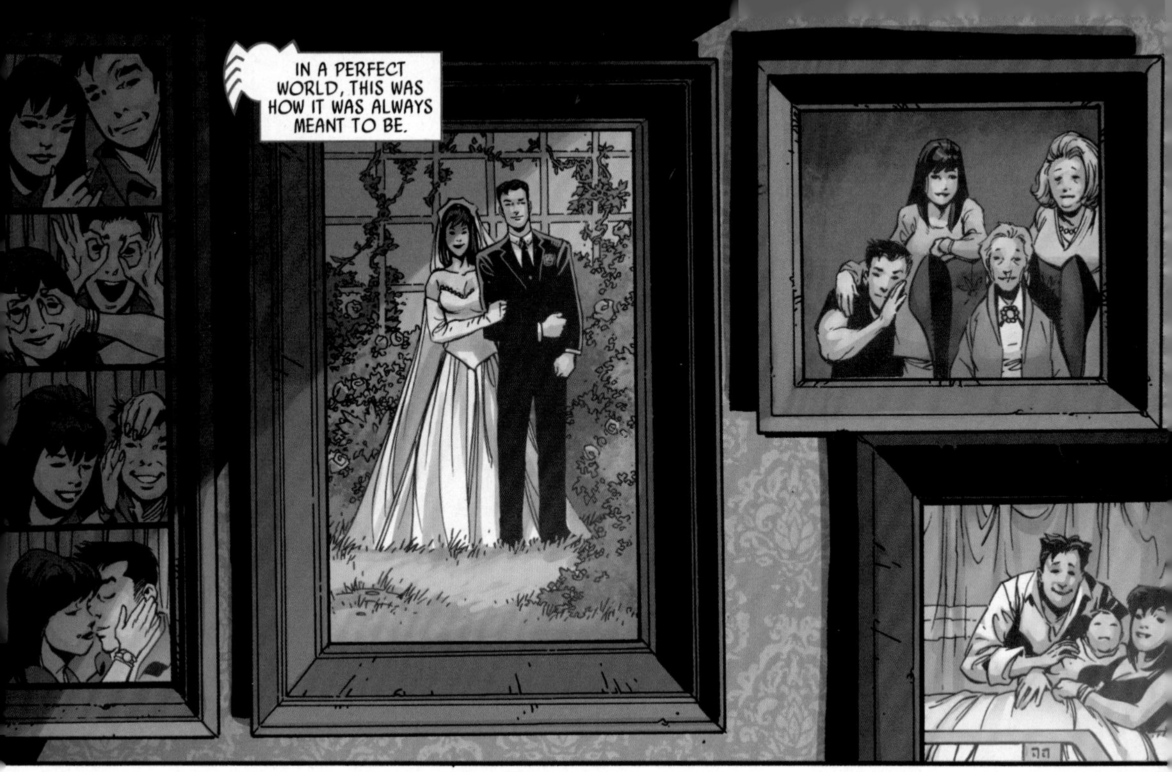
IN A PERFECT WORLD, THIS WAS HOW IT WAS ALWAYS MEANT TO BE.

Renew Your Vows

Part 1: Why We Can't Have Nice Things

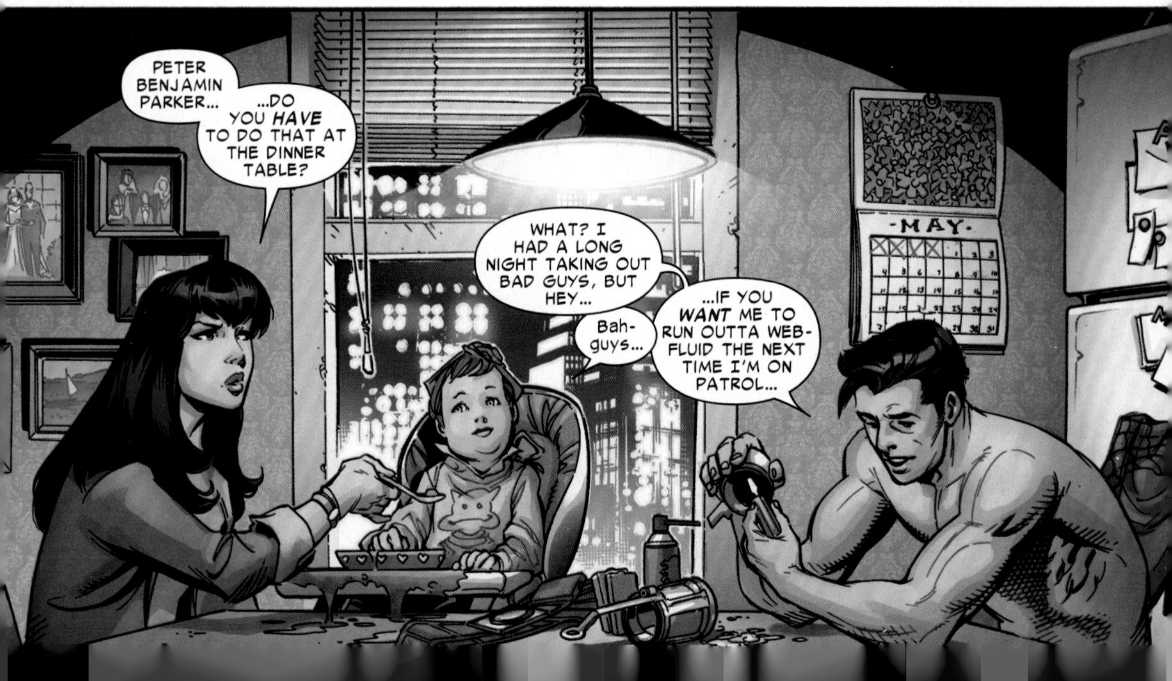
PETER BENJAMIN PARKER...
...DO YOU *HAVE* TO DO THAT AT THE DINNER TABLE?
WHAT? I HAD A LONG NIGHT TAKING OUT BAD GUYS, BUT HEY...
Bah-guys...
...IF YOU *WANT* ME TO RUN OUTTA WEB-FLUID THE NEXT TIME I'M ON PATROL...
-MAY-

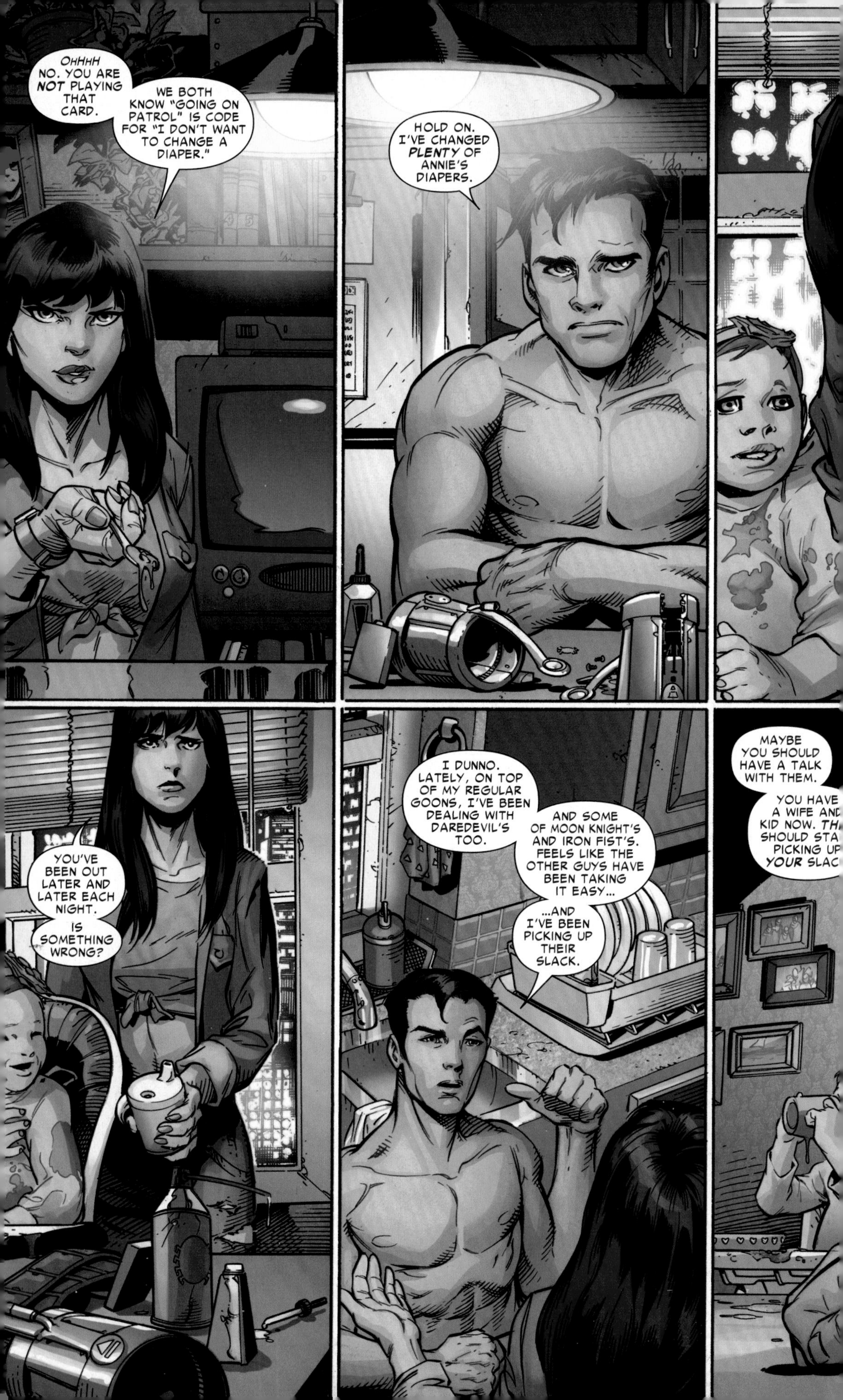

OHHHH NO. YOU ARE NOT PLAYING THAT CARD.
WE BOTH KNOW "GOING ON PATROL" IS CODE FOR "I DON'T WANT TO CHANGE A DIAPER."
HOLD ON. I'VE CHANGED PLENTY OF ANNIE'S DIAPERS.
YOU'VE BEEN OUT LATER AND LATER EACH NIGHT.
IS SOMETHING WRONG?
I DUNNO. LATELY, ON TOP OF MY REGULAR GOONS, I'VE BEEN DEALING WITH DAREDEVIL'S TOO.
AND SOME OF MOON KNIGHT'S AND IRON FIST'S. FEELS LIKE THE OTHER GUYS HAVE BEEN TAKING IT EASY...
...AND I'VE BEEN PICKING UP THEIR SLACK.
MAYBE YOU SHOULD HAVE A TALK WITH THEM.
YOU HAVE A WIFE AND KID NOW. TH SHOULD STA PICKING UP YOUR SLAC

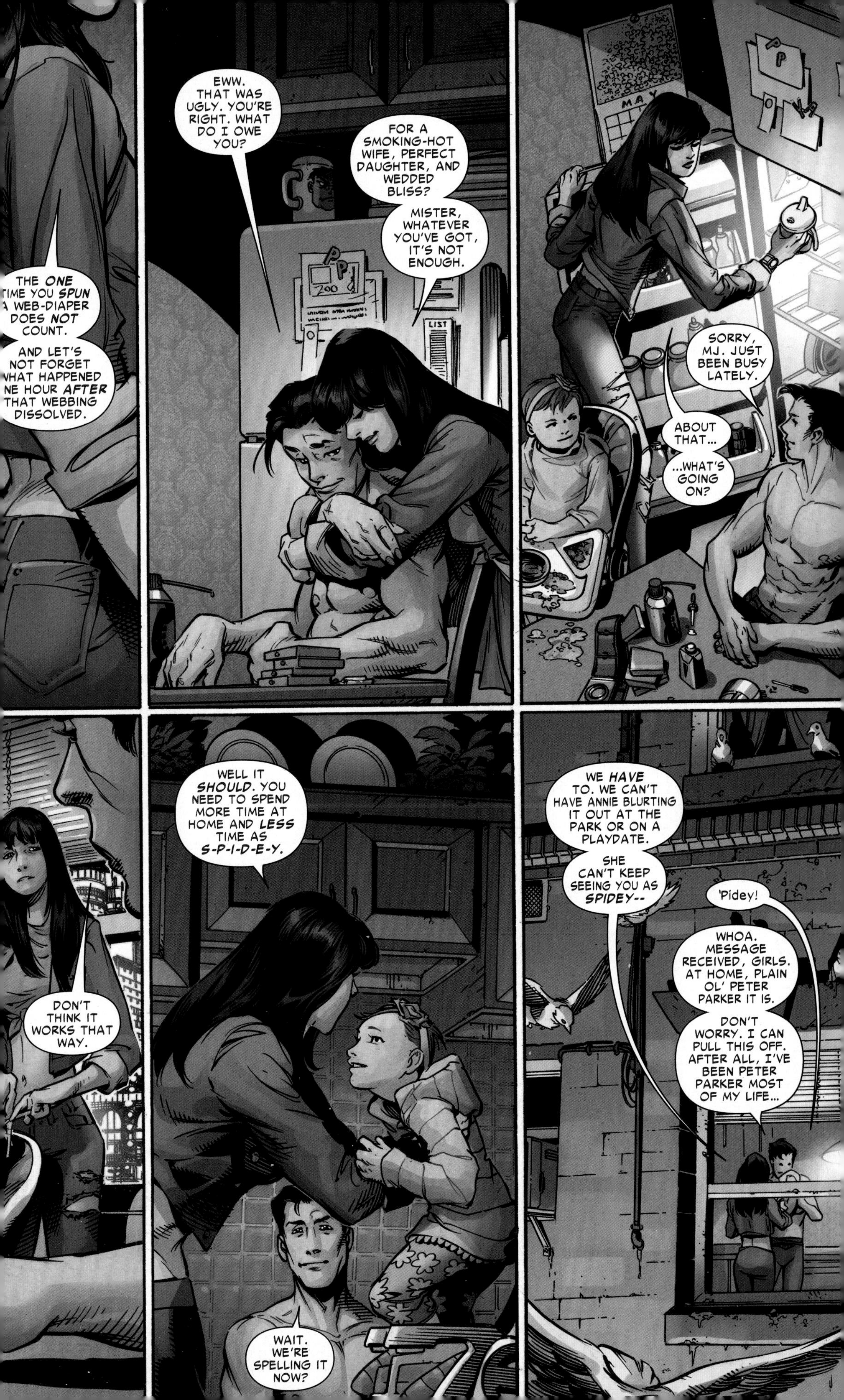
THE *ONE* TIME YOU *SPUN* A WEB-DIAPER DOES *NOT* COUNT.
AND LET'S NOT FORGET WHAT HAPPENED ONE HOUR *AFTER* THAT WEBBING DISSOLVED.
EWW. THAT WAS UGLY. YOU'RE RIGHT. WHAT DO I OWE YOU?
FOR A SMOKING-HOT WIFE, PERFECT DAUGHTER, AND WEDDED BLISS?
MISTER, WHATEVER YOU'VE GOT, IT'S NOT ENOUGH.
SORRY, MJ. JUST BEEN BUSY LATELY.
ABOUT THAT...
...WHAT'S GOING ON?
DON'T THINK IT WORKS THAT WAY.
WELL IT *SHOULD*. YOU NEED TO SPEND MORE TIME AT HOME AND *LESS* TIME AS *S-P-I-D-E-Y*.
WAIT. WE'RE SPELLING IT NOW?
WE *HAVE* TO. WE CAN'T HAVE ANNIE BLURTING IT OUT AT THE PARK OR ON A PLAYDATE.
SHE CAN'T KEEP SEEING YOU AS *SPIDEY*--
'Pidey!
WHOA. MESSAGE RECEIVED, GIRLS. AT HOME, PLAIN OL' PETER PARKER IT IS.
DON'T WORRY. I CAN PULL THIS OFF. AFTER ALL, I'VE BEEN PETER PARKER MOST OF MY LIFE...

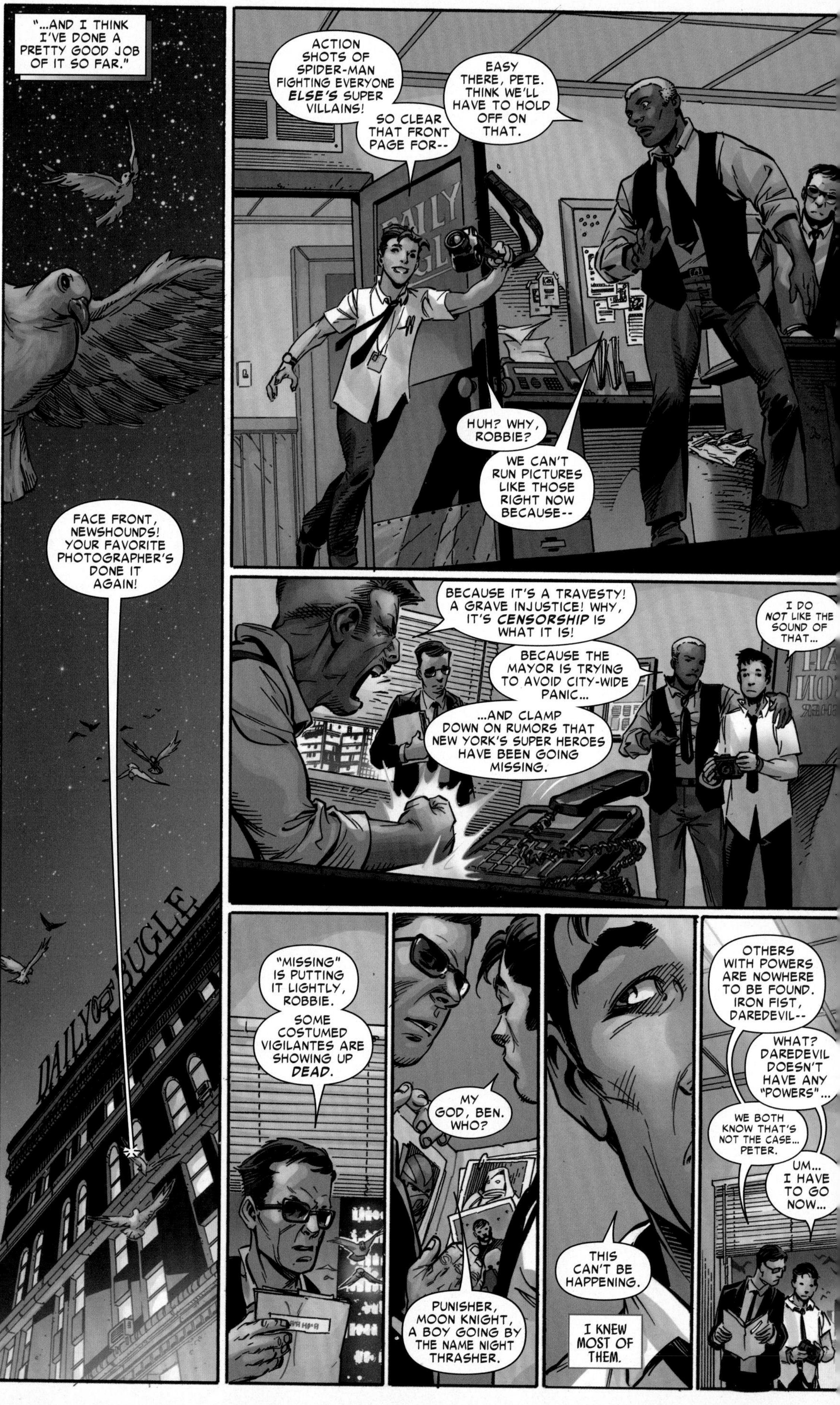

"...AND I THINK I'VE DONE A PRETTY GOOD JOB OF IT SO FAR."
FACE FRONT, NEWSHOUNDS! YOUR FAVORITE PHOTOGRAPHER'S DONE IT AGAIN!
DAILY BUGLE
ACTION SHOTS OF SPIDER-MAN FIGHTING EVERYONE ELSE'S SUPER VILLAINS!
SO CLEAR THAT FRONT PAGE FOR--
EASY THERE, PETE. THINK WE'LL HAVE TO HOLD OFF ON THAT.
HUH? WHY, ROBBIE?
WE CAN'T RUN PICTURES LIKE THOSE RIGHT NOW BECAUSE--
BECAUSE IT'S A TRAVESTY! A GRAVE INJUSTICE! WHY, IT'S CENSORSHIP IS WHAT IT IS!
BECAUSE THE MAYOR IS TRYING TO AVOID CITY-WIDE PANIC...
...AND CLAMP DOWN ON RUMORS THAT NEW YORK'S SUPER HEROES HAVE BEEN GOING MISSING.
I DO NOT LIKE THE SOUND OF THAT...
"MISSING" IS PUTTING IT LIGHTLY, ROBBIE.
SOME COSTUMED VIGILANTES ARE SHOWING UP DEAD.
MY GOD, BEN. WHO?
PUNISHER, MOON KNIGHT, A BOY GOING BY THE NAME NIGHT THRASHER.
THIS CAN'T BE HAPPENING.
I KNEW MOST OF THEM.
OTHERS WITH POWERS ARE NOWHERE TO BE FOUND. IRON FIST, DAREDEVIL--
WHAT? DAREDEVIL DOESN'T HAVE ANY "POWERS"...
WE BOTH KNOW THAT'S NOT THE CASE... PETER.
UM... I HAVE TO GO NOW...

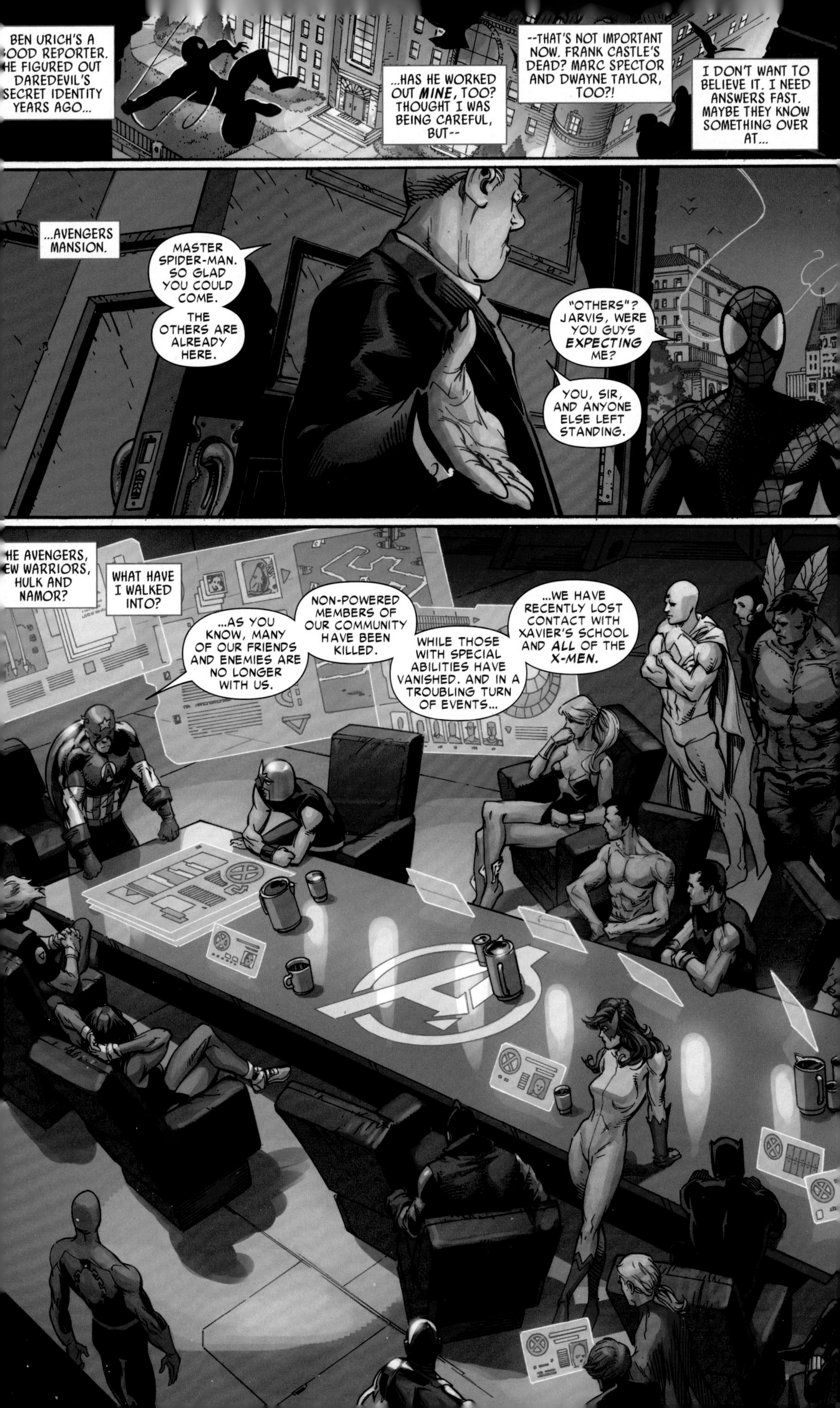

BEN URICH'S A GOOD REPORTER. HE FIGURED OUT DAREDEVIL'S SECRET IDENTITY YEARS AGO...
...HAS HE WORKED OUT MINE, TOO? THOUGHT I WAS BEING CAREFUL, BUT--
--THAT'S NOT IMPORTANT NOW. FRANK CASTLE'S DEAD? MARC SPECTOR AND DWAYNE TAYLOR, TOO?!
I DON'T WANT TO BELIEVE IT. I NEED ANSWERS FAST. MAYBE THEY KNOW SOMETHING OVER AT...
...AVENGERS MANSION.
MASTER SPIDER-MAN. SO GLAD YOU COULD COME.
THE OTHERS ARE ALREADY HERE.
"OTHERS"? JARVIS, WERE YOU GUYS EXPECTING ME?
YOU, SIR, AND ANYONE ELSE LEFT STANDING.
HE AVENGERS, EW WARRIORS, HULK AND NAMOR?
WHAT HAVE I WALKED INTO?
...AS YOU KNOW, MANY OF OUR FRIENDS AND ENEMIES ARE NO LONGER WITH US.
NON-POWERED MEMBERS OF OUR COMMUNITY HAVE BEEN KILLED.
WHILE THOSE WITH SPECIAL ABILITIES HAVE VANISHED. AND IN A TROUBLING TURN OF EVENTS...
...WE HAVE RECENTLY LOST CONTACT WITH XAVIER'S SCHOOL AND ALL OF THE X-MEN.

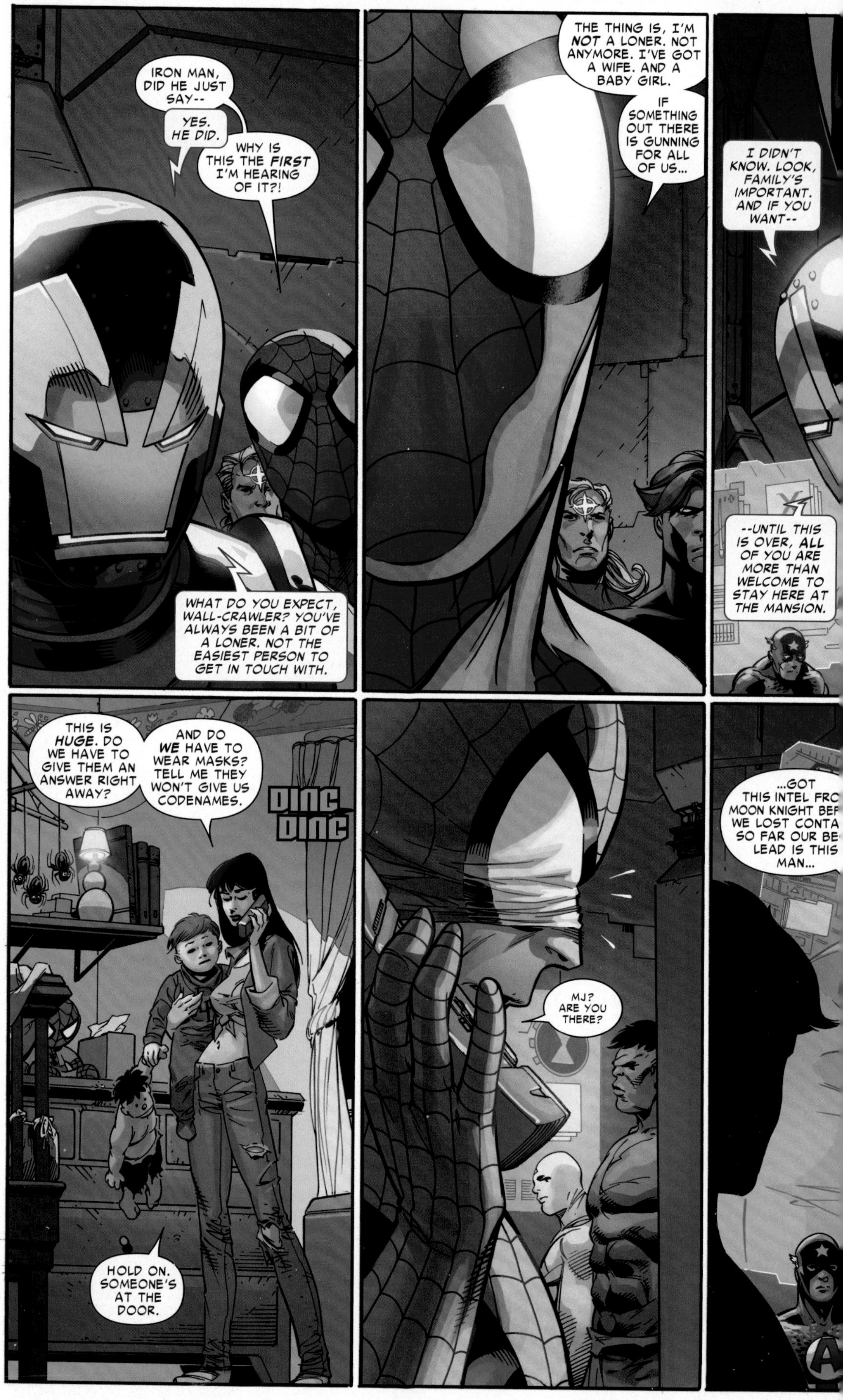
IRON MAN, DID HE JUST SAY--
YES. HE DID.
WHY IS THIS THE FIRST I'M HEARING OF IT?!
WHAT DO YOU EXPECT, WALL-CRAWLER? YOU'VE ALWAYS BEEN A BIT OF A LONER. NOT THE EASIEST PERSON TO GET IN TOUCH WITH.
THE THING IS, I'M NOT A LONER. NOT ANYMORE. I'VE GOT A WIFE. AND A BABY GIRL.
IF SOMETHING OUT THERE IS GUNNING FOR ALL OF US...
I DIDN'T KNOW. LOOK, FAMILY'S IMPORTANT. AND IF YOU WANT--
--UNTIL THIS IS OVER, ALL OF YOU ARE MORE THAN WELCOME TO STAY HERE AT THE MANSION.
THIS IS HUGE. DO WE HAVE TO GIVE THEM AN ANSWER RIGHT AWAY?
AND DO WE HAVE TO WEAR MASKS? TELL ME THEY WON'T GIVE US CODENAMES.
DING DING
HOLD ON. SOMEONE'S AT THE DOOR.
MJ? ARE YOU THERE?

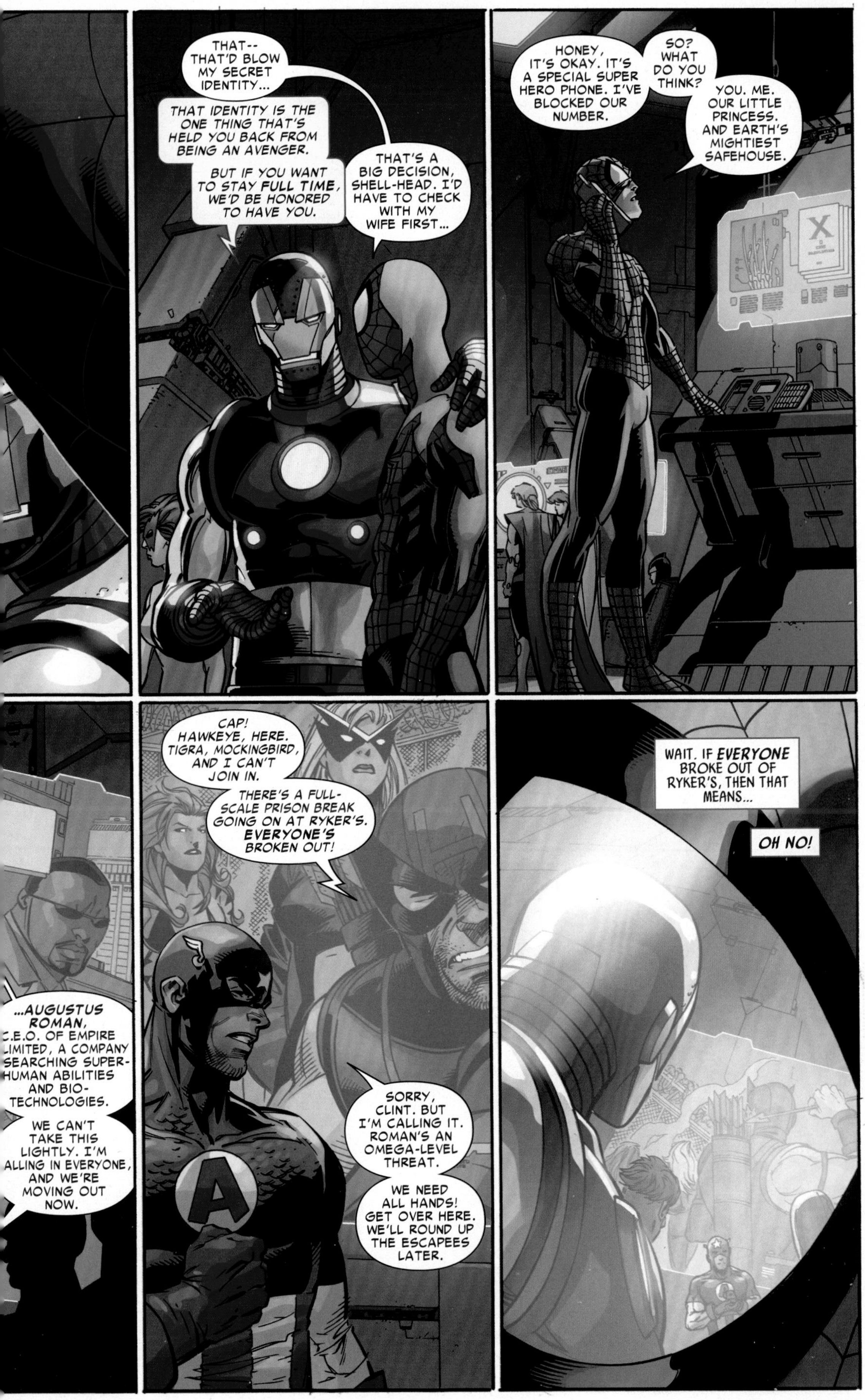

THAT-- THAT'D BLOW MY SECRET IDENTITY...
THAT IDENTITY IS THE ONE THING THAT'S HELD YOU BACK FROM BEING AN AVENGER.
BUT IF YOU WANT TO STAY FULL TIME, WE'D BE HONORED TO HAVE YOU.
THAT'S A BIG DECISION, SHELL-HEAD. I'D HAVE TO CHECK WITH MY WIFE FIRST...
HONEY, IT'S OKAY. IT'S A SPECIAL SUPER HERO PHONE. I'VE BLOCKED OUR NUMBER.
SO? WHAT DO YOU THINK?
YOU. ME. OUR LITTLE PRINCESS. AND EARTH'S MIGHTIEST SAFEHOUSE.
...AUGUSTUS ROMAN, C.E.O. OF EMPIRE LIMITED, A COMPANY SEARCHING SUPER-HUMAN ABILITIES AND BIO-TECHNOLOGIES.
WE CAN'T TAKE THIS LIGHTLY. I'M ALLING IN EVERYONE, AND WE'RE MOVING OUT NOW.
CAP! HAWKEYE, HERE. TIGRA, MOCKINGBIRD, AND I CAN'T JOIN IN.
THERE'S A FULL-SCALE PRISON BREAK GOING ON AT RYKER'S. EVERYONE'S BROKEN OUT!
SORRY, CLINT. BUT I'M CALLING IT. ROMAN'S AN OMEGA-LEVEL THREAT.
WE NEED ALL HANDS! GET OVER HERE. WE'LL ROUND UP THE ESCAPEES LATER.
WAIT. IF EVERYONE BROKE OUT OF RYKER'S, THEN THAT MEANS...
OH NO!

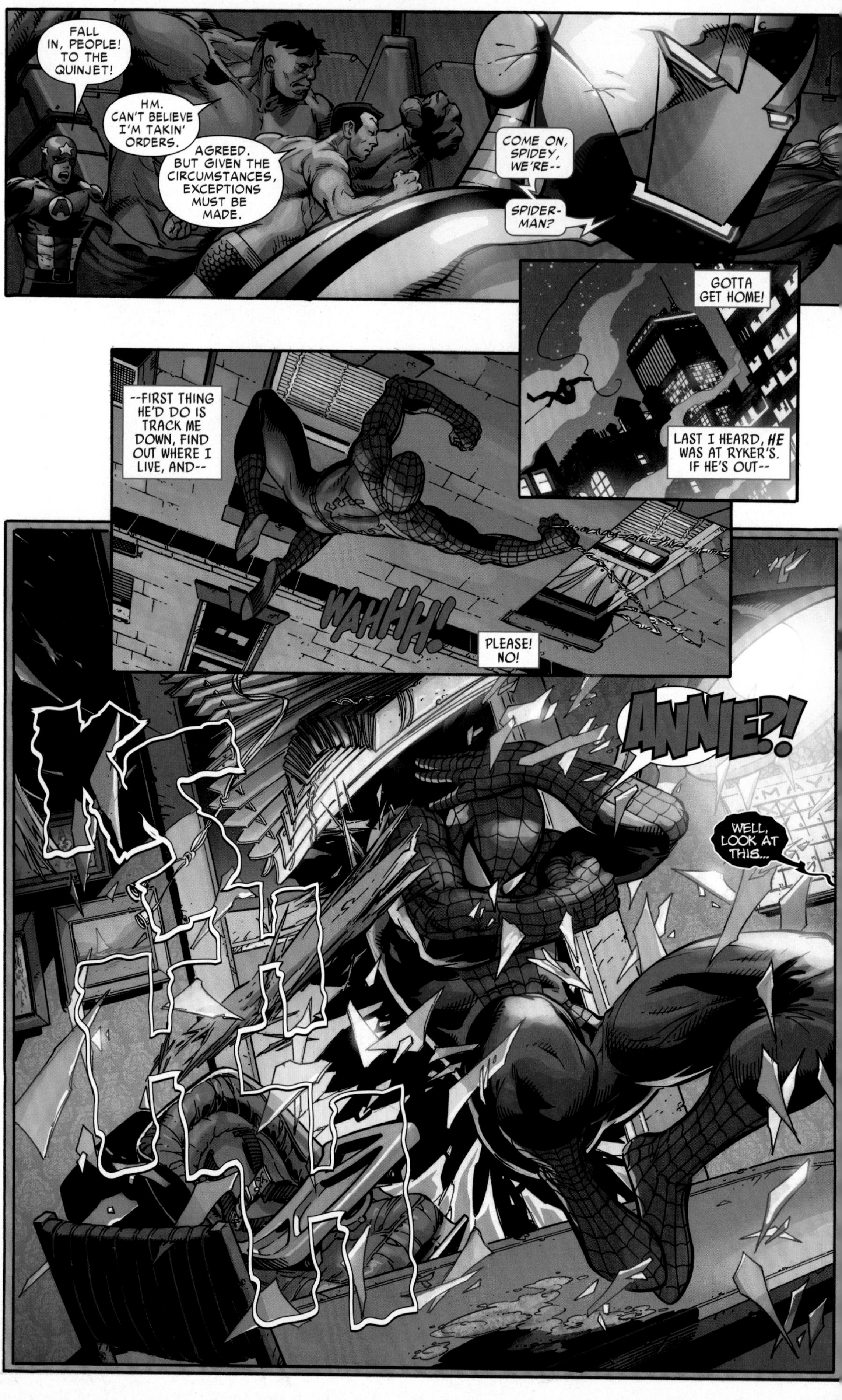
FALL IN, PEOPLE! TO THE QUINJET!
HM. CAN'T BELIEVE I'M TAKIN' ORDERS.
AGREED. BUT GIVEN THE CIRCUMSTANCES, EXCEPTIONS MUST BE MADE.
COME ON, SPIDEY, WE'RE--
SPIDER-MAN?
GOTTA GET HOME!
LAST I HEARD, HE WAS AT RYKER'S. IF HE'S OUT--
--FIRST THING HE'D DO IS TRACK ME DOWN, FIND OUT WHERE I LIVE, AND--
WAHHH!
PLEASE! NO!
ANNIE?!
WELL, LOOK AT THIS...

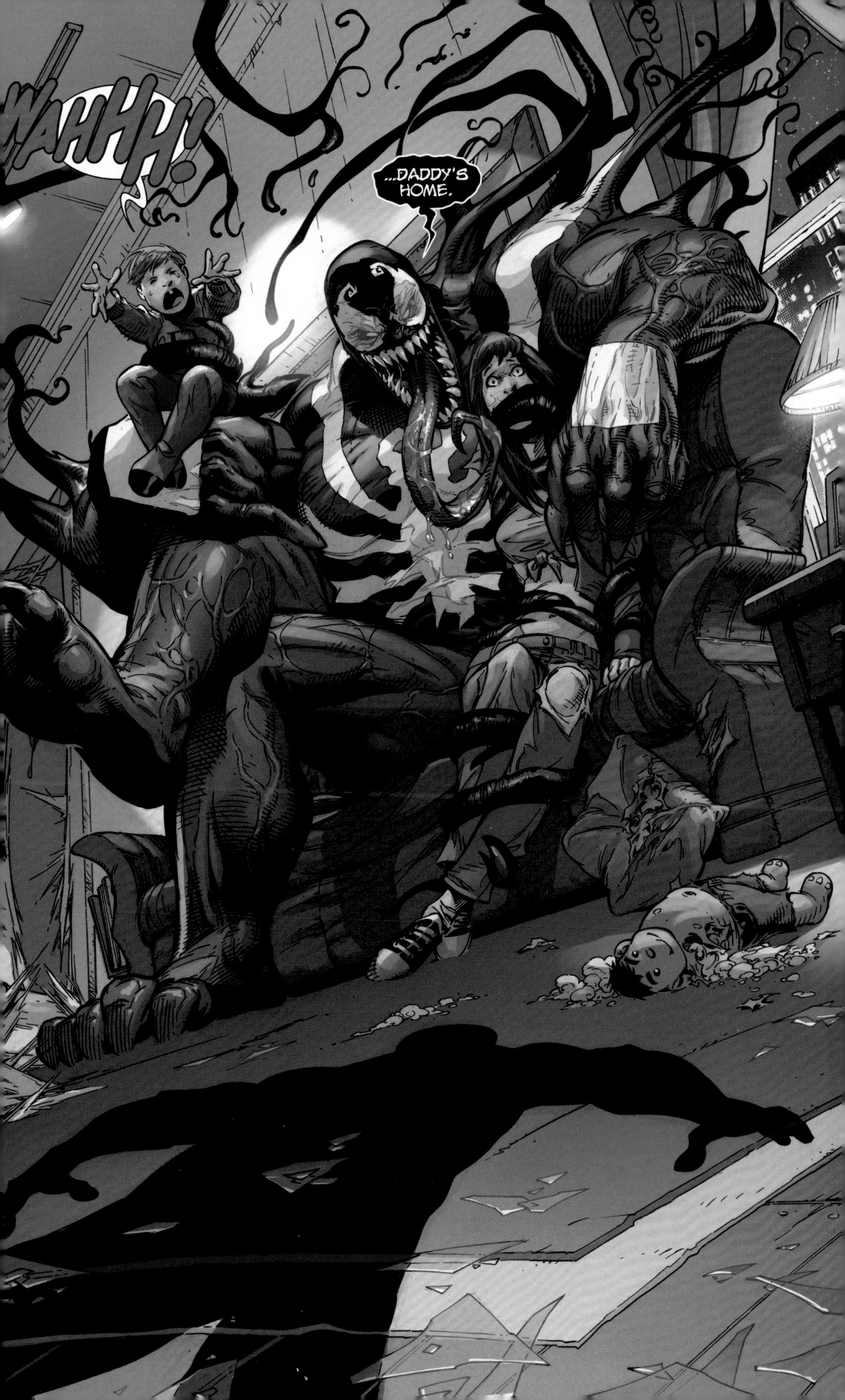
WAHHH!
...DADDY'S HOME.

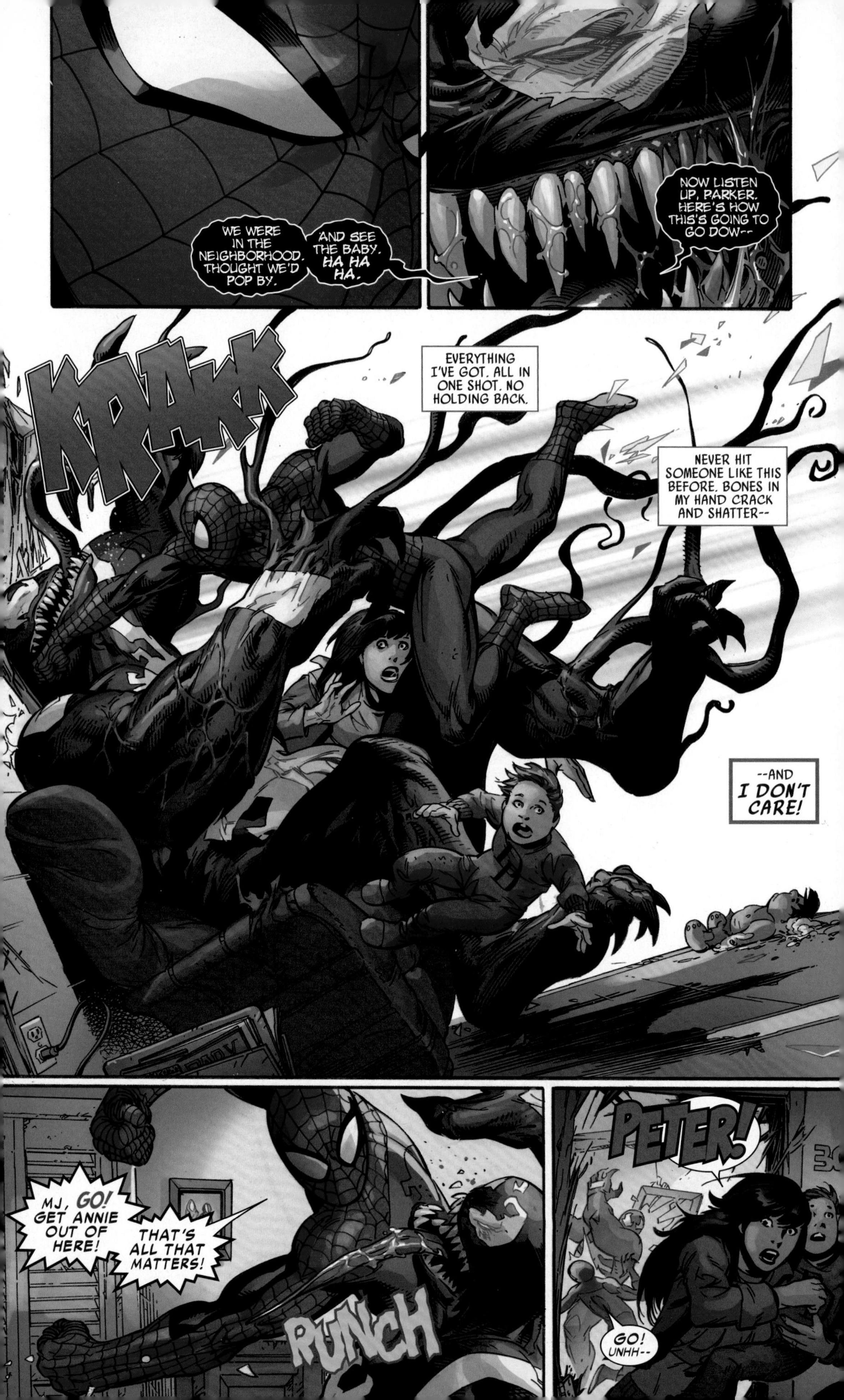

WE WERE IN THE NEIGHBORHOOD. THOUGHT WE'D POP BY.
AND SEE THE BABY. HA HA HA.
NOW LISTEN UP, PARKER. HERE'S HOW THIS'S GOING TO GO DOW--
KRAKK
EVERYTHING I'VE GOT. ALL IN ONE SHOT. NO HOLDING BACK.
NEVER HIT SOMEONE LIKE THIS BEFORE. BONES IN MY HAND CRACK AND SHATTER--
--AND I DON'T CARE!
MJ, GO! GET ANNIE OUT OF HERE!
THAT'S ALL THAT MATTERS!
RUNCH
PETER!
GO! UNHH--

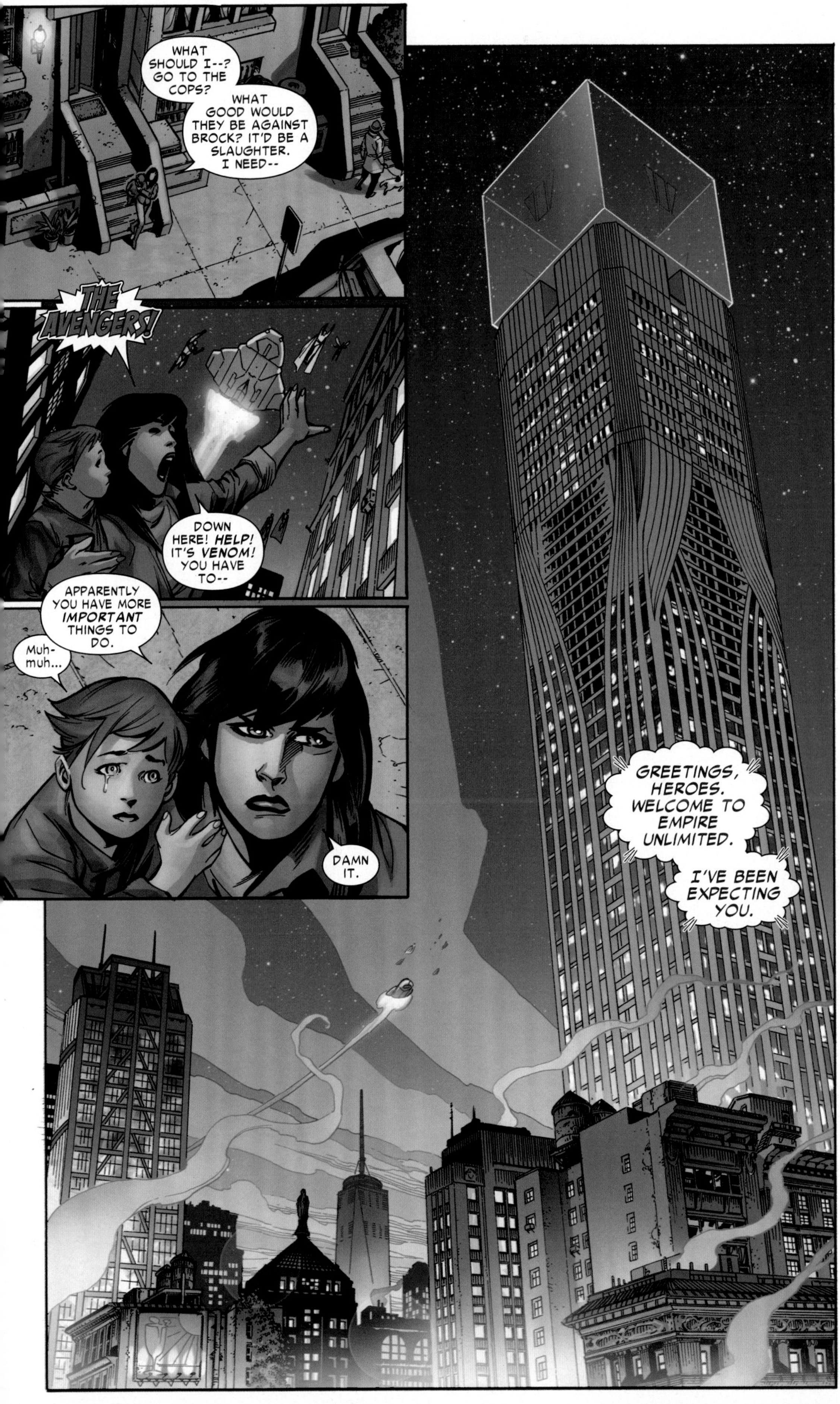
WHAT SHOULD I--? GO TO THE COPS?
WHAT GOOD WOULD THEY BE AGAINST BROCK? IT'D BE A SLAUGHTER. I NEED--
THE AVENGERS!
DOWN HERE! HELP! IT'S VENOM! YOU HAVE TO--
APPARENTLY YOU HAVE MORE IMPORTANT THINGS TO DO.
Muh-muh...
DAMN IT.
GREETINGS, HEROES. WELCOME TO EMPIRE UNLIMITED.
I'VE BEEN EXPECTING YOU.

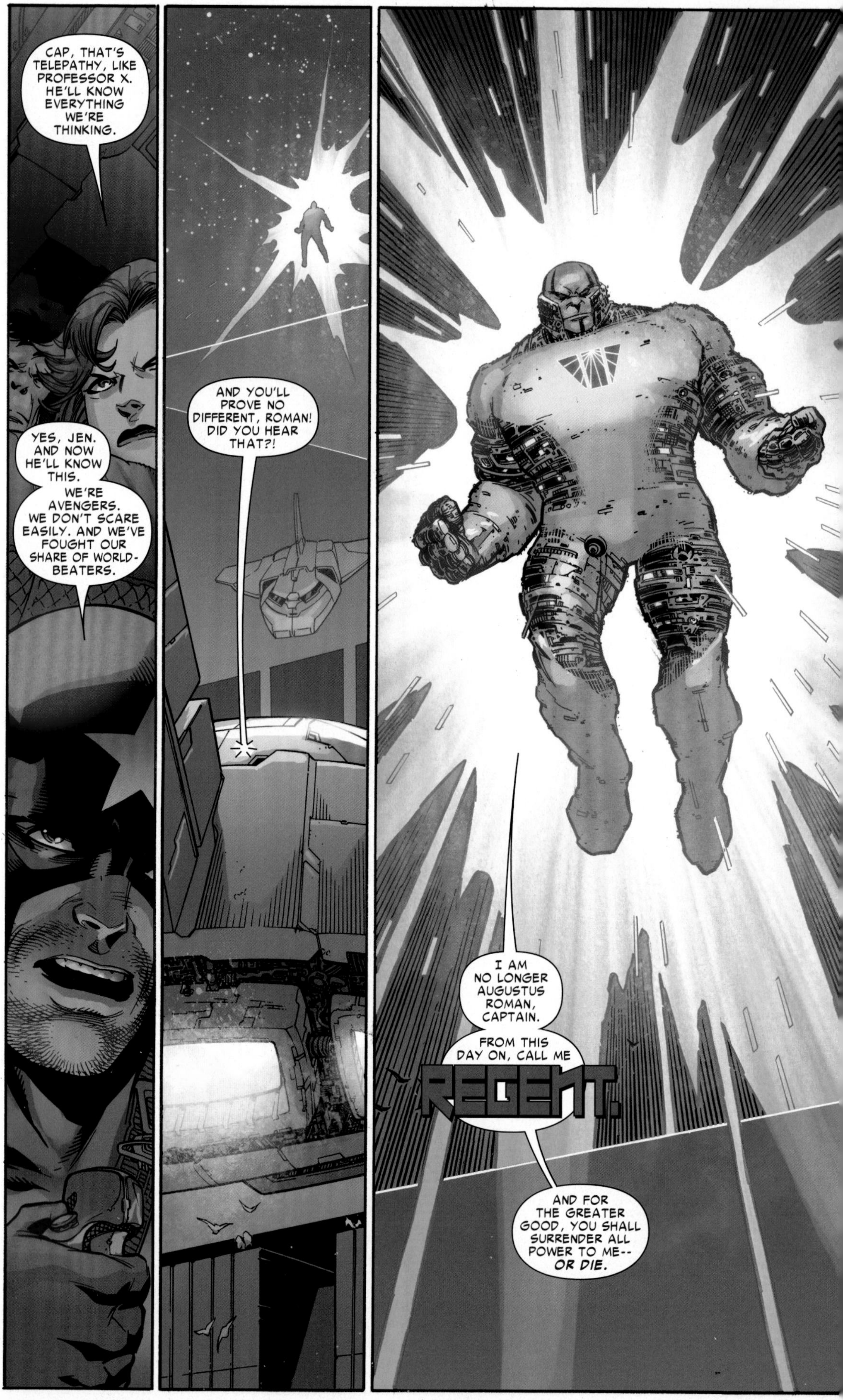
CAP, THAT'S TELEPATHY, LIKE PROFESSOR X. HE'LL KNOW EVERYTHING WE'RE THINKING.
YES, JEN. AND NOW HE'LL KNOW THIS.
WE'RE AVENGERS. WE DON'T SCARE EASILY. AND WE'VE FOUGHT OUR SHARE OF WORLD-BEATERS.
AND YOU'LL PROVE NO DIFFERENT, ROMAN! DID YOU HEAR THAT?!
I AM NO LONGER AUGUSTUS ROMAN, CAPTAIN.
FROM THIS DAY ON, CALL ME
REGENT.
AND FOR THE GREATER GOOD, YOU SHALL SURRENDER ALL POWER TO ME-- OR DIE.

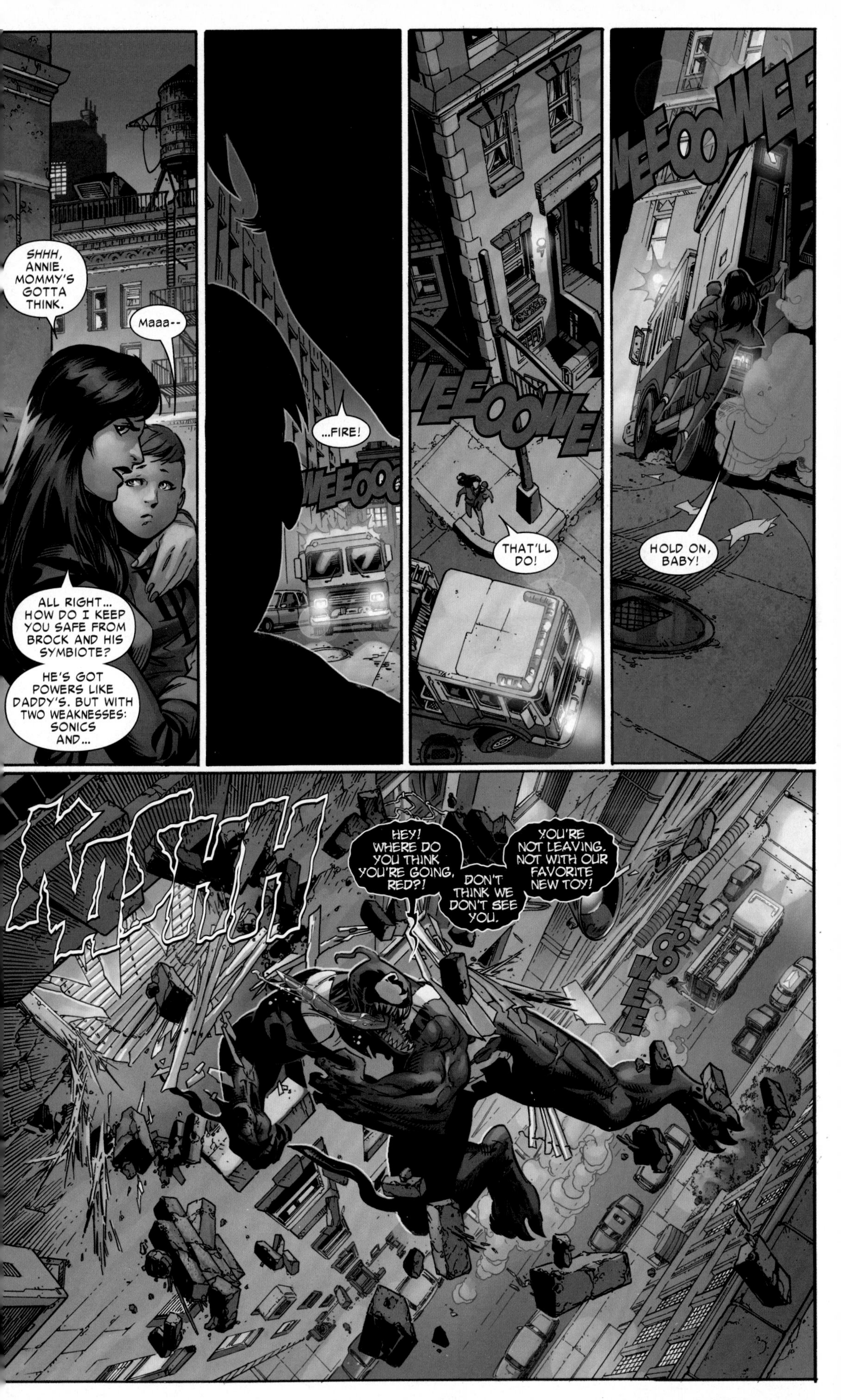
SHHH, ANNIE. MOMMY'S GOTTA THINK.
Maaa--
ALL RIGHT... HOW DO I KEEP YOU SAFE FROM BROCK AND HIS SYMBIOTE?
HE'S GOT POWERS LIKE DADDY'S. BUT WITH TWO WEAKNESSES: SONICS AND...
...FIRE!
WEEOOO
WEEOOWEE
THAT'LL DO!
WEEOOWEE
HOLD ON, BABY!
KRSSH
HEY! WHERE DO YOU THINK YOU'RE GOING, RED?!
DON'T THINK WE DON'T SEE YOU.
YOU'RE NOT LEAVING. NOT WITH OUR FAVORITE NEW TOY!
WEEOOWEE

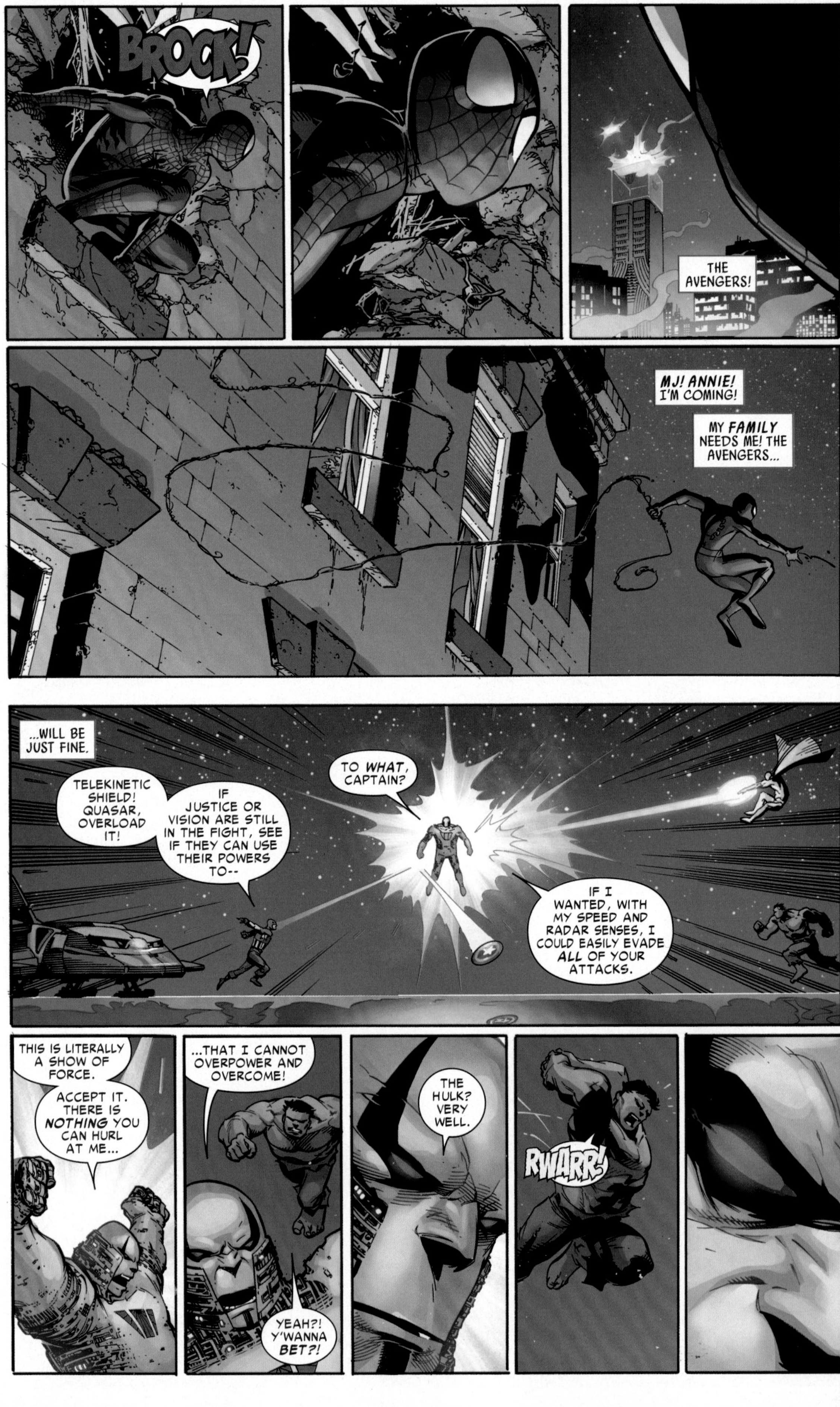
BROCK!
THE AVENGERS!
MJ! ANNIE! I'M COMING!
MY FAMILY NEEDS ME! THE AVENGERS...
...WILL BE JUST FINE.
TELEKINETIC SHIELD! QUASAR, OVERLOAD IT!
IF JUSTICE OR VISION ARE STILL IN THE FIGHT, SEE IF THEY CAN USE THEIR POWERS TO--
TO WHAT, CAPTAIN?
IF I WANTED, WITH MY SPEED AND RADAR SENSES, I COULD EASILY EVADE ALL OF YOUR ATTACKS.
THIS IS LITERALLY A SHOW OF FORCE.
ACCEPT IT. THERE IS NOTHING YOU CAN HURL AT ME...
...THAT I CANNOT OVERPOWER AND OVERCOME!
YEAH?! Y'WANNA BET?!
THE HULK? VERY WELL.
RWARR!

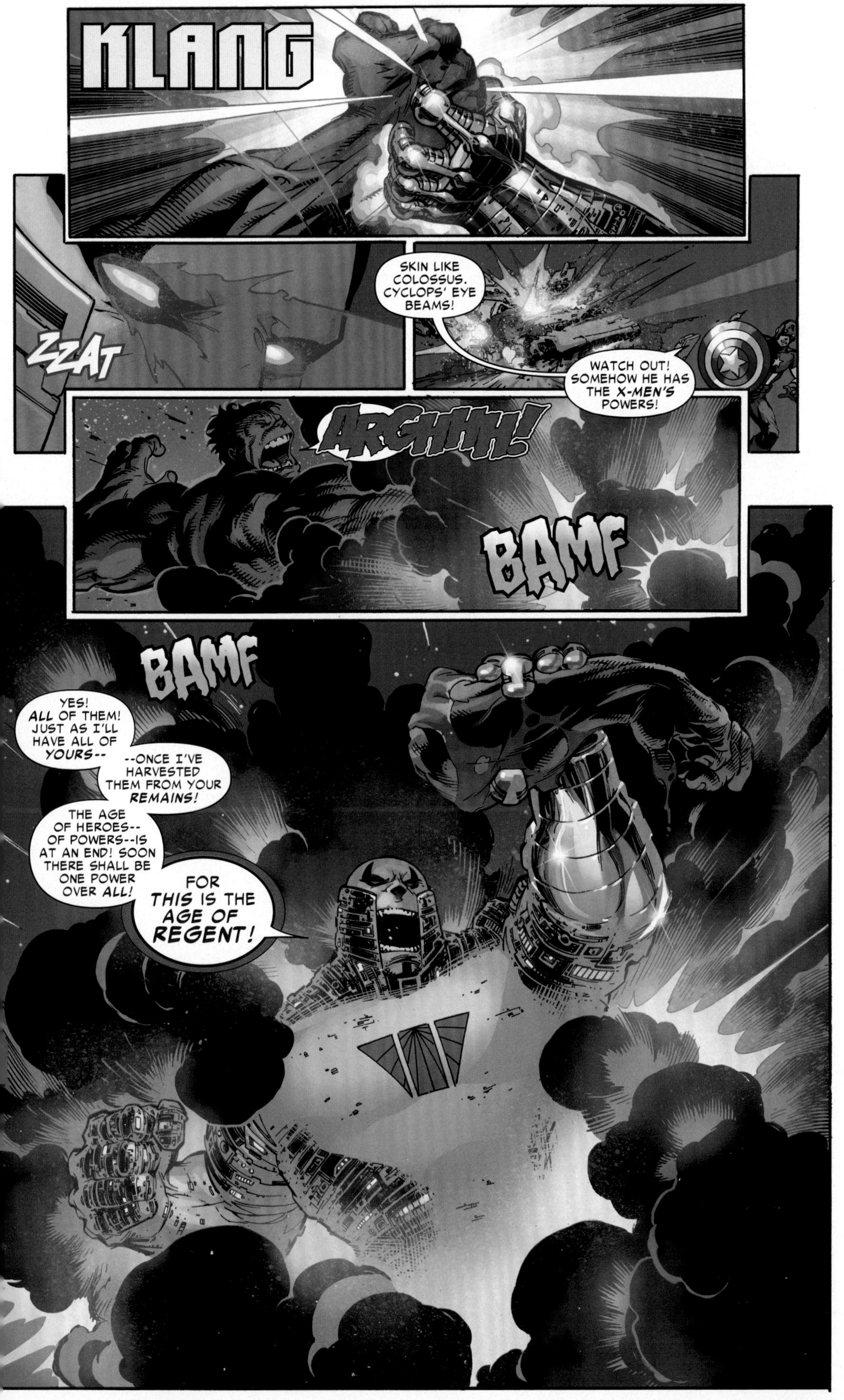
KLANG
ZZAT
SKIN LIKE COLOSSUS. CYCLOPS' EYE BEAMS!
WATCH OUT! SOMEHOW HE HAS THE X-MEN'S POWERS!
ARGHHH!
BAMF
BAMF
YES! ALL OF THEM! JUST AS I'LL HAVE ALL OF YOURS--
--ONCE I'VE HARVESTED THEM FROM YOUR REMAINS!
THE AGE OF HEROES-- OF POWERS--IS AT AN END! SOON THERE SHALL BE ONE POWER OVER ALL!
FOR THIS IS THE AGE OF REGENT!

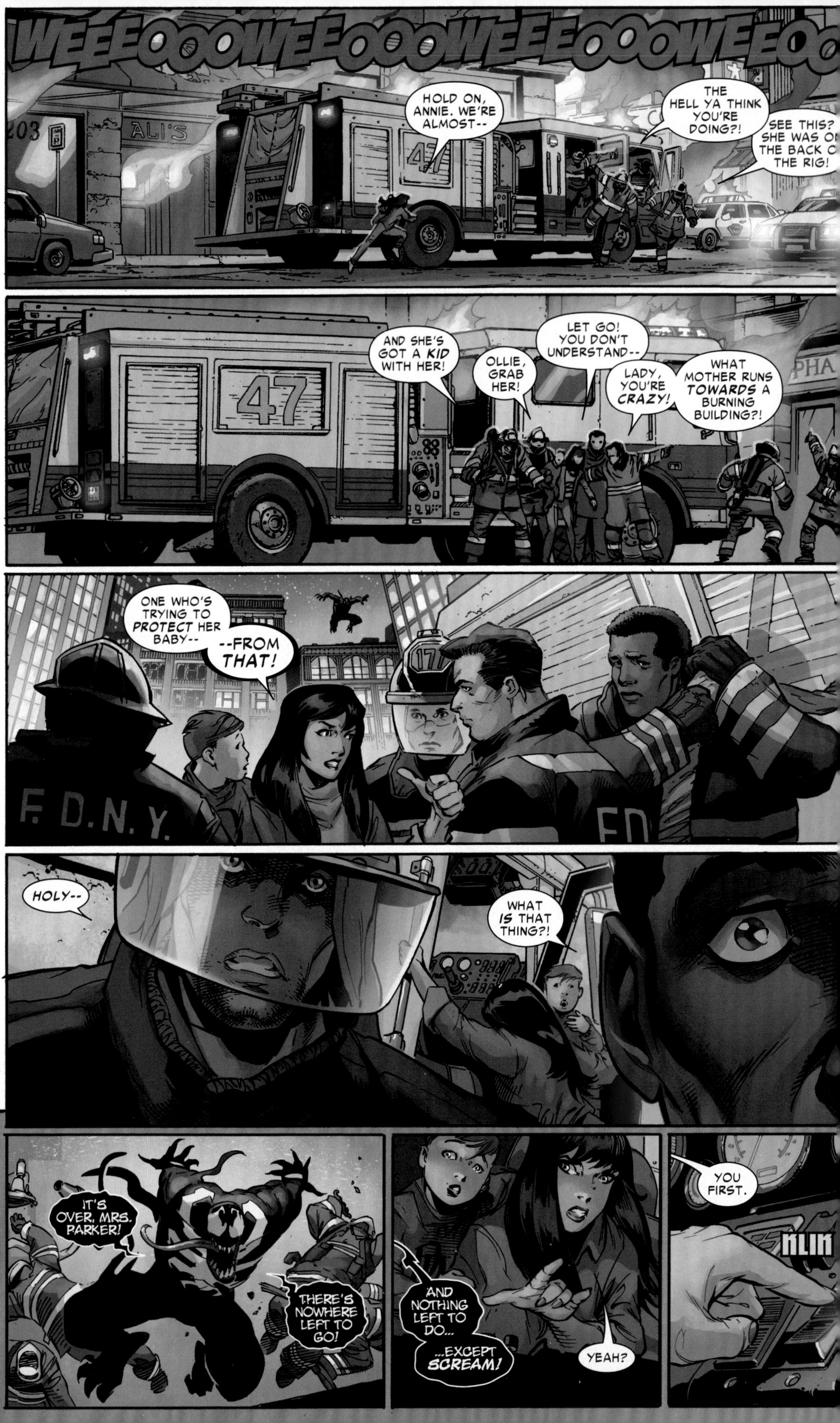
WEEEOOOWEEEOOOWEEEOOOWEEEO
HOLD ON, ANNIE. WE'RE ALMOST--
THE HELL YA THINK YOU'RE DOING?!
SEE THIS? SHE WAS ON THE BACK OF THE RIG!
AND SHE'S GOT A KID WITH HER!
OLLIE, GRAB HER!
LET GO! YOU DON'T UNDERSTAND--
LADY, YOU'RE CRAZY!
WHAT MOTHER RUNS TOWARDS A BURNING BUILDING?!
ONE WHO'S TRYING TO PROTECT HER BABY--
--FROM THAT!
HOLY--
WHAT IS THAT THING?!
IT'S OVER, MRS. PARKER!
THERE'S NOWHERE LEFT TO GO!
AND NOTHING LEFT TO DO...
...EXCEPT SCREAM!
YEAH?
YOU FIRST.
KLIK

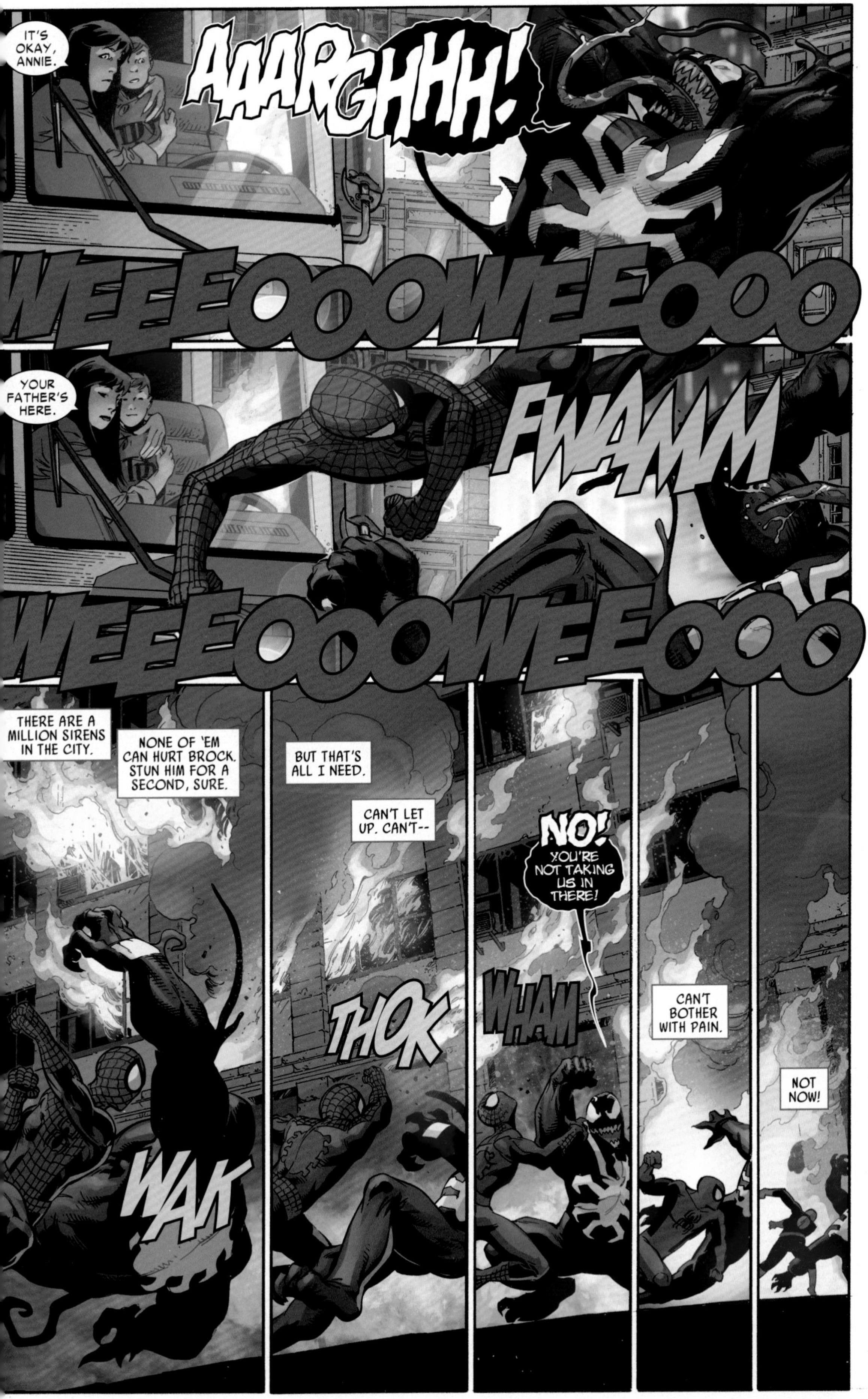
IT'S OKAY, ANNIE.
AAARGHHH!
WEEEOOOWEEOOO
YOUR FATHER'S HERE.
FWAMM
WEEEOOOWEEOOO
THERE ARE A MILLION SIRENS IN THE CITY.
NONE OF 'EM CAN HURT BROCK. STUN HIM FOR A SECOND, SURE.
WAK
BUT THAT'S ALL I NEED.
CAN'T LET UP. CAN'T--
THOK
NO! YOU'RE NOT TAKING US IN THERE!
WHAM
CAN'T BOTHER WITH PAIN.
NOT NOW!

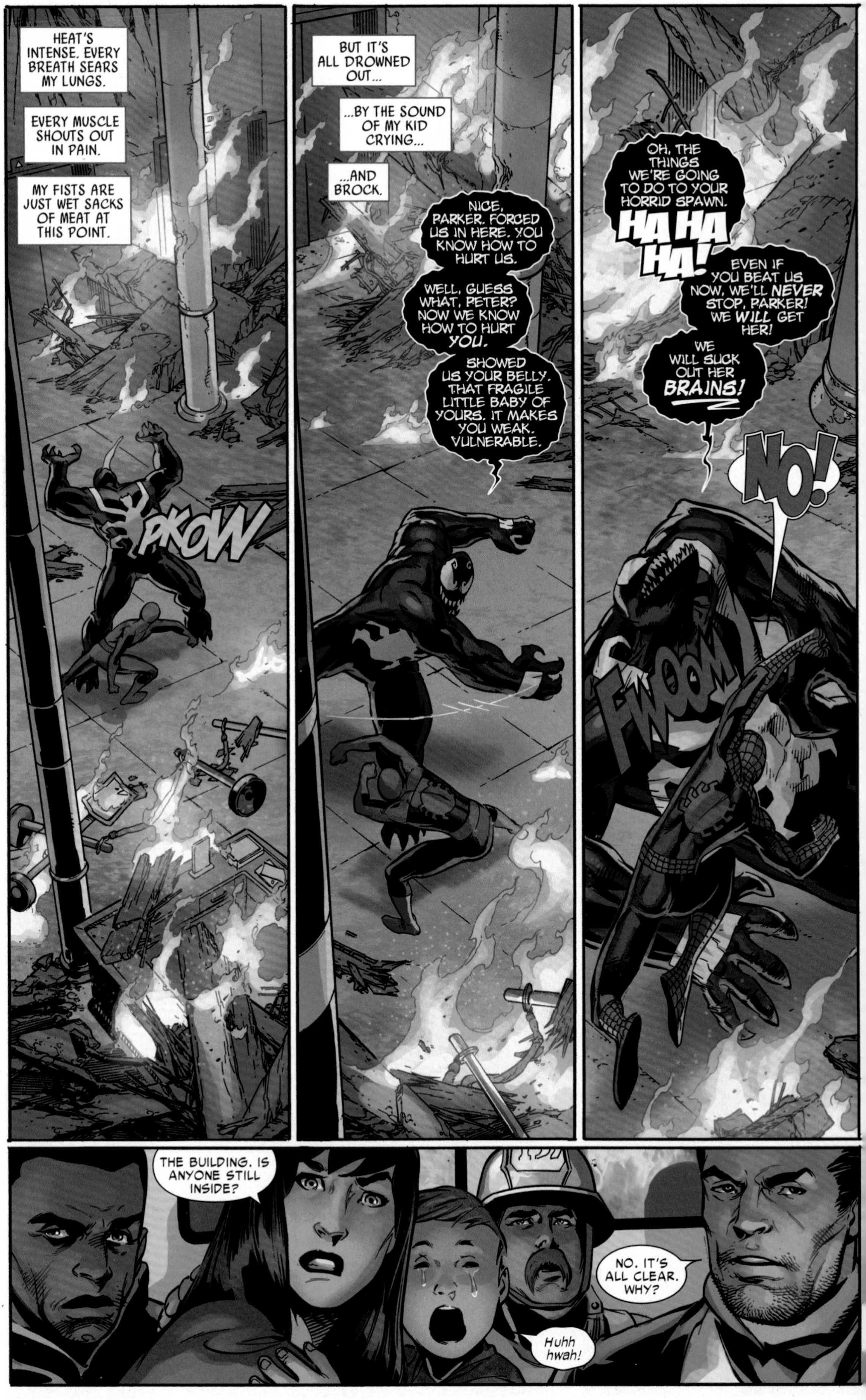
HEAT'S INTENSE. EVERY BREATH SEARS MY LUNGS.
EVERY MUSCLE SHOUTS OUT IN PAIN.
MY FISTS ARE JUST WET SACKS OF MEAT AT THIS POINT.
PKOW
BUT IT'S ALL DROWNED OUT...
...BY THE SOUND OF MY KID CRYING...
...AND BROCK.
NICE, PARKER. FORCED US IN HERE. YOU KNOW HOW TO HURT US.
WELL, GUESS WHAT, PETER? NOW WE KNOW HOW TO HURT YOU.
SHOWED US YOUR BELLY. THAT FRAGILE LITTLE BABY OF YOURS. IT MAKES YOU WEAK. VULNERABLE.
OH, THE THINGS WE'RE GOING TO DO TO YOUR HORRID SPAWN.
HA HA HA!
EVEN IF YOU BEAT US NOW, WE'LL NEVER STOP, PARKER! WE WILL GET HER!
WE WILL SUCK OUT HER BRAINS!
NO!
FWOOM
THE BUILDING. IS ANYONE STILL INSIDE?
NO. IT'S ALL CLEAR. WHY?
Huhh hwah!

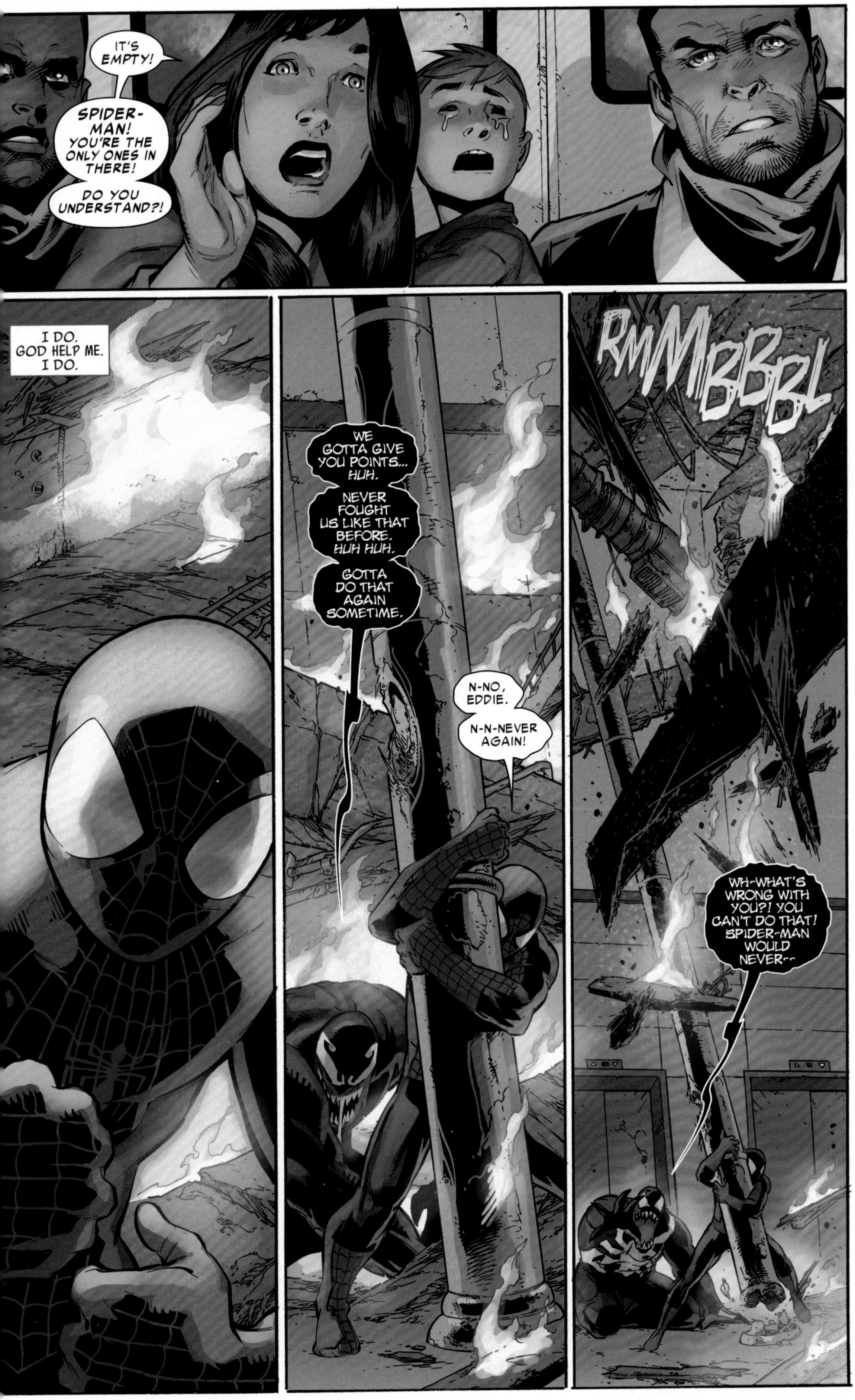

IT'S EMPTY!
SPIDER-MAN! YOU'RE THE ONLY ONES IN THERE!
DO YOU UNDERSTAND?!
I DO. GOD HELP ME. I DO.
WE GOTTA GIVE YOU POINTS... HUH.
NEVER FOUGHT US LIKE THAT BEFORE. HUH HUH.
GOTTA DO THAT AGAIN SOMETIME.
N-NO, EDDIE.
N-N-NEVER AGAIN!
RMMBBBL
WH-WHAT'S WRONG WITH YOU?! YOU CAN'T DO THAT! SPIDER-MAN WOULD NEVER--

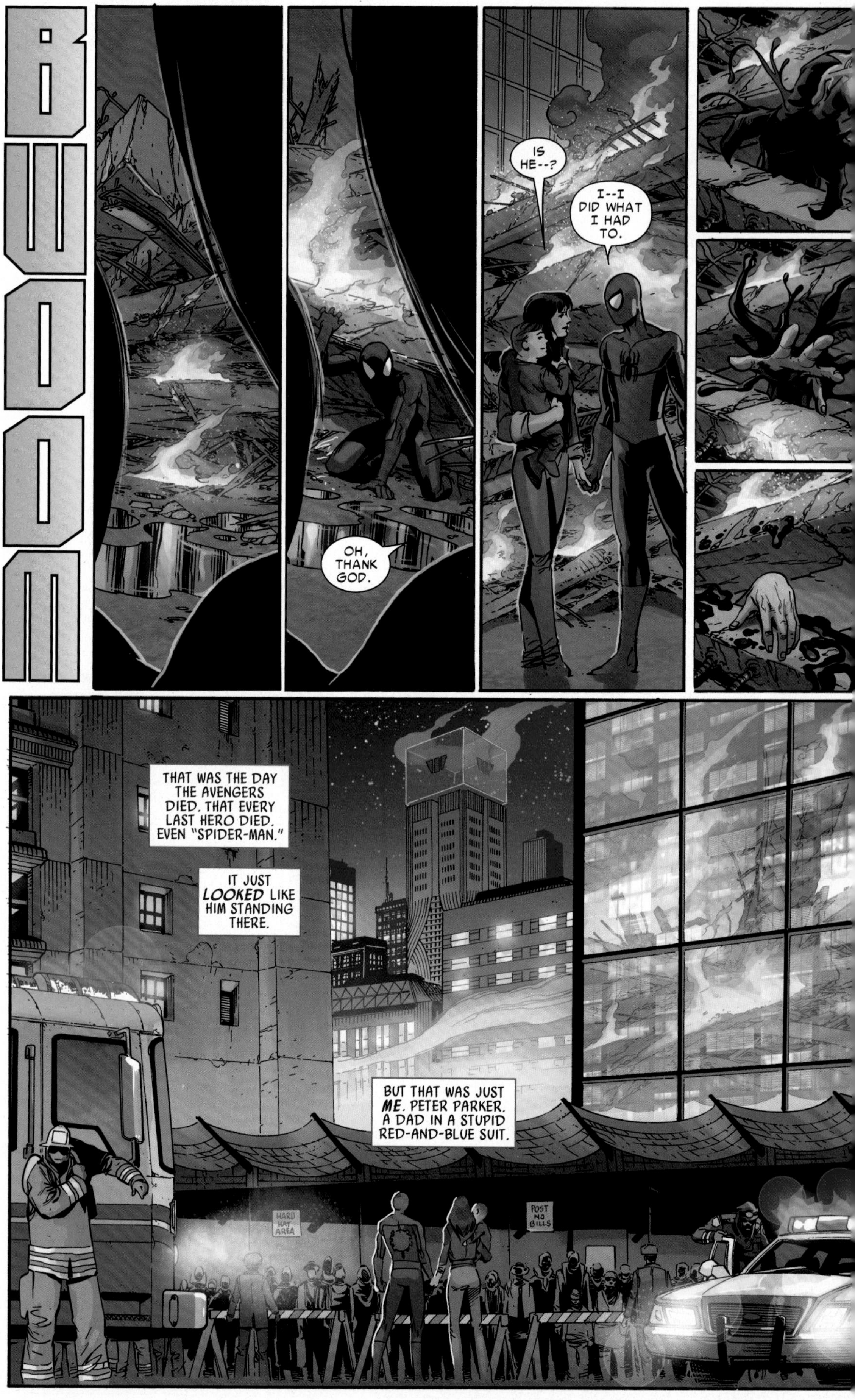
BOOM
OH, THANK GOD.
IS HE--?
I--I DID WHAT I HAD TO.
THAT WAS THE DAY THE AVENGERS DIED. THAT EVERY LAST HERO DIED. EVEN "SPIDER-MAN."
IT JUST LOOKED LIKE HIM STANDING THERE.
BUT THAT WAS JUST ME. PETER PARKER. A DAD IN A STUPID RED-AND-BLUE SUIT.
HARD HAT AREA
POST NO BILLS

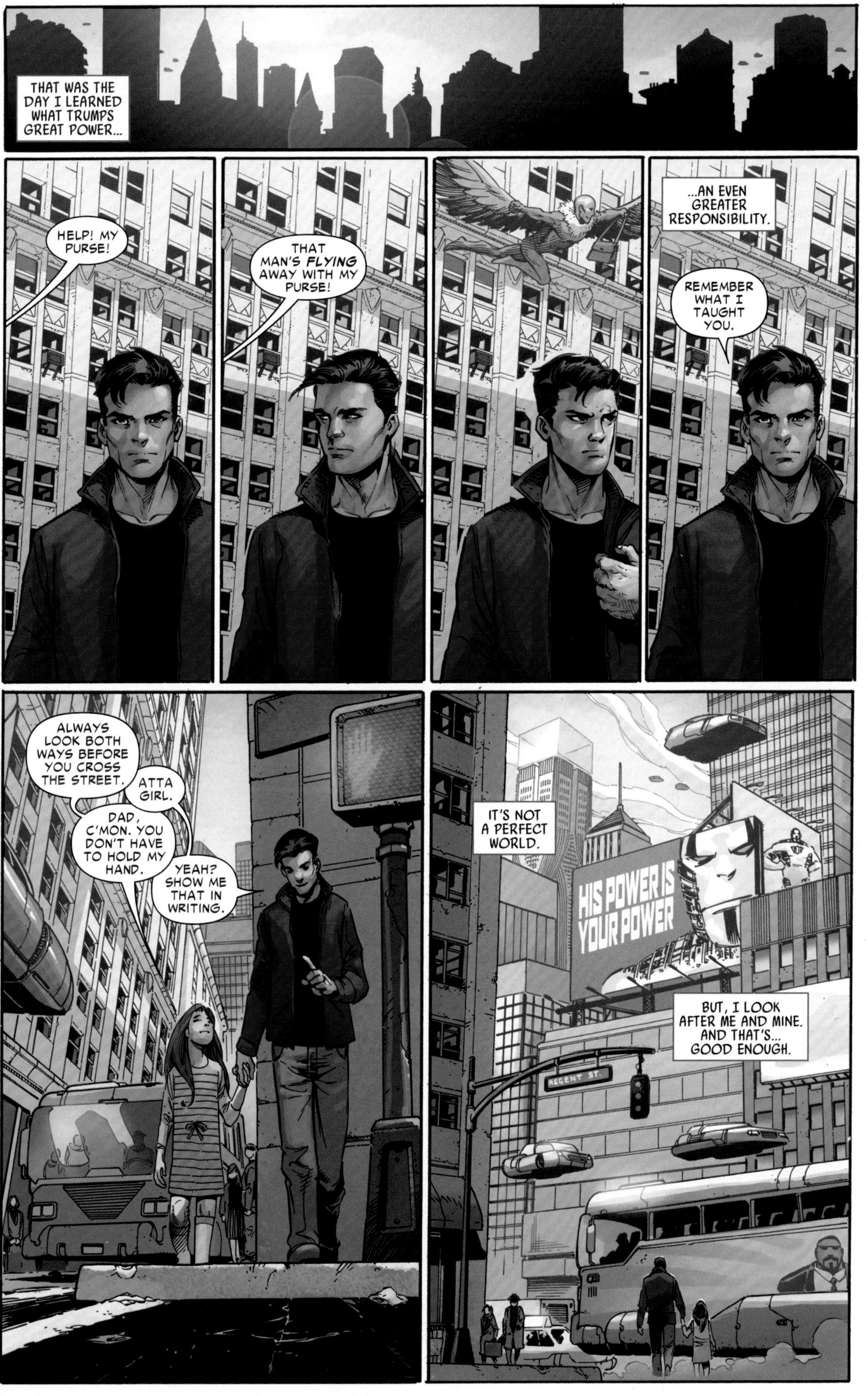
THAT WAS THE DAY I LEARNED WHAT TRUMPS GREAT POWER...
HELP! MY PURSE!
THAT MAN'S FLYING AWAY WITH MY PURSE!
...AN EVEN GREATER RESPONSIBILITY.
REMEMBER WHAT I TAUGHT YOU.
ALWAYS LOOK BOTH WAYS BEFORE YOU CROSS THE STREET.
ATTA GIRL.
DAD, C'MON. YOU DON'T HAVE TO HOLD MY HAND.
YEAH? SHOW ME THAT IN WRITING.
IT'S NOT A PERFECT WORLD.
HIS POWER IS YOUR POWER
BUT, I LOOK AFTER ME AND MINE. AND THAT'S... GOOD ENOUGH.
REGENT ST.

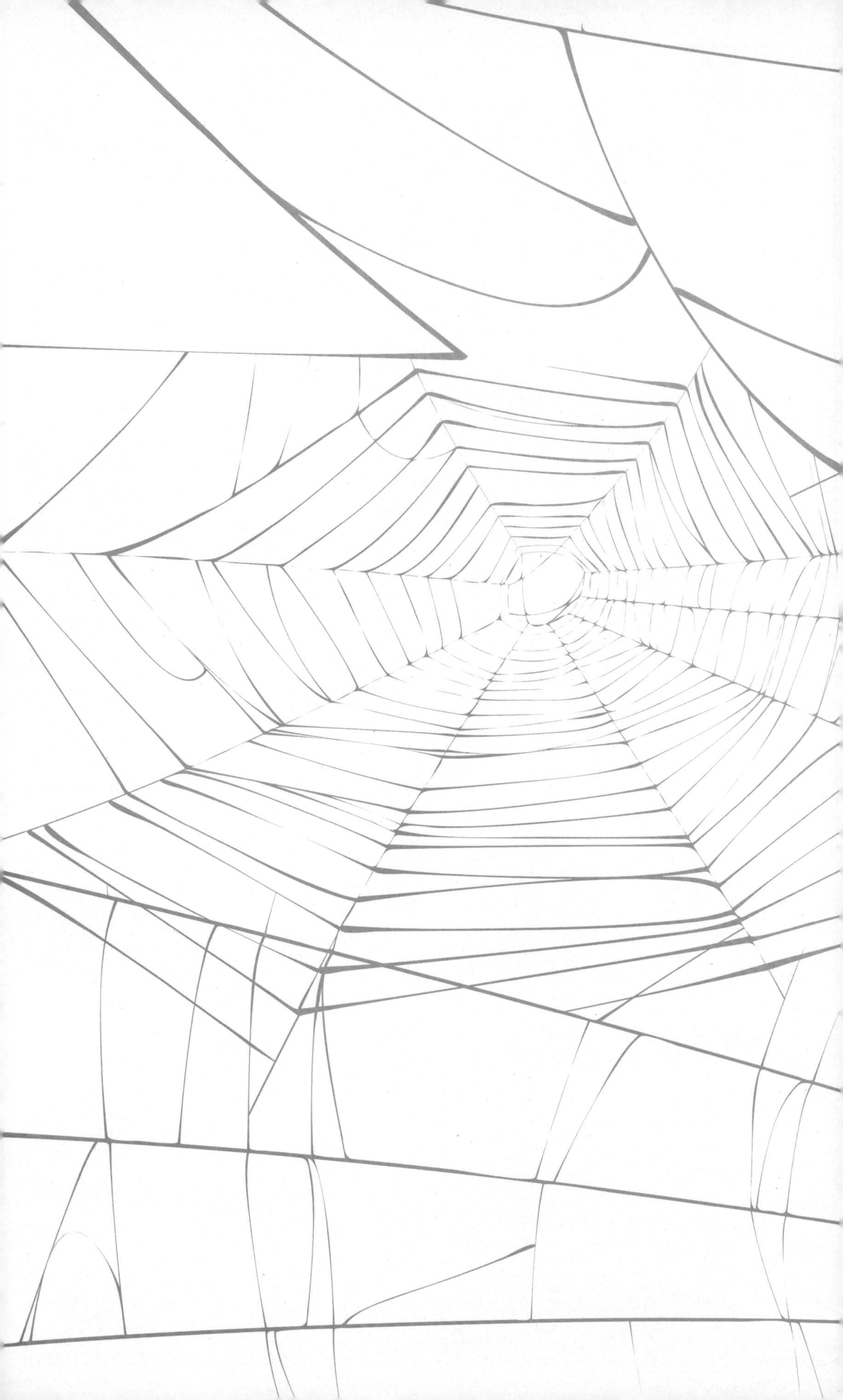

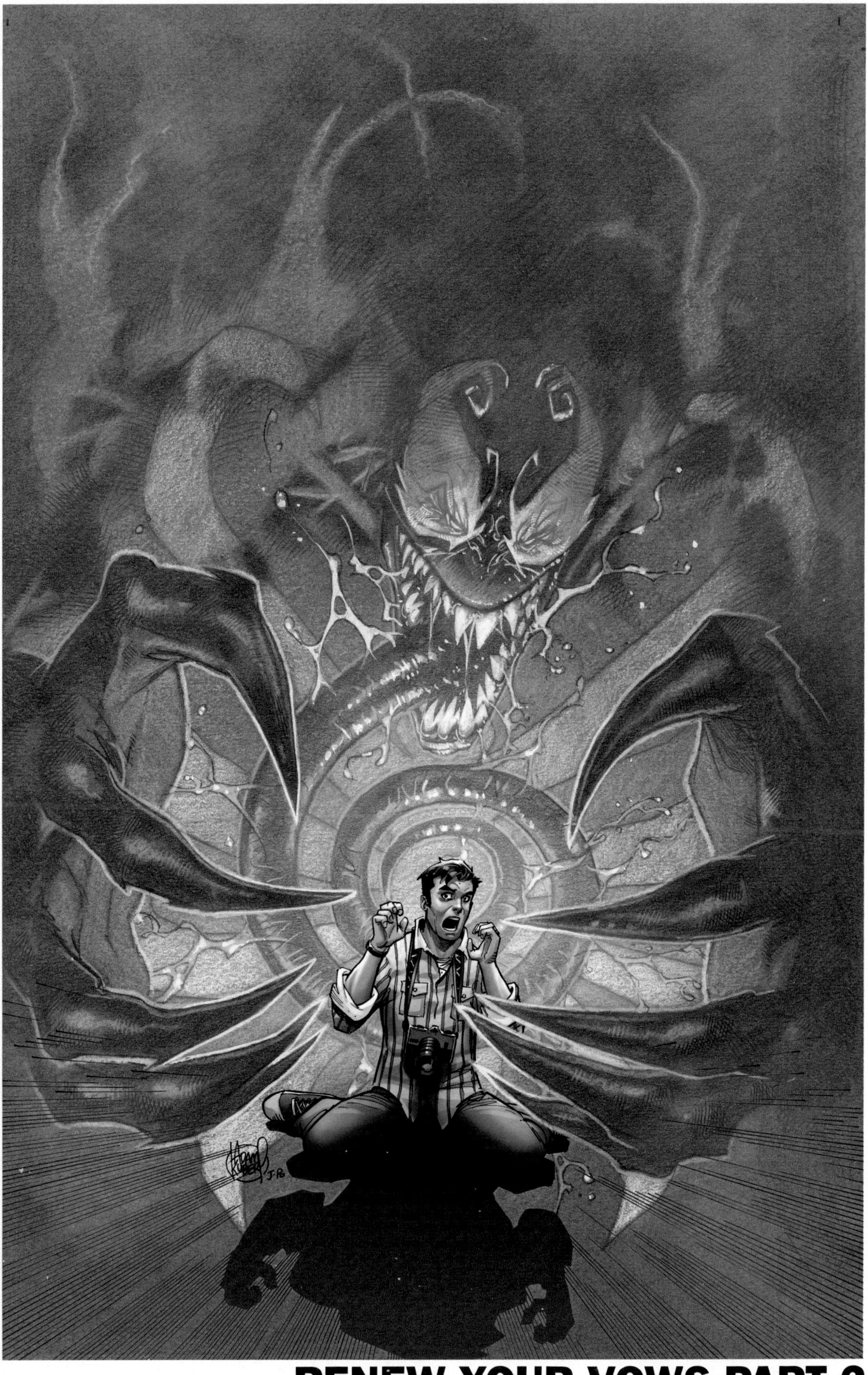

RENEW YOUR VOWS PART 2

"BECAUSE WE SAID SO, THAT'S WHY"

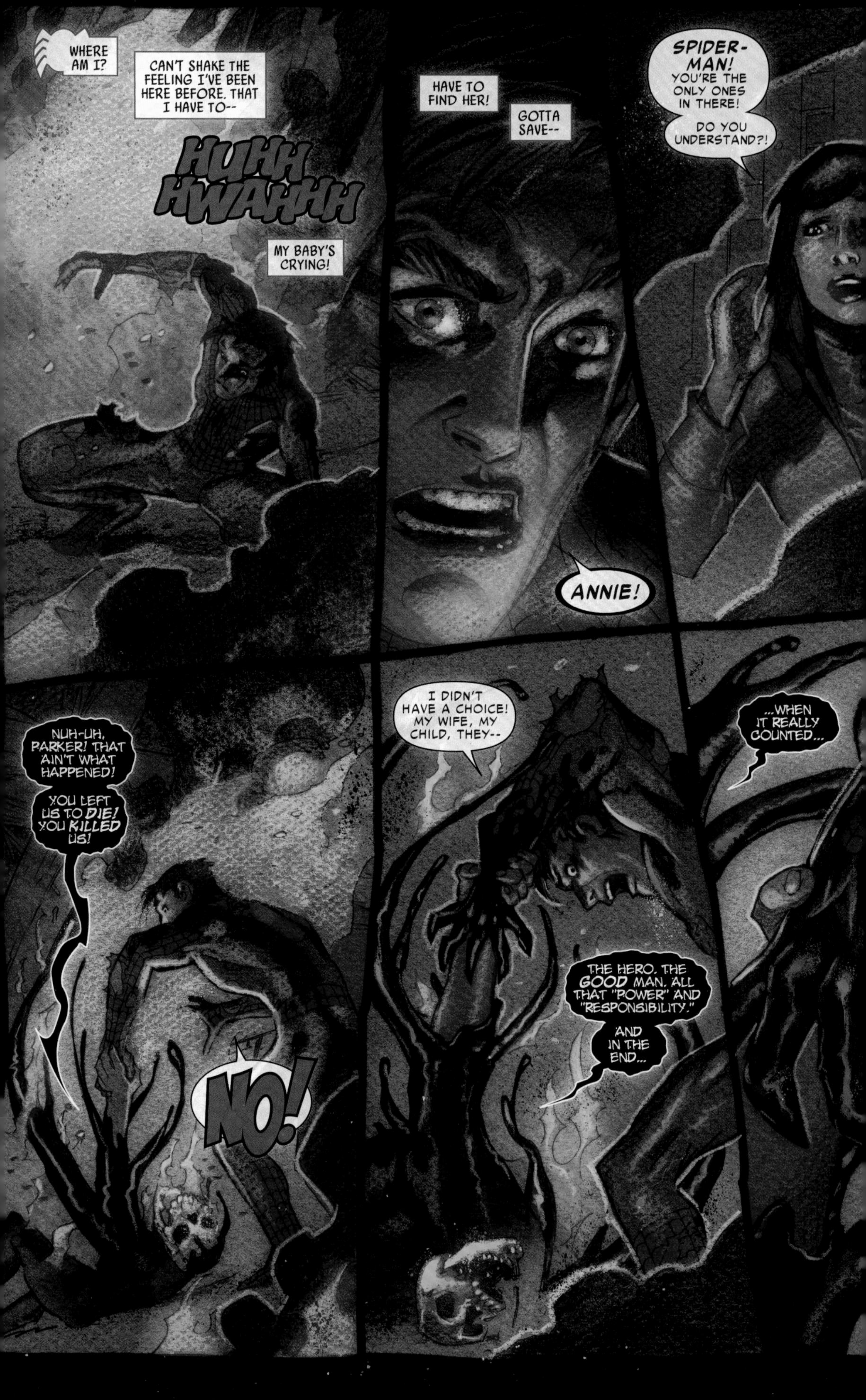
WHERE AM I?
CAN'T SHAKE THE FEELING I'VE BEEN HERE BEFORE. THAT I HAVE TO--
HUHH HWAHHH
MY BABY'S CRYING!
HAVE TO FIND HER!
GOTTA SAVE--
ANNIE!
SPIDER-MAN! YOU'RE THE ONLY ONES IN THERE!
DO YOU UNDERSTAND?!
NUH-UH, PARKER! THAT AIN'T WHAT HAPPENED!
YOU LEFT US TO DIE! YOU KILLED US!
NO!
I DIDN'T HAVE A CHOICE! MY WIFE, MY CHILD, THEY--
THE HERO. THE GOOD MAN. ALL THAT "POWER" AND "RESPONSIBILITY."
AND IN THE END...
...WHEN IT REALLY COUNTED...

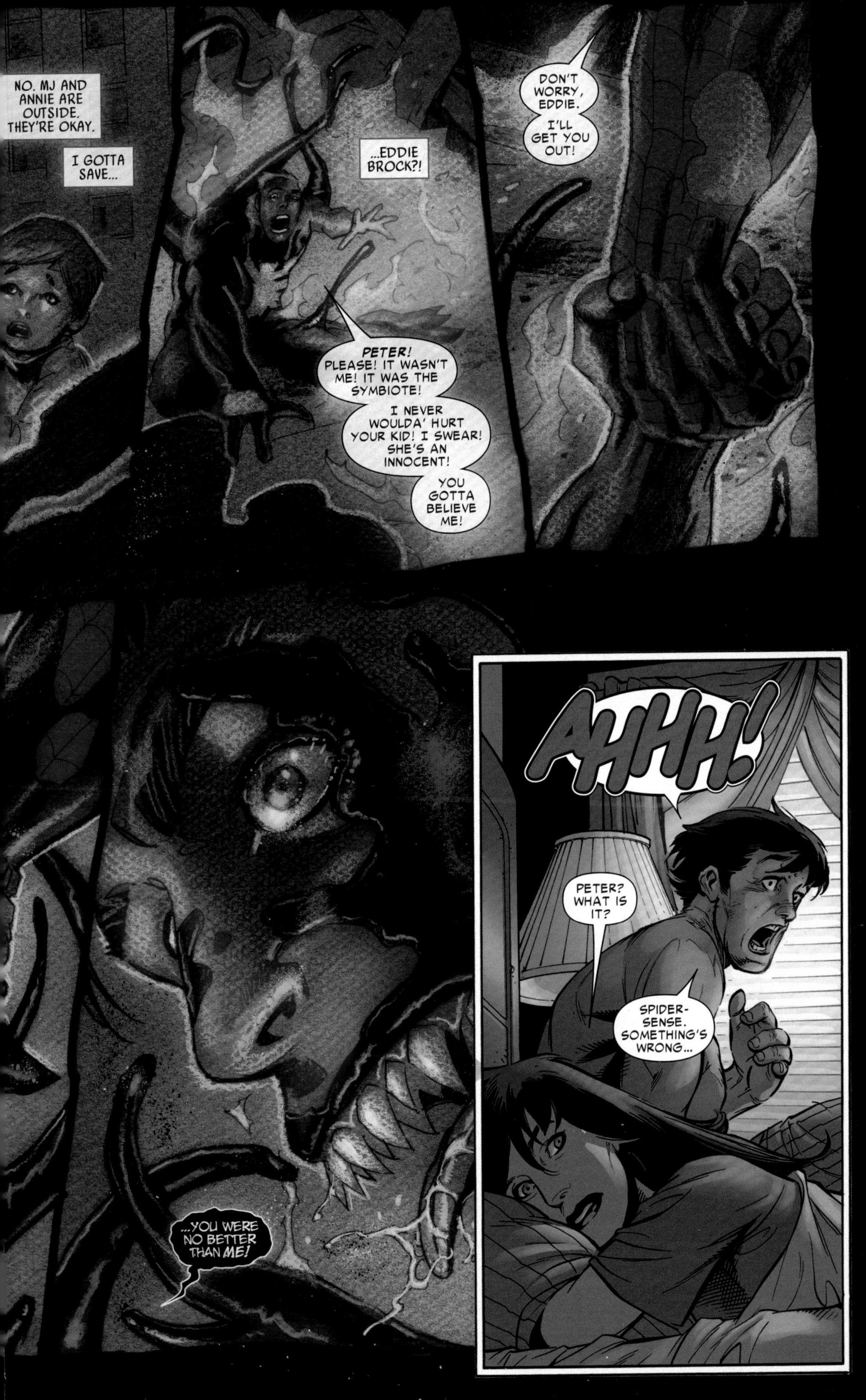
NO. MJ AND ANNIE ARE OUTSIDE. THEY'RE OKAY.
I GOTTA SAVE...
...EDDIE BROCK?!
PETER! PLEASE! IT WASN'T ME! IT WAS THE SYMBIOTE!
I NEVER WOULDA' HURT YOUR KID! I SWEAR! SHE'S AN INNOCENT!
YOU GOTTA BELIEVE ME!
DON'T WORRY, EDDIE.
I'LL GET YOU OUT!
...YOU WERE NO BETTER THAN ME!
AHHH!
PETER? WHAT IS IT?
SPIDER-SENSE. SOMETHING'S WRONG...

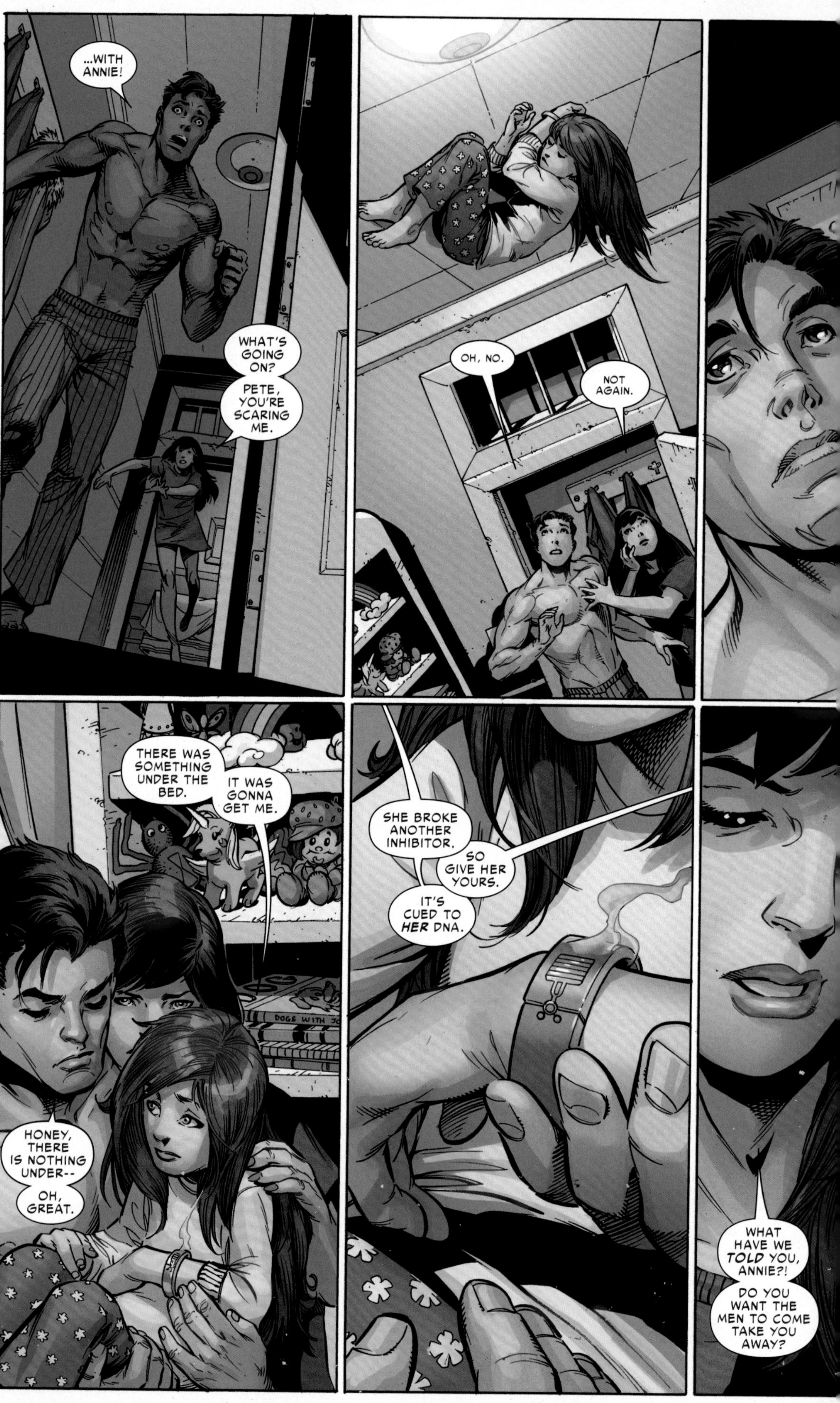
...WITH ANNIE!
WHAT'S GOING ON?
PETE, YOU'RE SCARING ME.
OH, NO.
NOT AGAIN.
THERE WAS SOMETHING UNDER THE BED.
IT WAS GONNA GET ME.
HONEY, THERE IS NOTHING UNDER--
OH, GREAT.
SHE BROKE ANOTHER INHIBITOR.
SO GIVE HER YOURS.
IT'S CUED TO *HER* DNA.
WHAT HAVE WE *TOLD* YOU, ANNIE?!
DO YOU WANT THE MEN TO COME TAKE YOU AWAY?

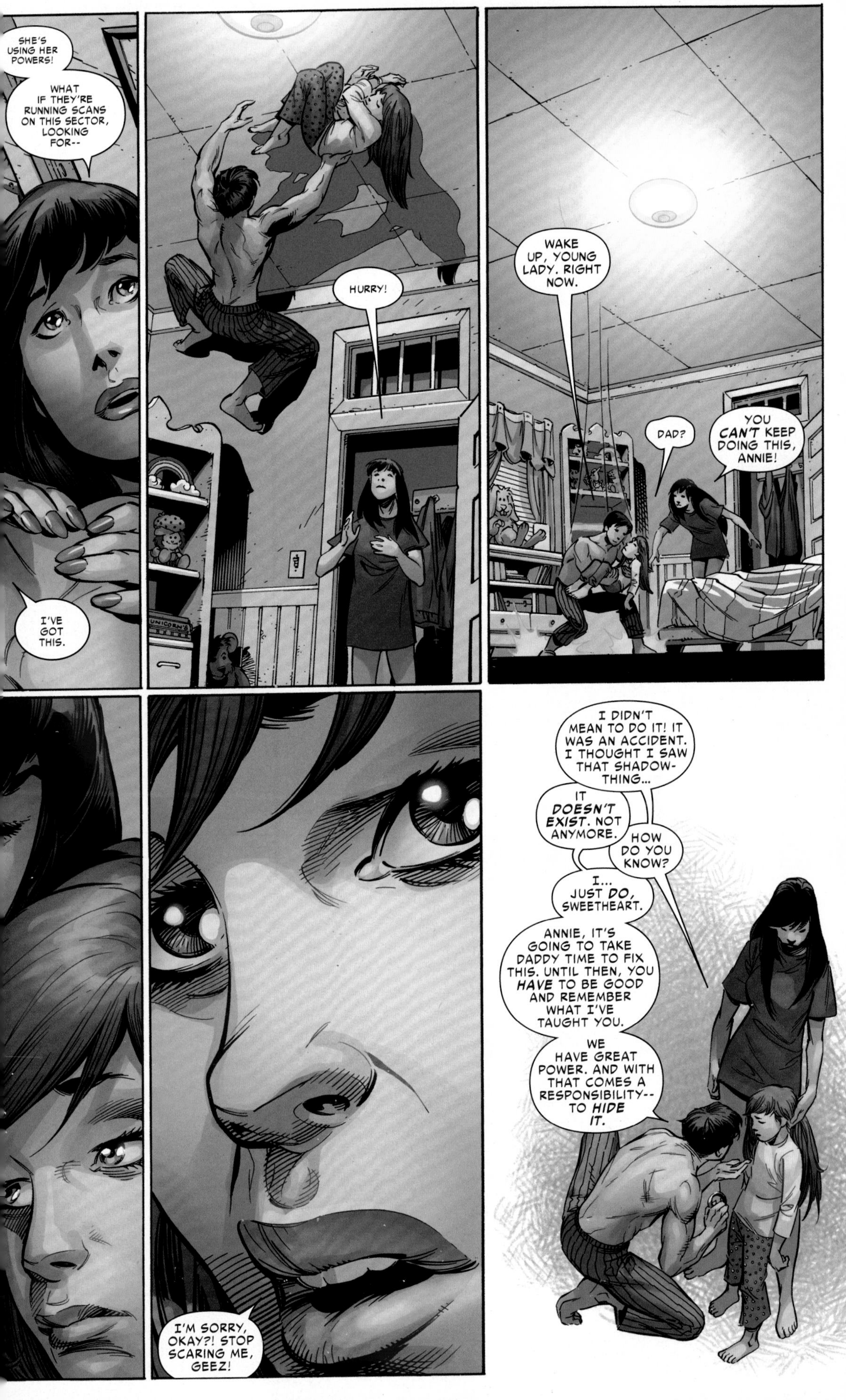
SHE'S USING HER POWERS!
WHAT IF THEY'RE RUNNING SCANS ON THIS SECTOR, LOOKING FOR--
I'VE GOT THIS.
HURRY!
WAKE UP, YOUNG LADY. RIGHT NOW.
DAD?
YOU CAN'T KEEP DOING THIS, ANNIE!
I'M SORRY, OKAY?! STOP SCARING ME, GEEZ!
I DIDN'T MEAN TO DO IT! IT WAS AN ACCIDENT. I THOUGHT I SAW THAT SHADOW-THING...
IT DOESN'T EXIST. NOT ANYMORE.
HOW DO YOU KNOW?
I... JUST DO, SWEETHEART.
ANNIE, IT'S GOING TO TAKE DADDY TIME TO FIX THIS. UNTIL THEN, YOU HAVE TO BE GOOD AND REMEMBER WHAT I'VE TAUGHT YOU.
WE HAVE GREAT POWER. AND WITH THAT COMES A RESPONSIBILITY-- TO HIDE IT.

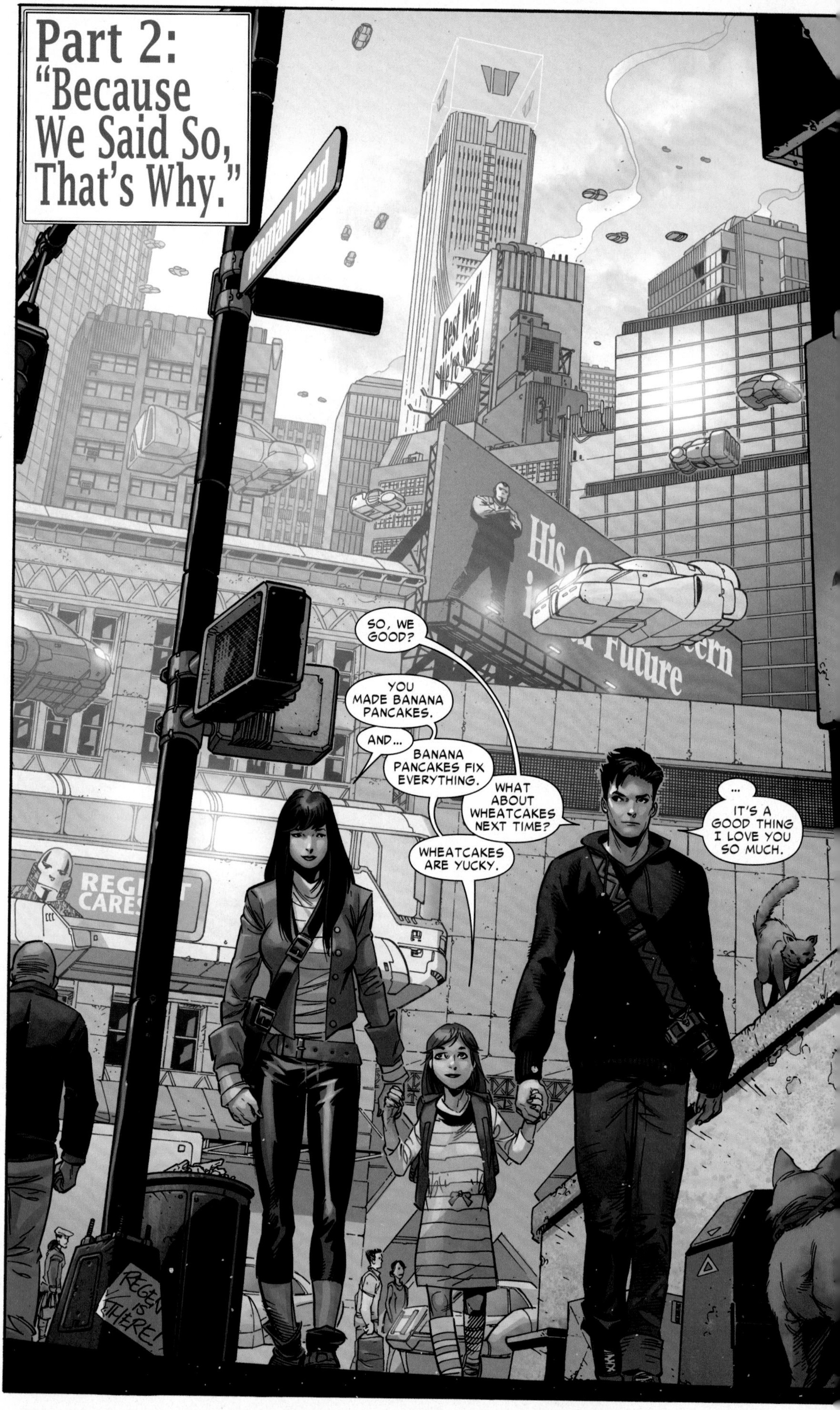
Part 2: "Because We Said So, That's Why."
Roman Blvd
SO, WE GOOD?
YOU MADE BANANA PANCAKES.
AND... BANANA PANCAKES FIX EVERYTHING.
WHAT ABOUT WHEATCAKES NEXT TIME?
WHEATCAKES ARE YUCKY.
...
IT'S A GOOD THING I LOVE YOU SO MUCH.

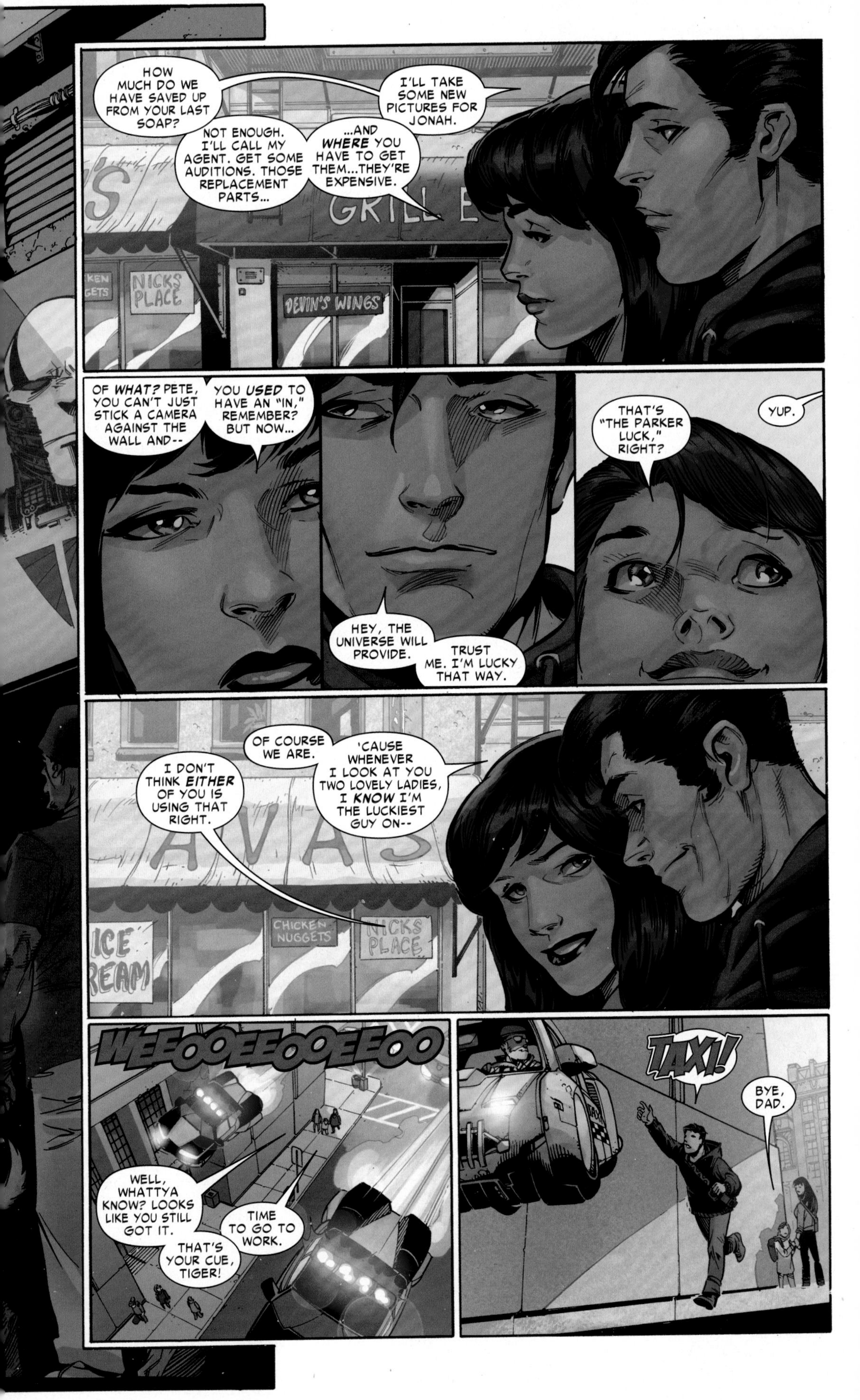
HOW MUCH DO WE HAVE SAVED UP FROM YOUR LAST SOAP?
I'LL TAKE SOME NEW PICTURES FOR JONAH.
NOT ENOUGH. I'LL CALL MY AGENT. GET SOME AUDITIONS. THOSE REPLACEMENT PARTS...
...AND WHERE YOU HAVE TO GET THEM...THEY'RE EXPENSIVE.
GRILL
NICKS PLACE
DEVIN'S WINGS
OF WHAT? PETE, YOU CAN'T JUST STICK A CAMERA AGAINST THE WALL AND--
YOU USED TO HAVE AN "IN," REMEMBER? BUT NOW...
HEY, THE UNIVERSE WILL PROVIDE.
TRUST ME. I'M LUCKY THAT WAY.
THAT'S "THE PARKER LUCK," RIGHT?
YUP.
I DON'T THINK EITHER OF YOU IS USING THAT RIGHT.
OF COURSE WE ARE.
'CAUSE WHENEVER I LOOK AT YOU TWO LOVELY LADIES, I KNOW I'M THE LUCKIEST GUY ON--
CHICKEN NUGGETS
NICKS PLACE
WEEOOEEOOEEOO
WELL, WHATTYA KNOW? LOOKS LIKE YOU STILL GOT IT.
TIME TO GO TO WORK.
THAT'S YOUR CUE, TIGER!
TAXI!
BYE, DAD.

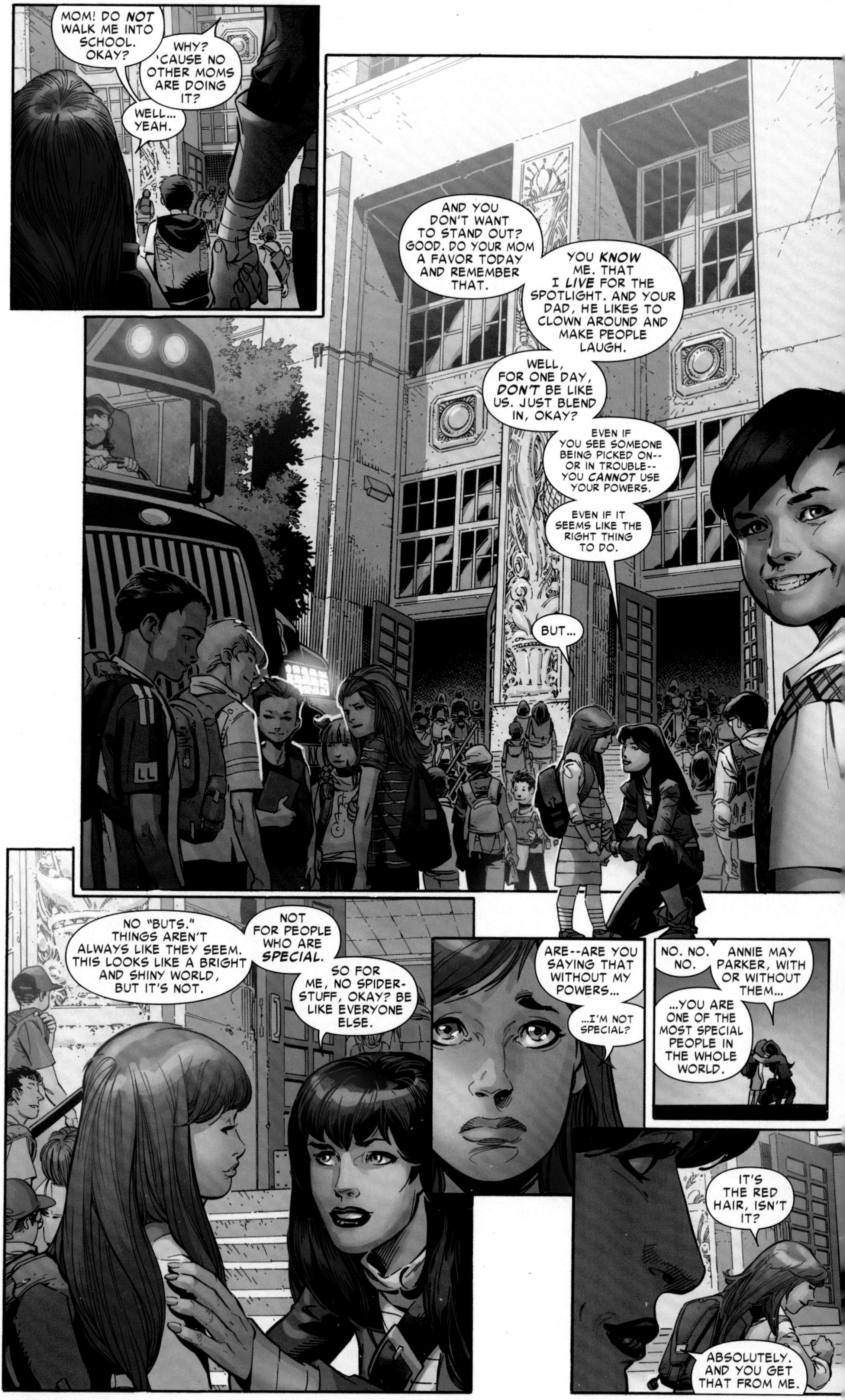
MOM! DO NOT WALK ME INTO SCHOOL. OKAY?
WHY? 'CAUSE NO OTHER MOMS ARE DOING IT?
WELL... YEAH.
AND YOU DON'T WANT TO STAND OUT? GOOD. DO YOUR MOM A FAVOR TODAY AND REMEMBER THAT.
YOU KNOW ME. THAT I LIVE FOR THE SPOTLIGHT. AND YOUR DAD, HE LIKES TO CLOWN AROUND AND MAKE PEOPLE LAUGH.
WELL, FOR ONE DAY, DON'T BE LIKE US. JUST BLEND IN, OKAY?
EVEN IF YOU SEE SOMEONE BEING PICKED ON--OR IN TROUBLE--YOU CANNOT USE YOUR POWERS.
EVEN IF IT SEEMS LIKE THE RIGHT THING TO DO.
BUT...
NO "BUTS." THINGS AREN'T ALWAYS LIKE THEY SEEM. THIS LOOKS LIKE A BRIGHT AND SHINY WORLD, BUT IT'S NOT.
NOT FOR PEOPLE WHO ARE SPECIAL.
SO FOR ME, NO SPIDER-STUFF, OKAY? BE LIKE EVERYONE ELSE.
ARE--ARE YOU SAYING THAT WITHOUT MY POWERS...
...I'M NOT SPECIAL?
NO. NO. NO.
ANNIE MAY PARKER, WITH OR WITHOUT THEM...
...YOU ARE ONE OF THE MOST SPECIAL PEOPLE IN THE WHOLE WORLD.
IT'S THE RED HAIR, ISN'T IT?
ABSOLUTELY. AND YOU GET THAT FROM ME.

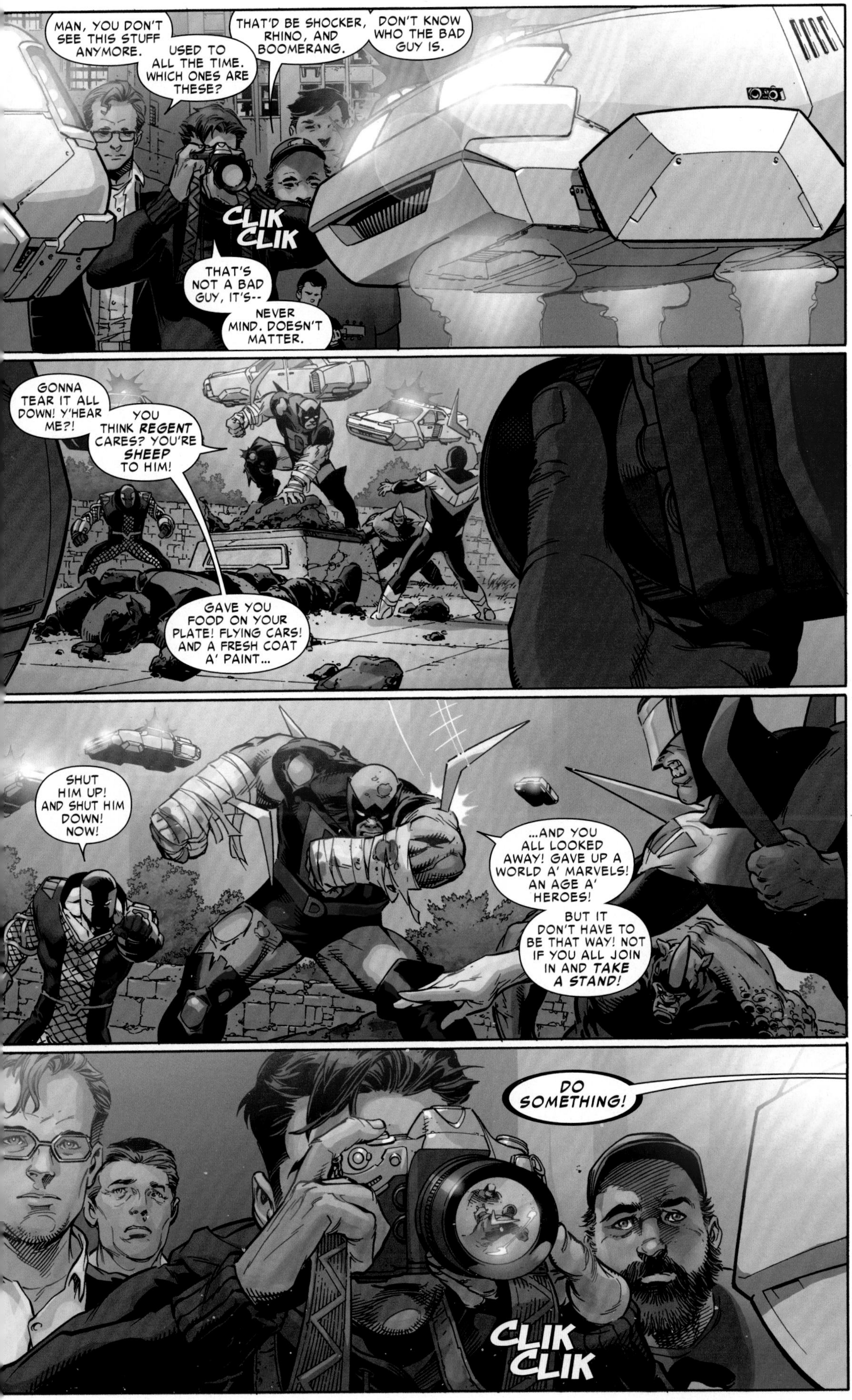

MAN, YOU DON'T SEE THIS STUFF ANYMORE.
USED TO ALL THE TIME. WHICH ONES ARE THESE?
THAT'D BE SHOCKER, RHINO, AND BOOMERANG.
DON'T KNOW WHO THE BAD GUY IS.
CLIK CLIK
THAT'S NOT A BAD GUY, IT'S--
NEVER MIND. DOESN'T MATTER.
GONNA TEAR IT ALL DOWN! Y'HEAR ME?!
YOU THINK REGENT CARES? YOU'RE SHEEP TO HIM!
GAVE YOU FOOD ON YOUR PLATE! FLYING CARS! AND A FRESH COAT A' PAINT...
SHUT HIM UP! AND SHUT HIM DOWN! NOW!
...AND YOU ALL LOOKED AWAY! GAVE UP A WORLD A' MARVELS! AN AGE A' HEROES!
BUT IT DON'T HAVE TO BE THAT WAY! NOT IF YOU ALL JOIN IN AND TAKE A STAND!
DO SOMETHING!
CLIK CLIK

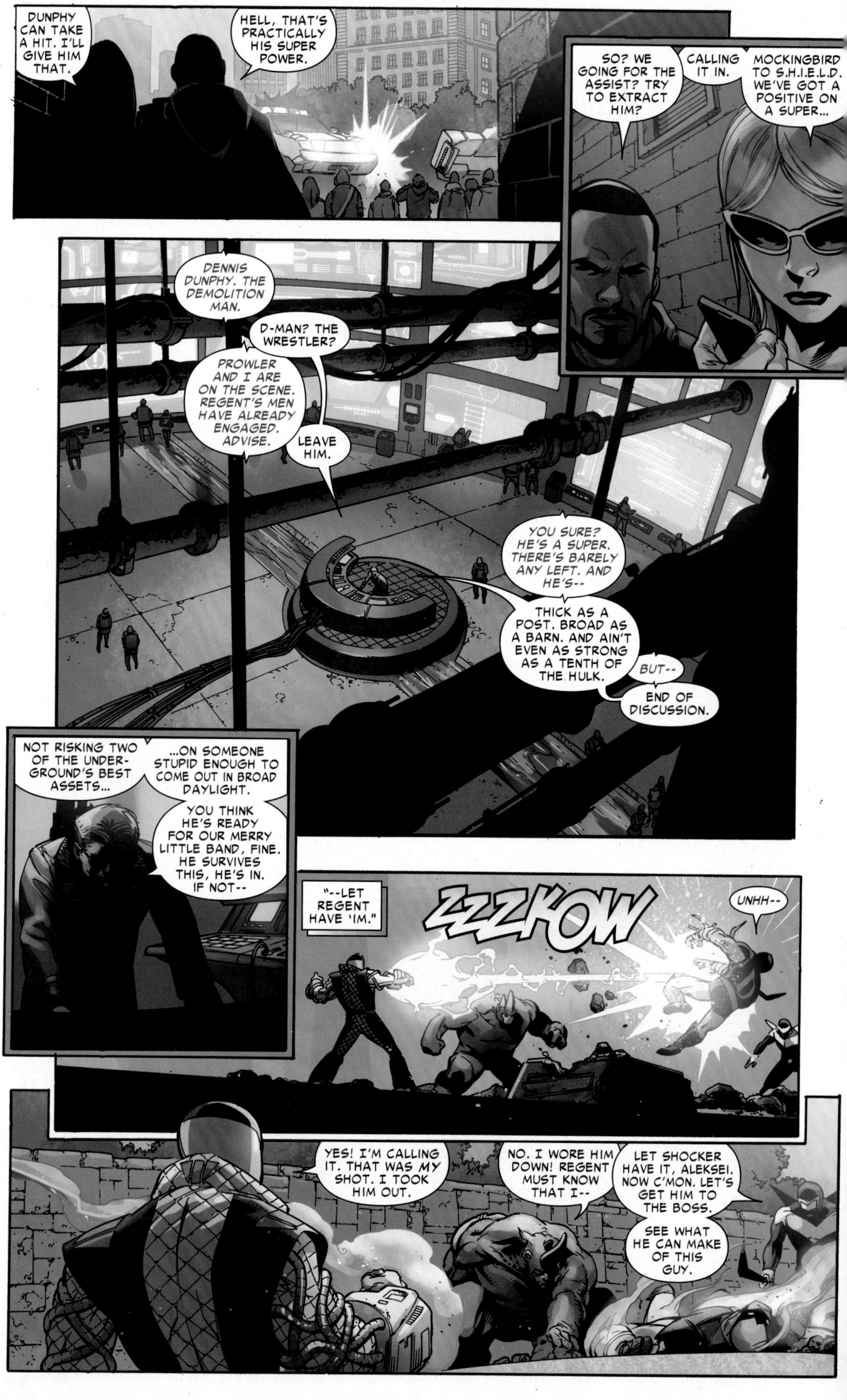
DUNPHY CAN TAKE A HIT. I'LL GIVE HIM THAT.
HELL, THAT'S PRACTICALLY HIS SUPER POWER.
SO? WE GOING FOR THE ASSIST? TRY TO EXTRACT HIM?
CALLING IT IN.
MOCKINGBIRD TO S.H.I.E.L.D. WE'VE GOT A POSITIVE ON A SUPER...
DENNIS DUNPHY. THE DEMOLITION MAN.
D-MAN? THE WRESTLER?
PROWLER AND I ARE ON THE SCENE. REGENT'S MEN HAVE ALREADY ENGAGED. ADVISE.
LEAVE HIM.
YOU SURE? HE'S A SUPER. THERE'S BARELY ANY LEFT. AND HE'S--
THICK AS A POST. BROAD AS A BARN. AND AIN'T EVEN AS STRONG AS A TENTH OF THE HULK.
BUT--
END OF DISCUSSION.
NOT RISKING TWO OF THE UNDERGROUND'S BEST ASSETS...
...ON SOMEONE STUPID ENOUGH TO COME OUT IN BROAD DAYLIGHT.
YOU THINK HE'S READY FOR OUR MERRY LITTLE BAND, FINE. HE SURVIVES THIS, HE'S IN. IF NOT--
"--LET REGENT HAVE 'IM."
ZZZKOW
UNHH--
YES! I'M CALLING IT. THAT WAS MY SHOT. I TOOK HIM OUT.
NO. I WORE HIM DOWN! REGENT MUST KNOW THAT I--
LET SHOCKER HAVE IT, ALEKSEI. NOW C'MON. LET'S GET HIM TO THE BOSS.
SEE WHAT HE CAN MAKE OF THIS GUY.

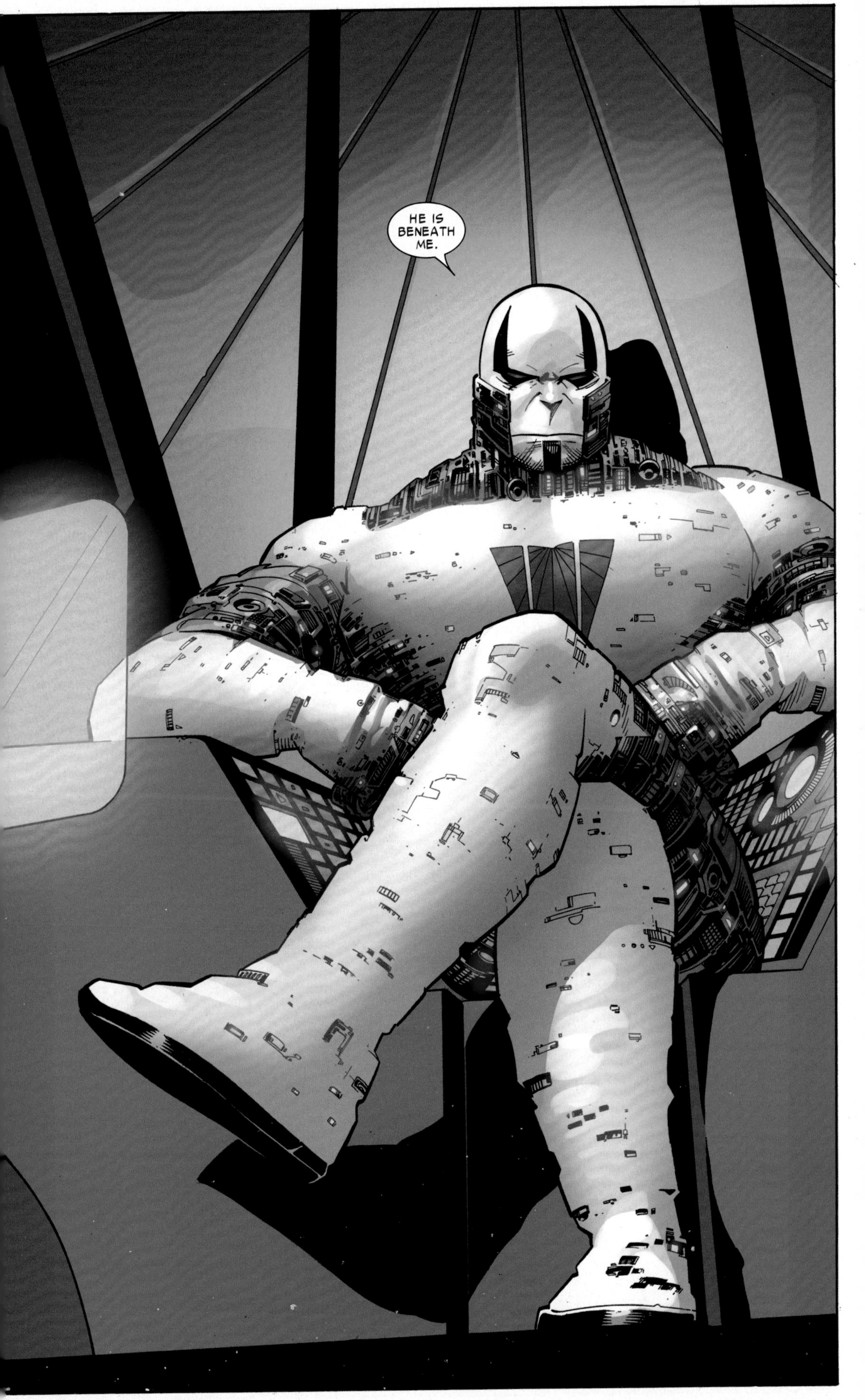
HE IS BENEATH ME.

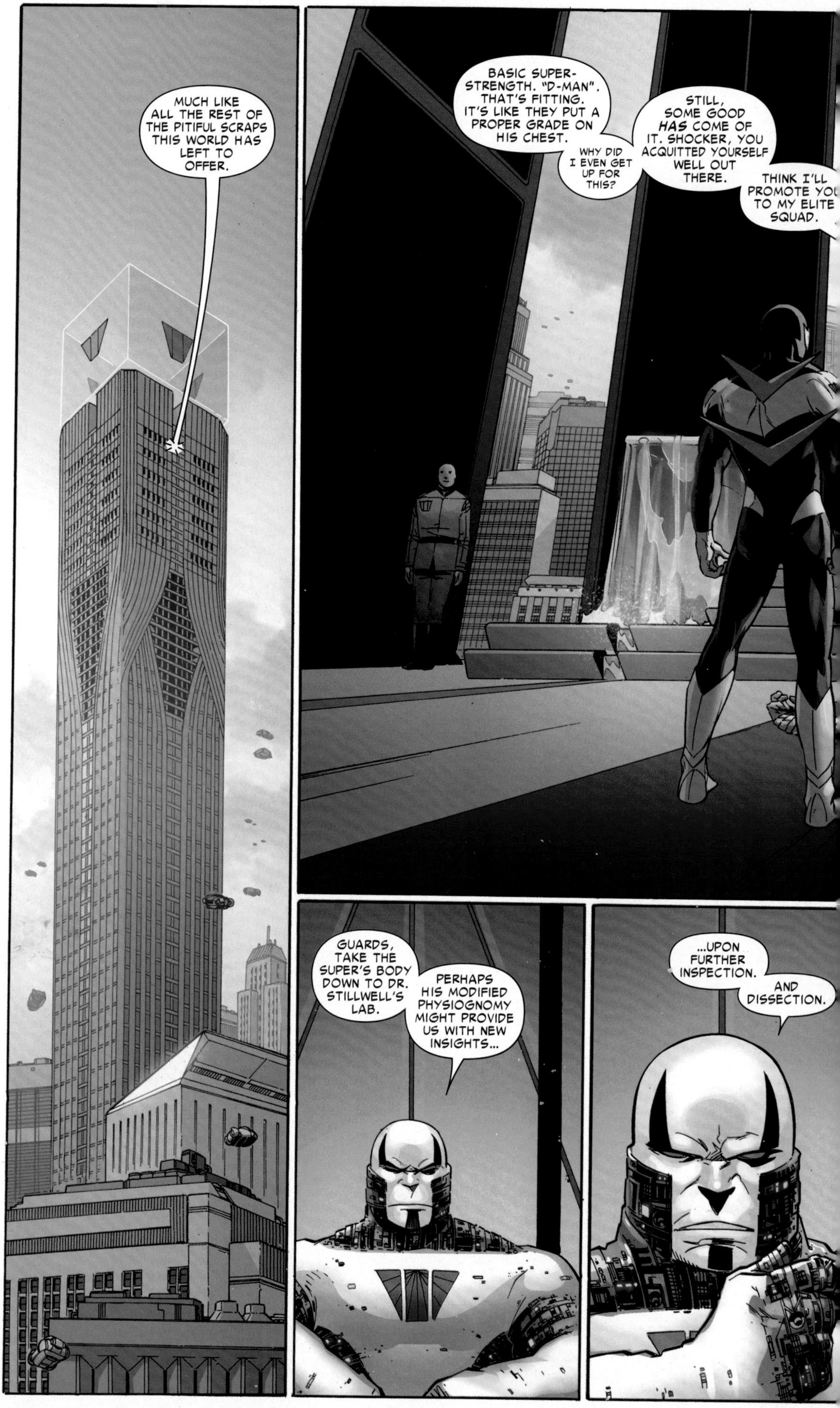

MUCH LIKE ALL THE REST OF THE PITIFUL SCRAPS THIS WORLD HAS LEFT TO OFFER.
BASIC SUPER-STRENGTH. "D-MAN". THAT'S FITTING. IT'S LIKE THEY PUT A PROPER GRADE ON HIS CHEST.
WHY DID I EVEN GET UP FOR THIS?
STILL, SOME GOOD HAS COME OF IT. SHOCKER, YOU ACQUITTED YOURSELF WELL OUT THERE.
THINK I'LL PROMOTE YOU TO MY ELITE SQUAD.
GUARDS, TAKE THE SUPER'S BODY DOWN TO DR. STILLWELL'S LAB.
PERHAPS HIS MODIFIED PHYSIOGNOMY MIGHT PROVIDE US WITH NEW INSIGHTS...
...UPON FURTHER INSPECTION.
AND DISSECTION.

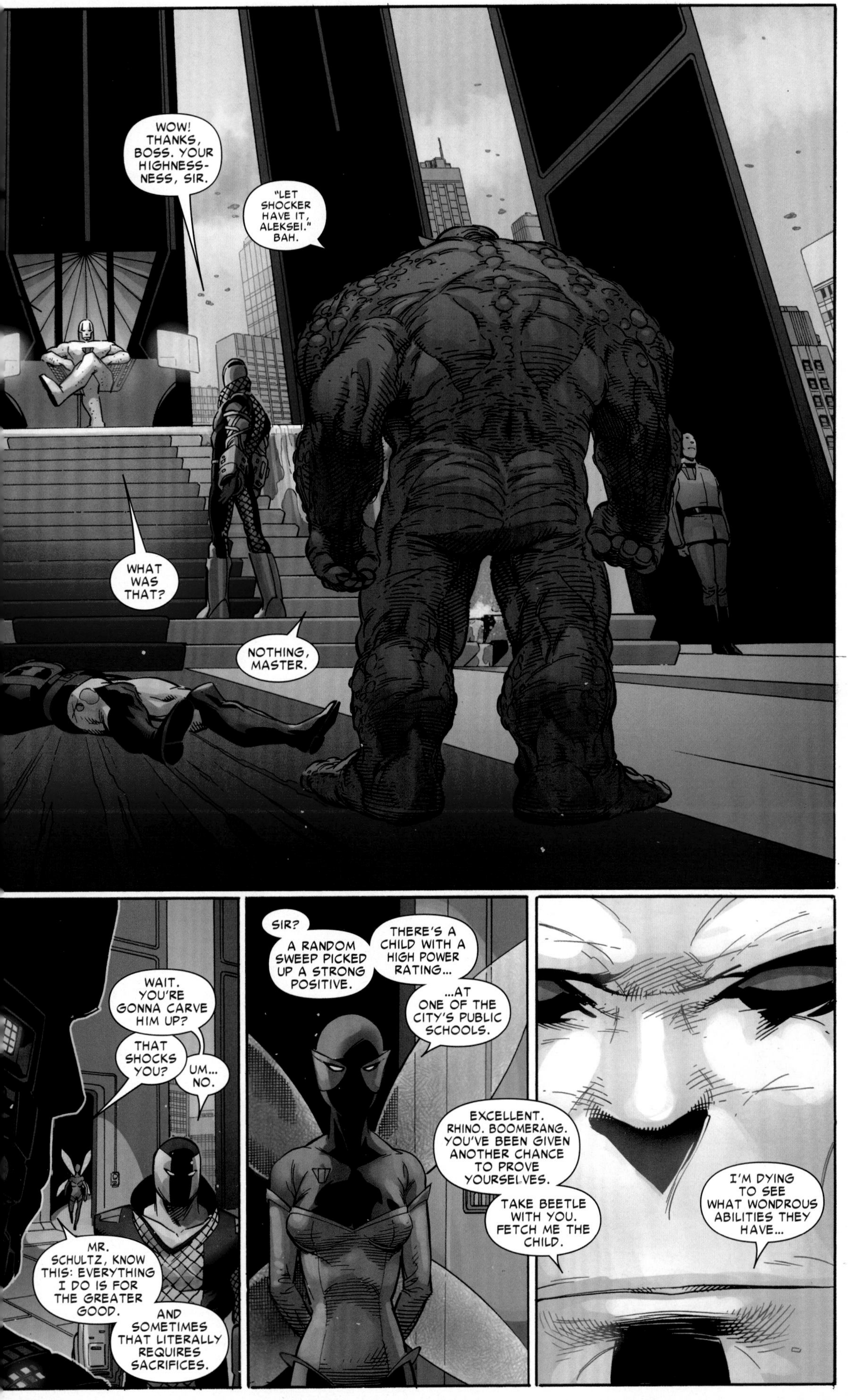
WOW! THANKS, BOSS. YOUR HIGHNESS-NESS, SIR.
"LET SHOCKER HAVE IT, ALEKSEI." BAH.
WHAT WAS THAT?
NOTHING, MASTER.
WAIT. YOU'RE GONNA CARVE HIM UP?
THAT SHOCKS YOU?
UM... NO.
MR. SCHULTZ, KNOW THIS: EVERYTHING I DO IS FOR THE GREATER GOOD.
AND SOMETIMES THAT LITERALLY REQUIRES SACRIFICES.
SIR?
A RANDOM SWEEP PICKED UP A STRONG POSITIVE.
THERE'S A CHILD WITH A HIGH POWER RATING...
...AT ONE OF THE CITY'S PUBLIC SCHOOLS.
EXCELLENT. RHINO. BOOMERANG. YOU'VE BEEN GIVEN ANOTHER CHANCE TO PROVE YOURSELVES.
TAKE BEETLE WITH YOU. FETCH ME THE CHILD.
I'M DYING TO SEE WHAT WONDROUS ABILITIES THEY HAVE...

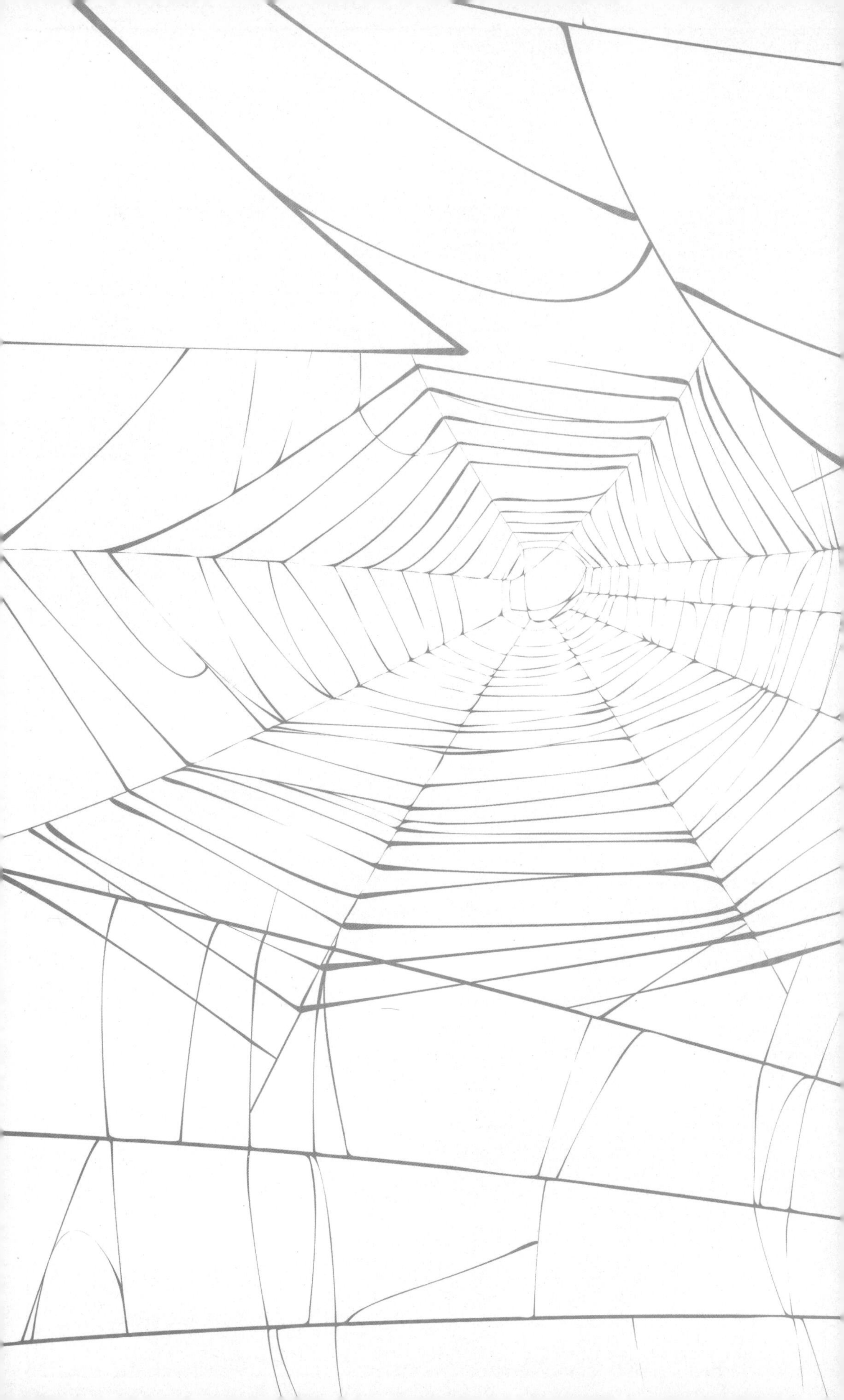

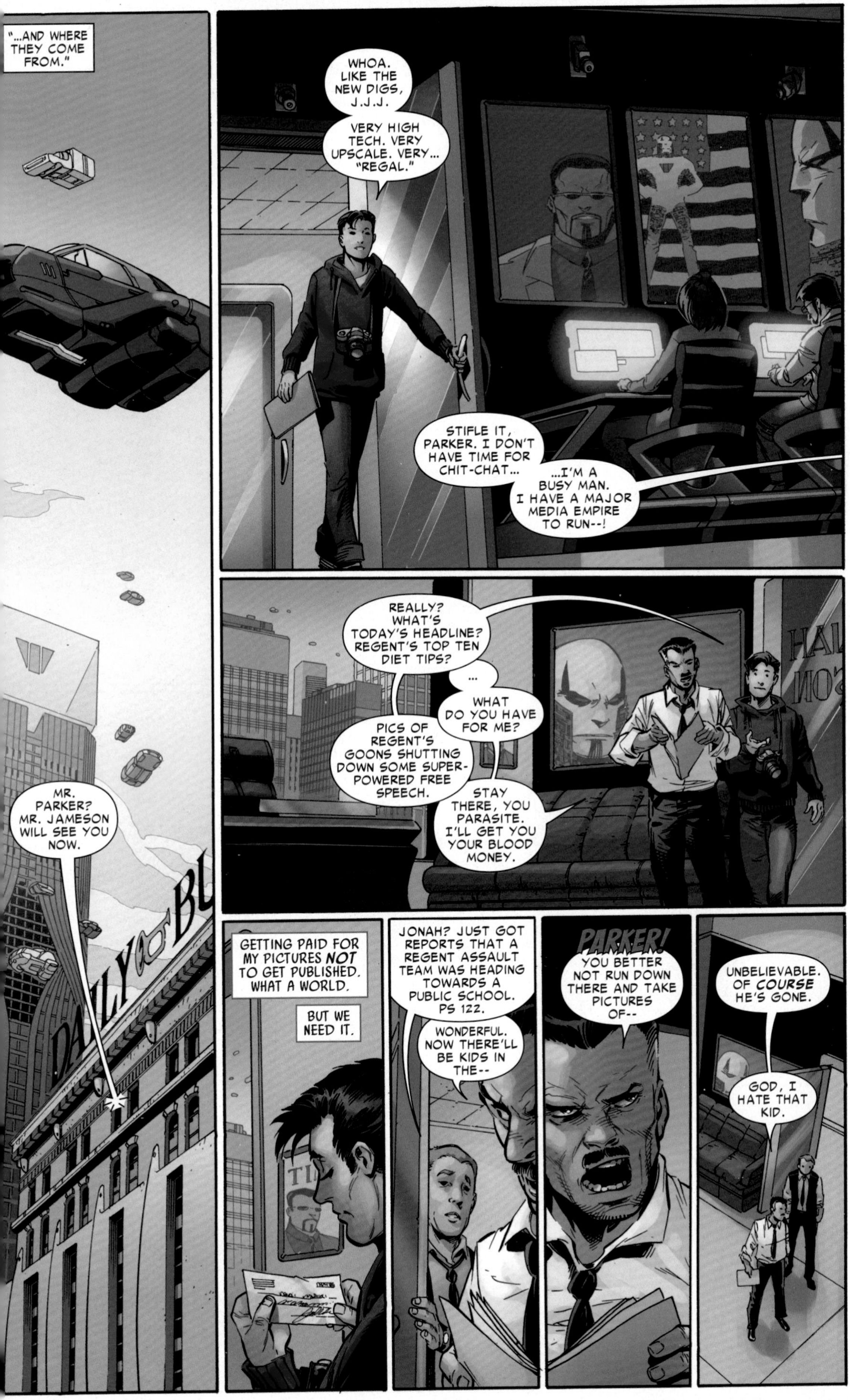
"...AND WHERE THEY COME FROM."
MR. PARKER? MR. JAMESON WILL SEE YOU NOW.
DAILY BU
WHOA. LIKE THE NEW DIGS, J.J.J.
VERY HIGH TECH. VERY UPSCALE. VERY... "REGAL."
STIFLE IT, PARKER. I DON'T HAVE TIME FOR CHIT-CHAT...
...I'M A BUSY MAN. I HAVE A MAJOR MEDIA EMPIRE TO RUN--!
REALLY? WHAT'S TODAY'S HEADLINE? REGENT'S TOP TEN DIET TIPS?
...
WHAT DO YOU HAVE FOR ME?
PICS OF REGENT'S GOONS SHUTTING DOWN SOME SUPER-POWERED FREE SPEECH.
STAY THERE, YOU PARASITE. I'LL GET YOU YOUR BLOOD MONEY.
GETTING PAID FOR MY PICTURES NOT TO GET PUBLISHED. WHAT A WORLD.
BUT WE NEED IT.
JONAH? JUST GOT REPORTS THAT A REGENT ASSAULT TEAM WAS HEADING TOWARDS A PUBLIC SCHOOL. PS 122.
WONDERFUL. NOW THERE'LL BE KIDS IN THE--
PARKER!
YOU BETTER NOT RUN DOWN THERE AND TAKE PICTURES OF--
UNBELIEVABLE. OF COURSE HE'S GONE.
GOD, I HATE THAT KID.

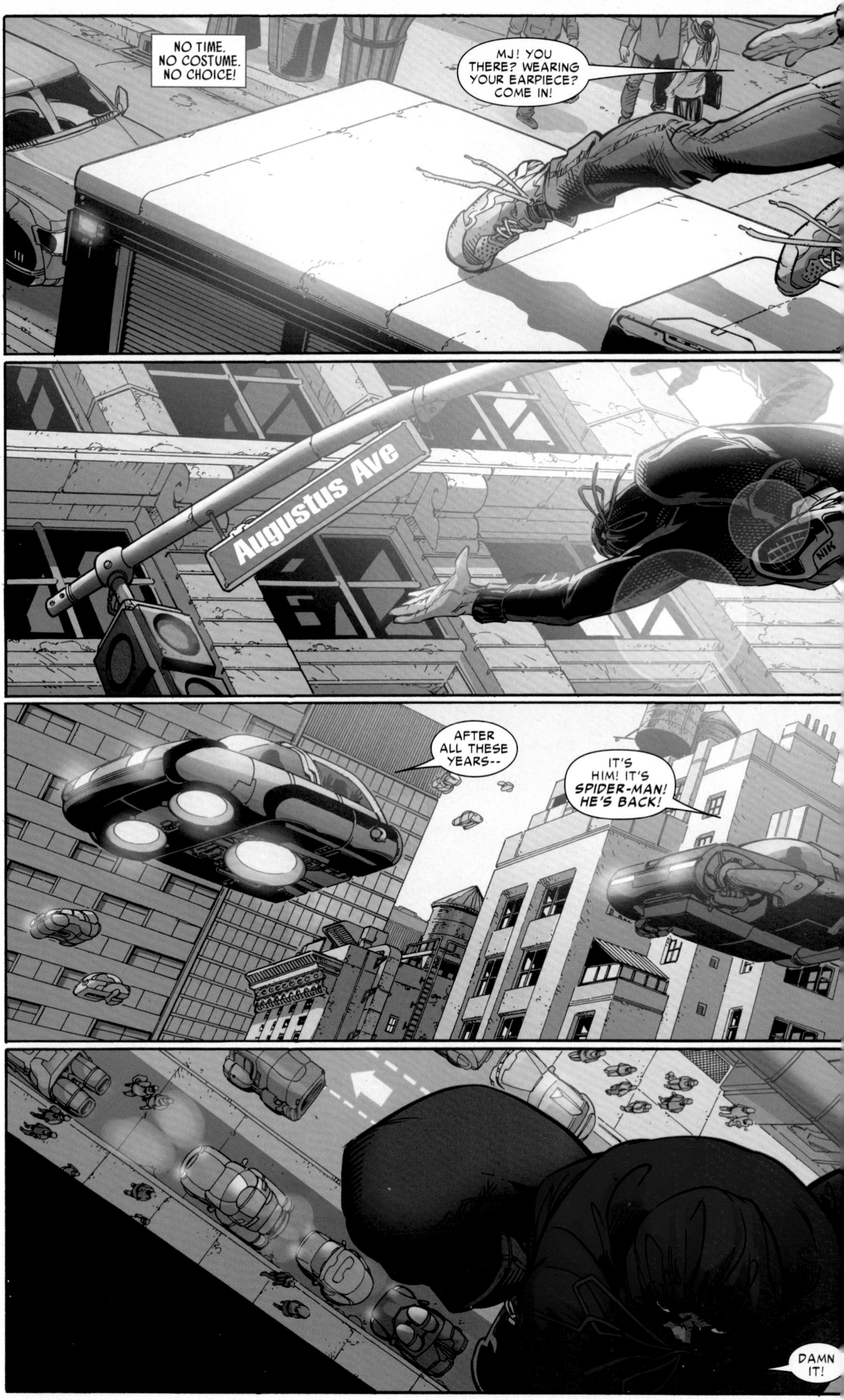
NO TIME. NO COSTUME. NO CHOICE!
MJ! YOU THERE? WEARING YOUR EARPIECE? COME IN!
Augustus Ave
AFTER ALL THESE YEARS--
IT'S HIM! IT'S SPIDER-MAN! HE'S BACK!
DAMN IT!

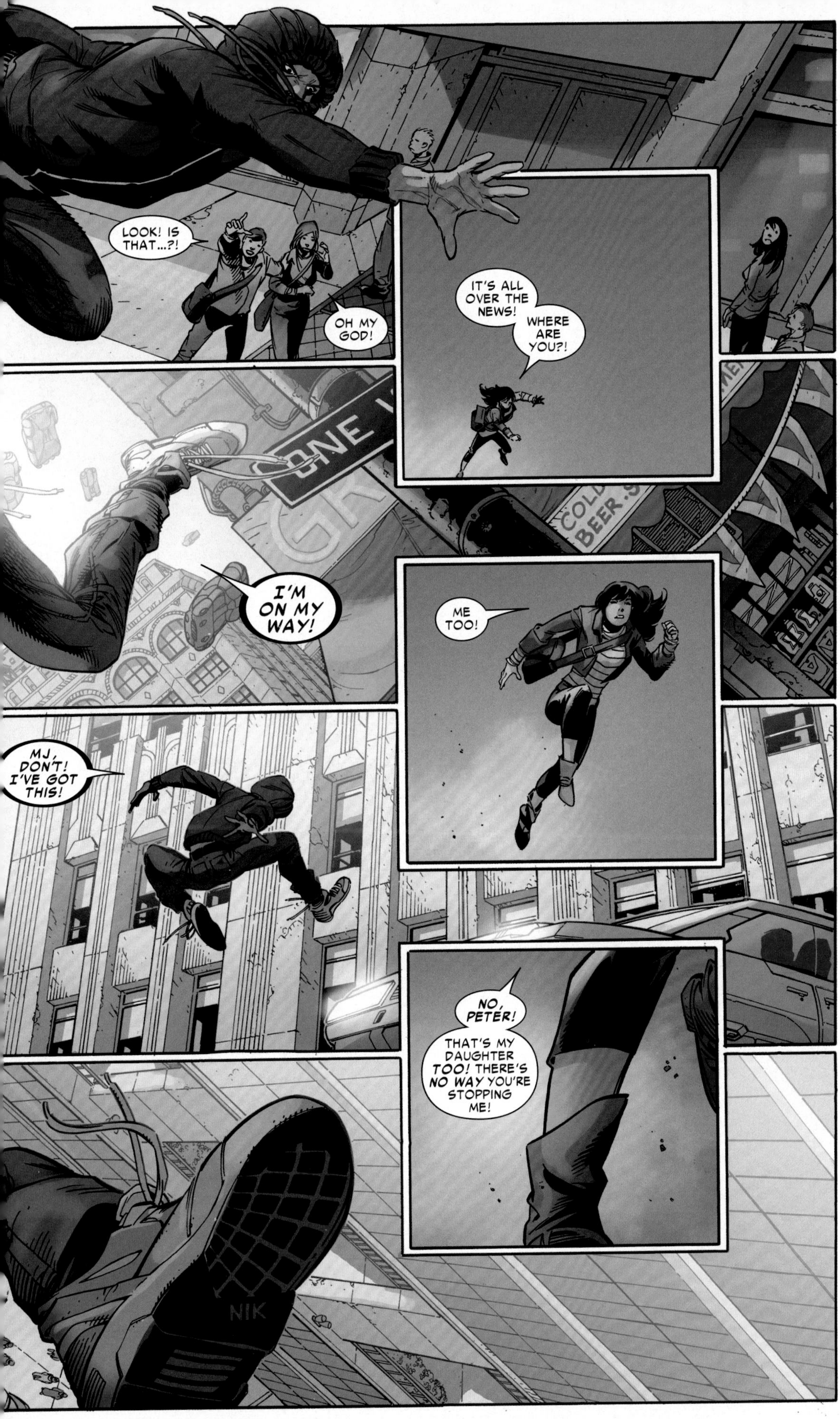
LOOK! IS THAT...?!
OH MY GOD!
IT'S ALL OVER THE NEWS!
WHERE ARE YOU?!
ONE
COLD BEER
I'M ON MY WAY!
ME TOO!
MJ, DON'T! I'VE GOT THIS!
NO, PETER!
THAT'S MY DAUGHTER TOO! THERE'S NO WAY YOU'RE STOPPING ME!
NIK

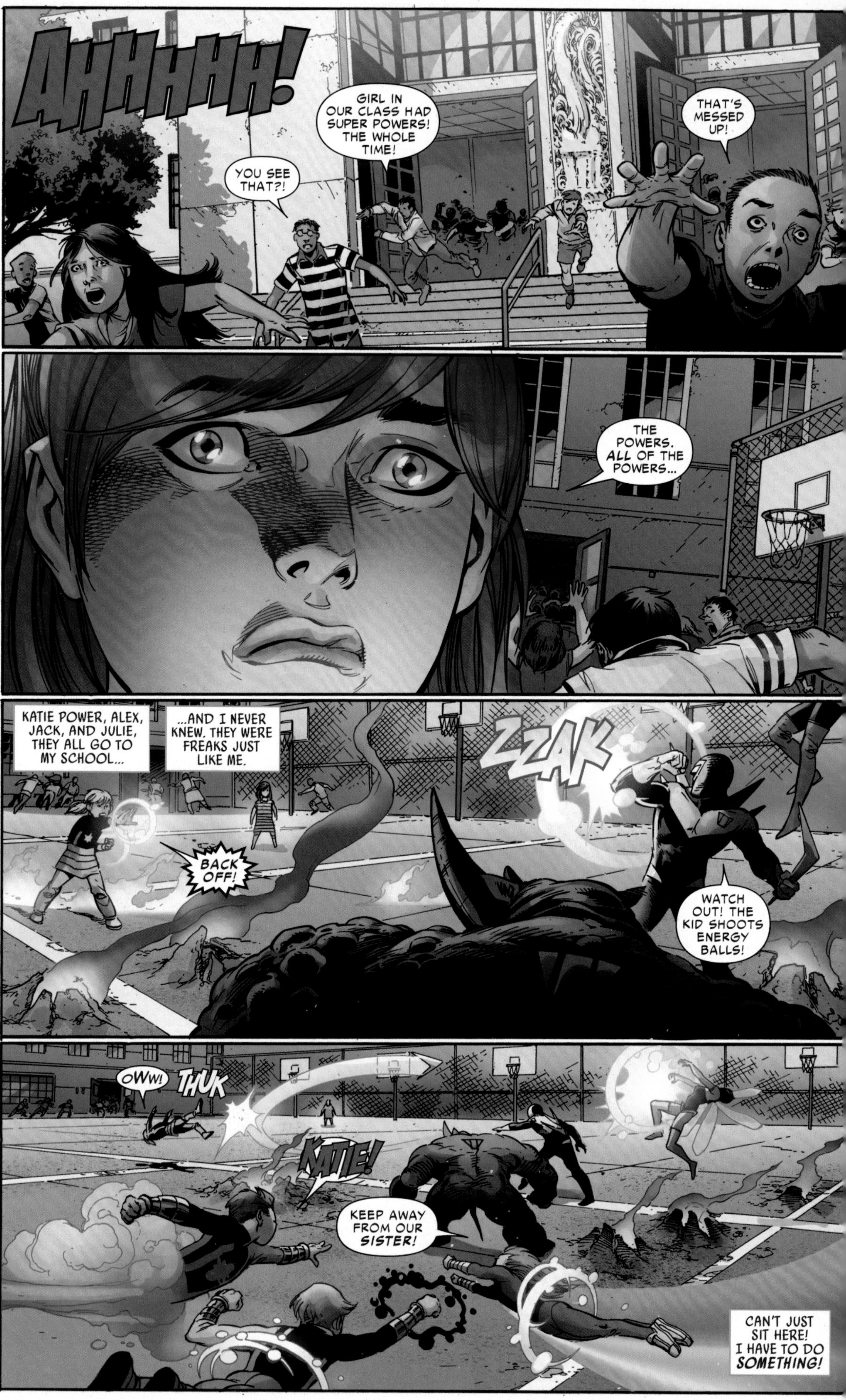
AHHHHHH!
GIRL IN OUR CLASS HAD SUPER POWERS! THE WHOLE TIME!
YOU SEE THAT?!
THAT'S MESSED UP!
THE POWERS. ALL OF THE POWERS...
KATIE POWER, ALEX, JACK, AND JULIE, THEY ALL GO TO MY SCHOOL...
...AND I NEVER KNEW. THEY WERE FREAKS JUST LIKE ME.
ZZAK
BACK OFF!
WATCH OUT! THE KID SHOOTS ENERGY BALLS!
OWW!
THUK
KATIE!
KEEP AWAY FROM OUR SISTER!
CAN'T JUST SIT HERE! I HAVE TO DO SOMETHING!

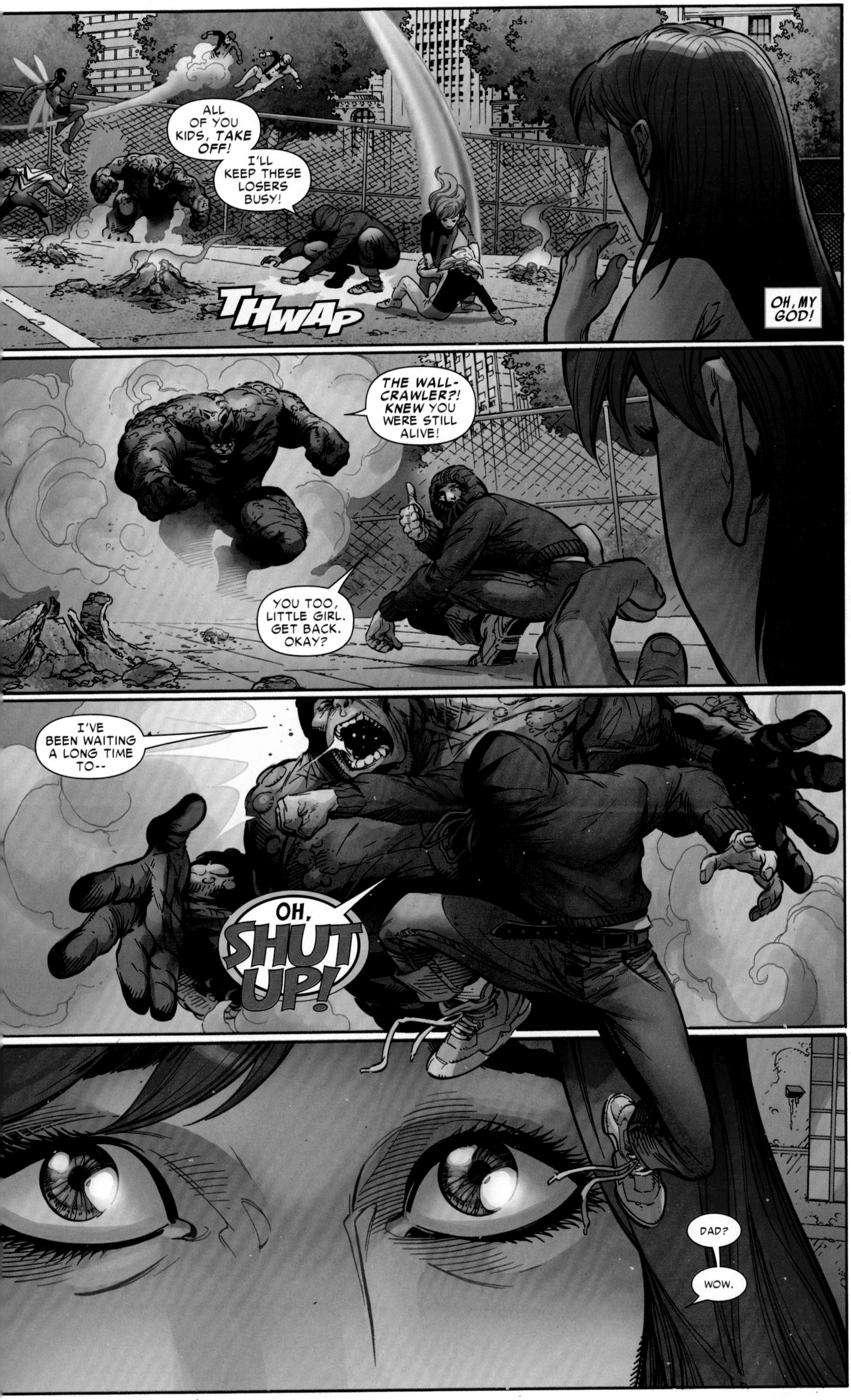
ALL OF YOU KIDS, TAKE OFF!
I'LL KEEP THESE LOSERS BUSY!
THWAP
OH, MY GOD!
THE WALL-CRAWLER?! KNEW YOU WERE STILL ALIVE!
YOU TOO, LITTLE GIRL. GET BACK. OKAY?
I'VE BEEN WAITING A LONG TIME TO--
OH, SHUT UP!
DAD?
WOW.

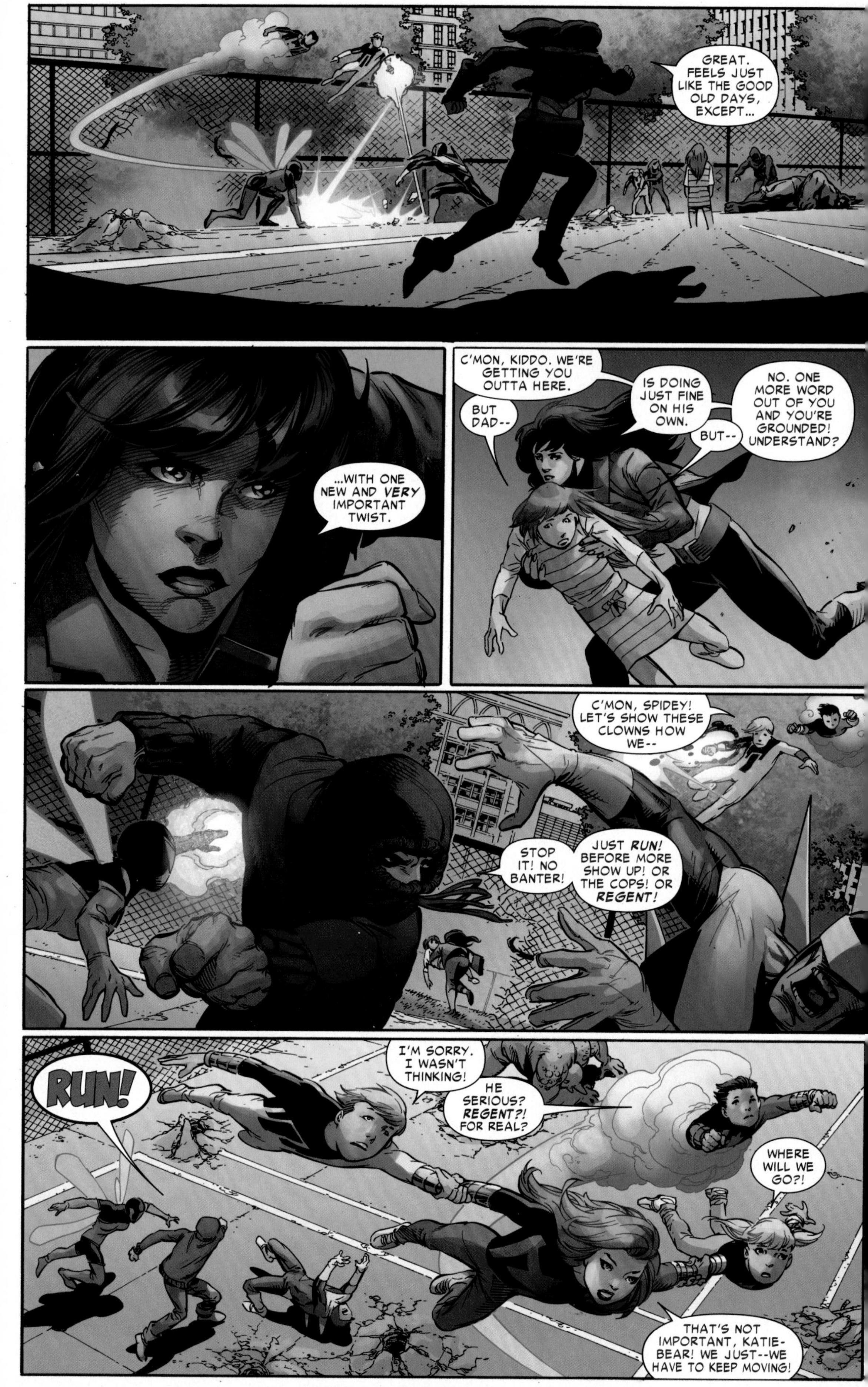

GREAT. FEELS JUST LIKE THE GOOD OLD DAYS, EXCEPT...
...WITH ONE NEW AND VERY IMPORTANT TWIST.
C'MON, KIDDO. WE'RE GETTING YOU OUTTA HERE.
BUT DAD--
IS DOING JUST FINE ON HIS OWN.
BUT--
NO. ONE MORE WORD OUT OF YOU AND YOU'RE GROUNDED! UNDERSTAND?
C'MON, SPIDEY! LET'S SHOW THESE CLOWNS HOW WE--
STOP IT! NO BANTER!
JUST RUN! BEFORE MORE SHOW UP! OR THE COPS! OR REGENT!
RUN!
I'M SORRY. I WASN'T THINKING!
HE SERIOUS? REGENT?! FOR REAL?
WHERE WILL WE GO?!
THAT'S NOT IMPORTANT, KATIE-BEAR! WE JUST--WE HAVE TO KEEP MOVING!

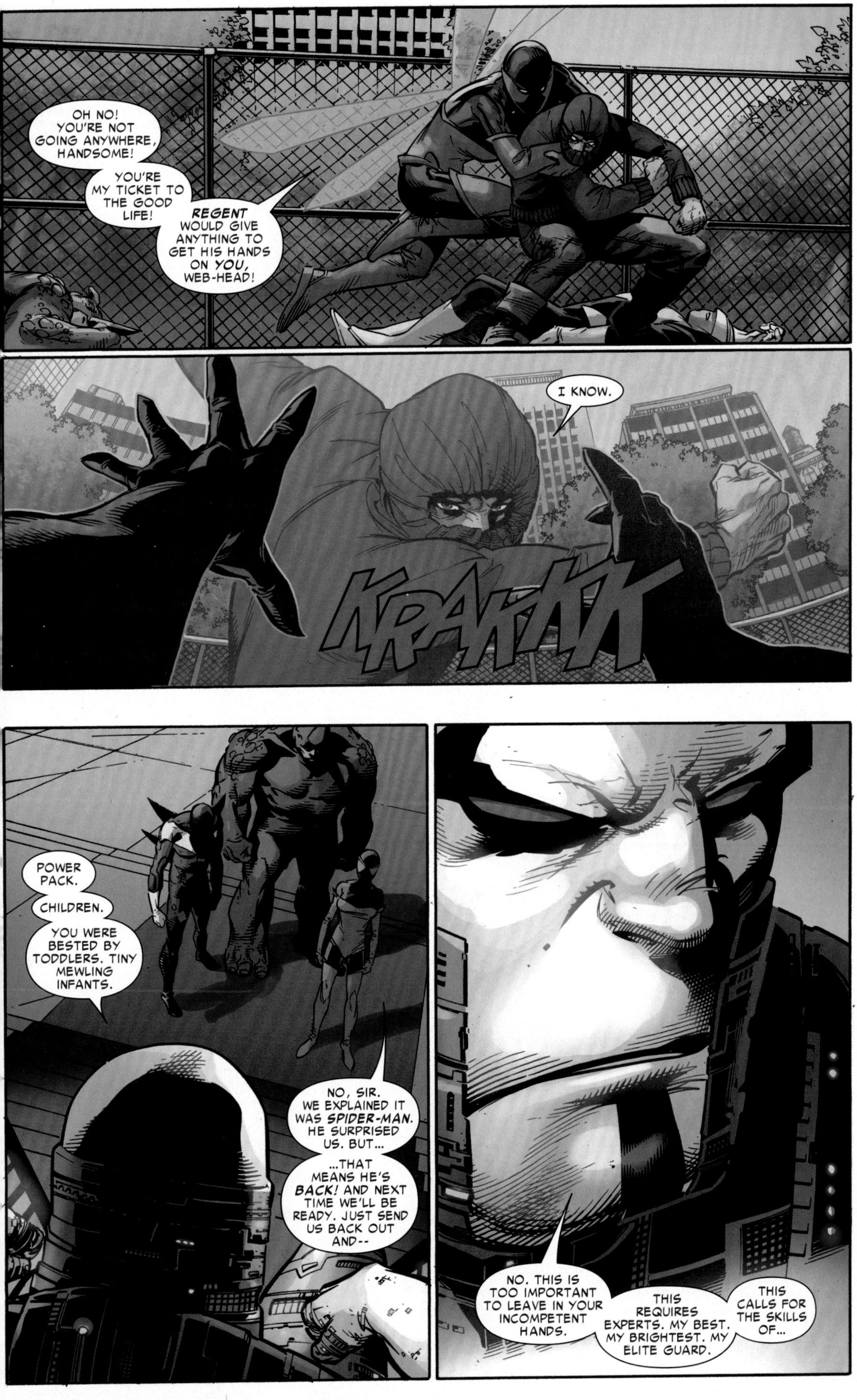
OH NO! YOU'RE NOT GOING ANYWHERE, HANDSOME!
YOU'RE MY TICKET TO THE GOOD LIFE!
REGENT WOULD GIVE ANYTHING TO GET HIS HANDS ON YOU, WEB-HEAD!
I KNOW.
KRAKAKK
POWER PACK.
CHILDREN.
YOU WERE BESTED BY TODDLERS. TINY MEWLING INFANTS.
NO, SIR. WE EXPLAINED IT WAS SPIDER-MAN. HE SURPRISED US. BUT...
...THAT MEANS HE'S BACK! AND NEXT TIME WE'LL BE READY. JUST SEND US BACK OUT AND--
NO. THIS IS TOO IMPORTANT TO LEAVE IN YOUR INCOMPETENT HANDS.
THIS REQUIRES EXPERTS. MY BEST. MY BRIGHTEST. MY ELITE GUARD.
THIS CALLS FOR THE SKILLS OF...

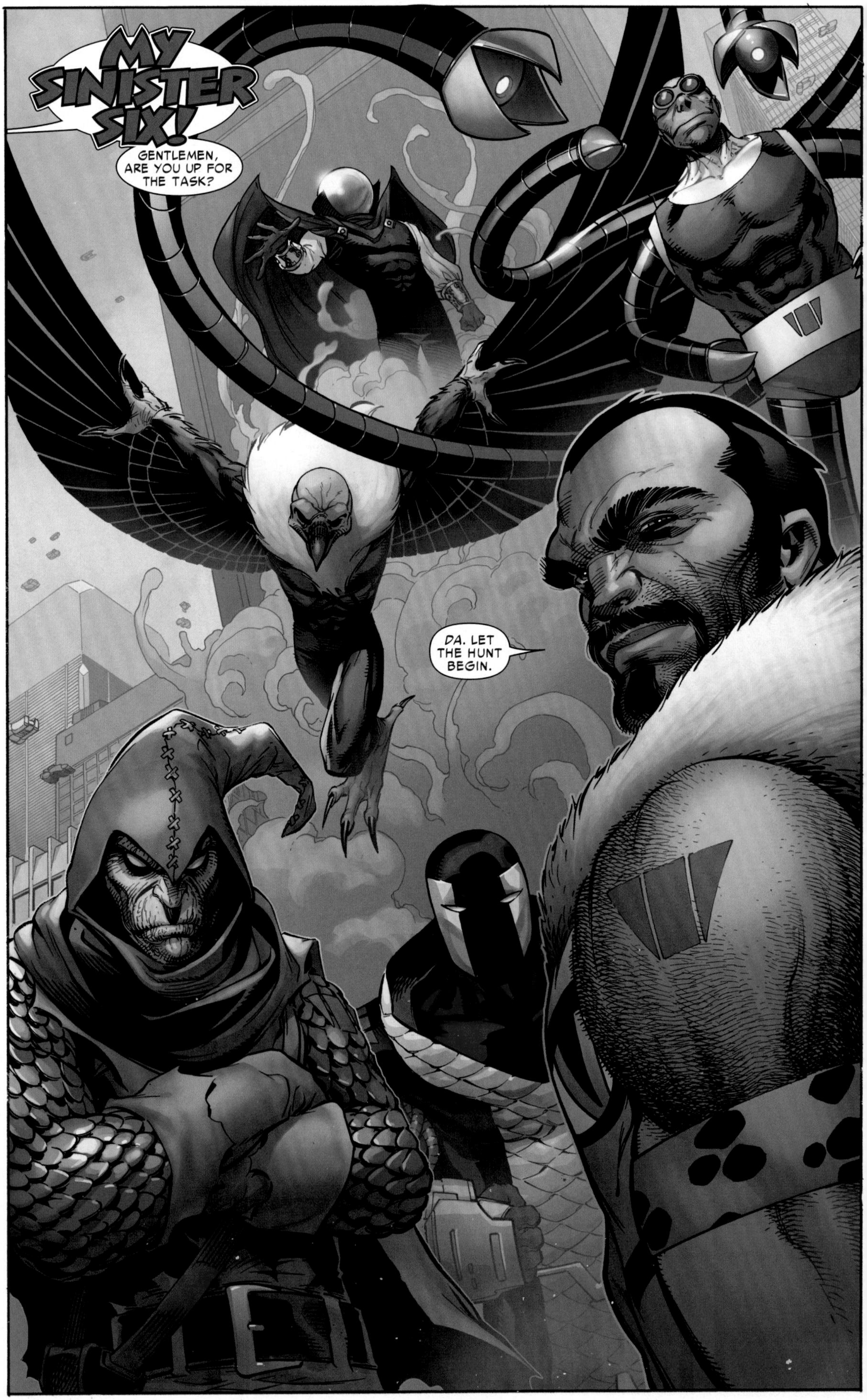
MY SINISTER SIX!
GENTLEMEN, ARE YOU UP FOR THE TASK?
DA. LET THE HUNT BEGIN.

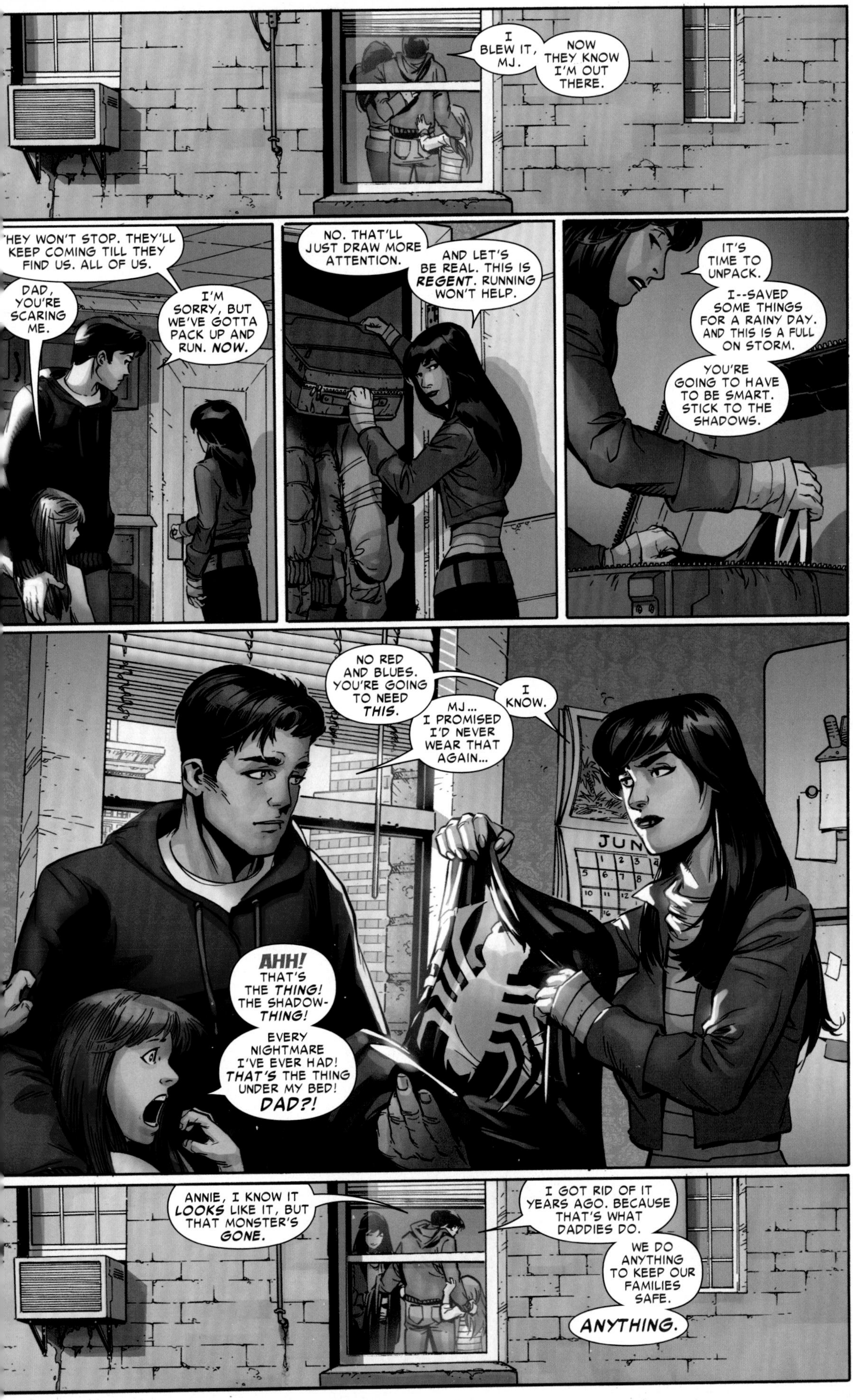

I BLEW IT, MJ.
NOW THEY KNOW I'M OUT THERE.
THEY WON'T STOP. THEY'LL KEEP COMING TILL THEY FIND US. ALL OF US.
DAD, YOU'RE SCARING ME.
I'M SORRY, BUT WE'VE GOTTA PACK UP AND RUN. NOW.
NO. THAT'LL JUST DRAW MORE ATTENTION.
AND LET'S BE REAL. THIS IS REGENT. RUNNING WON'T HELP.
IT'S TIME TO UNPACK.
I--SAVED SOME THINGS FOR A RAINY DAY. AND THIS IS A FULL ON STORM.
YOU'RE GOING TO HAVE TO BE SMART. STICK TO THE SHADOWS.
NO RED AND BLUES. YOU'RE GOING TO NEED THIS.
I KNOW.
MJ... I PROMISED I'D NEVER WEAR THAT AGAIN...
AHH! THAT'S THE THING! THE SHADOW-THING!
EVERY NIGHTMARE I'VE EVER HAD! THAT'S THE THING UNDER MY BED! DAD?!
ANNIE, I KNOW IT LOOKS LIKE IT, BUT THAT MONSTER'S GONE.
I GOT RID OF IT YEARS AGO. BECAUSE THAT'S WHAT DADDIES DO.
WE DO ANYTHING TO KEEP OUR FAMILIES SAFE.
ANYTHING.

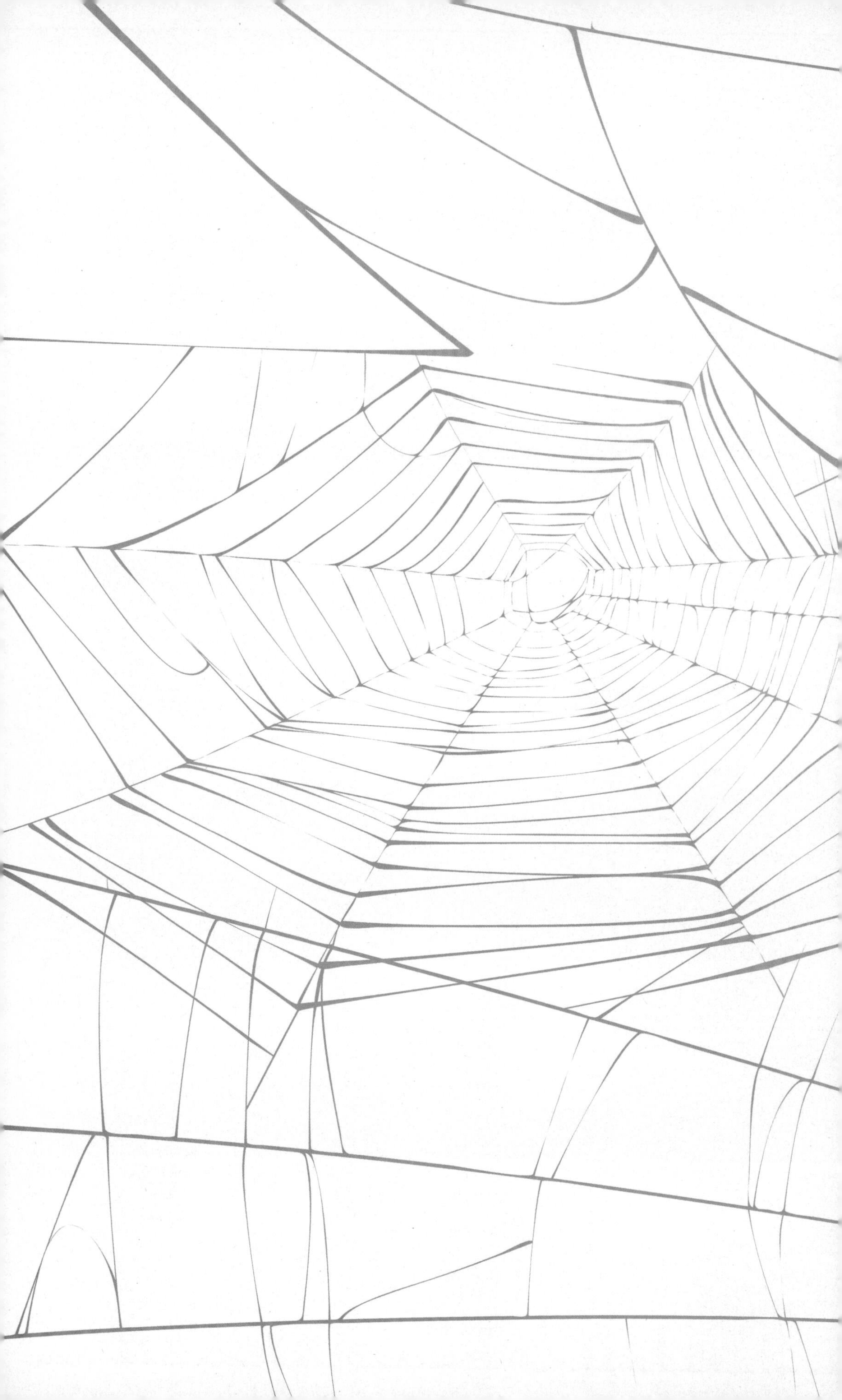

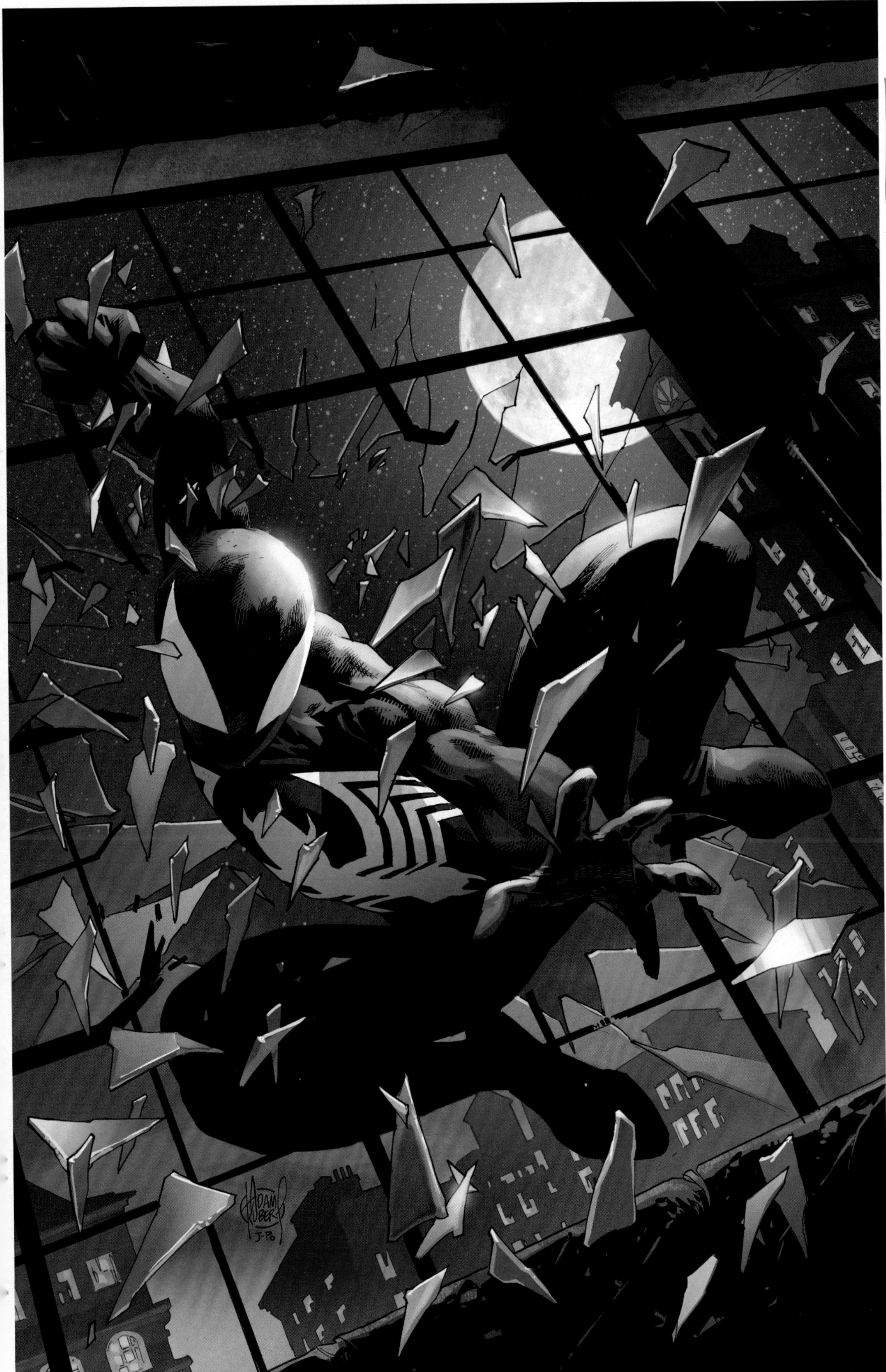

RENEW YOUR VOWS PART 3

"CALLING A FAMILY MEETING"

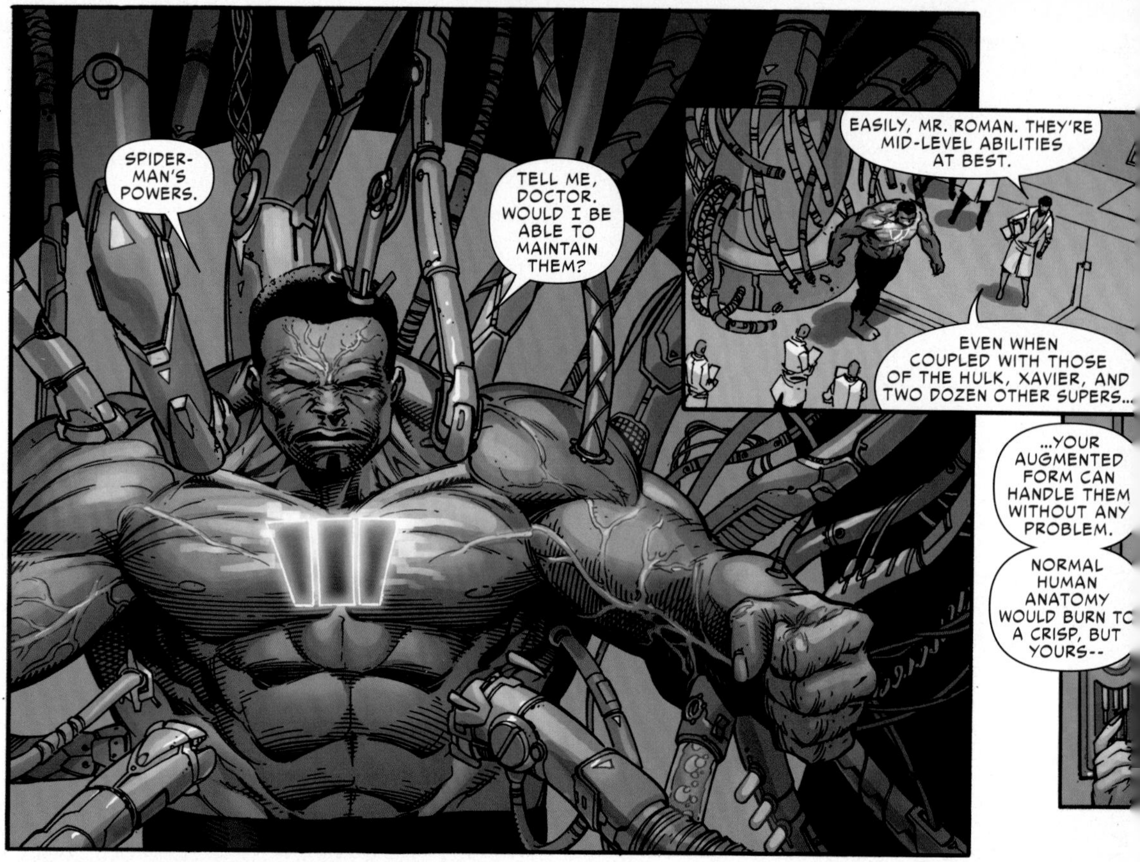
SPIDER-MAN'S POWERS.
TELL ME, DOCTOR. WOULD I BE ABLE TO MAINTAIN THEM?
EASILY, MR. ROMAN. THEY'RE MID-LEVEL ABILITIES AT BEST.
EVEN WHEN COUPLED WITH THOSE OF THE HULK, XAVIER, AND TWO DOZEN OTHER SUPERS...
...YOUR AUGMENTED FORM CAN HANDLE THEM WITHOUT ANY PROBLEM.
NORMAL HUMAN ANATOMY WOULD BURN TO A CRISP, BUT YOURS--

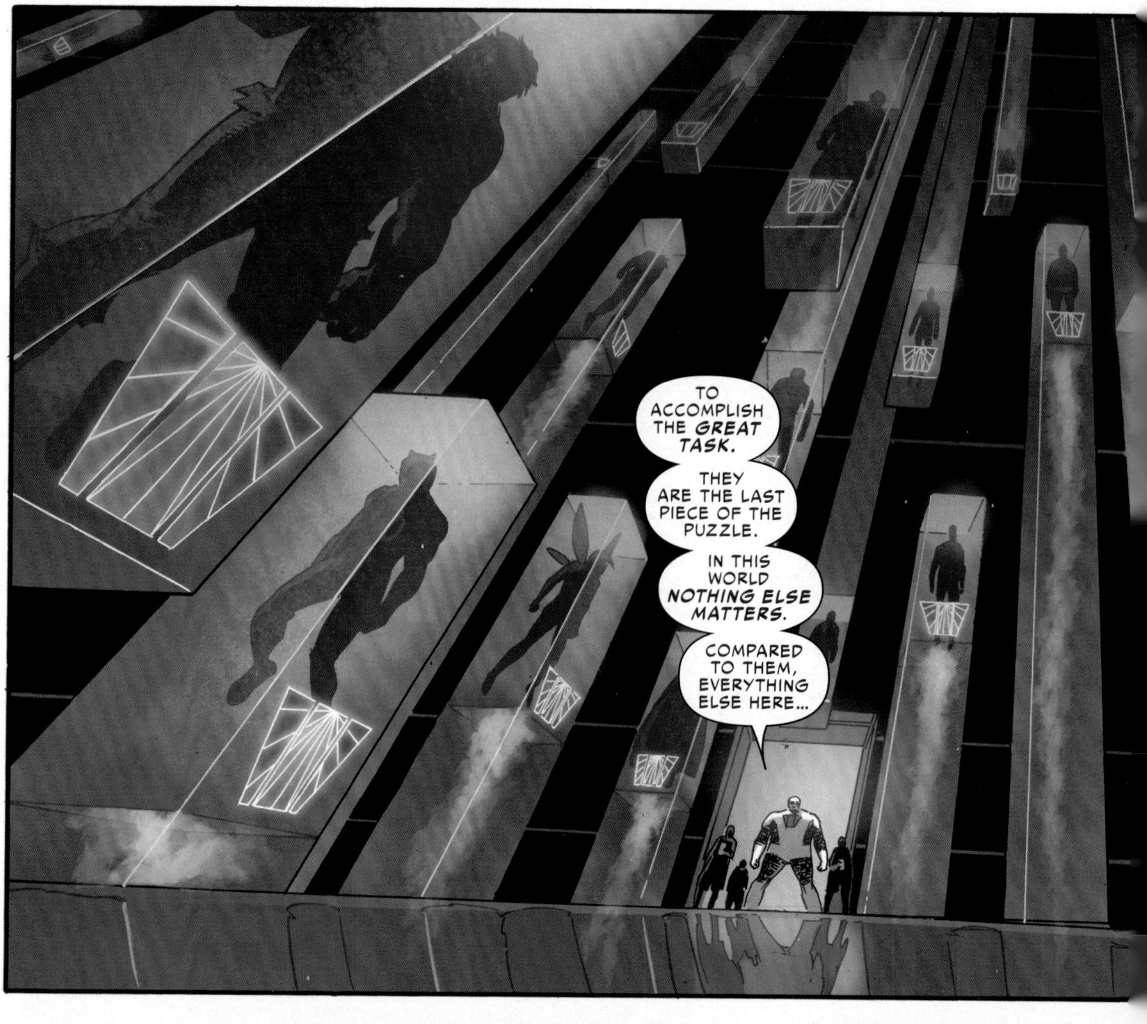
TO ACCOMPLISH THE GREAT TASK.
THEY ARE THE LAST PIECE OF THE PUZZLE.
IN THIS WORLD NOTHING ELSE MATTERS.
COMPARED TO THEM, EVERYTHING ELSE HERE...

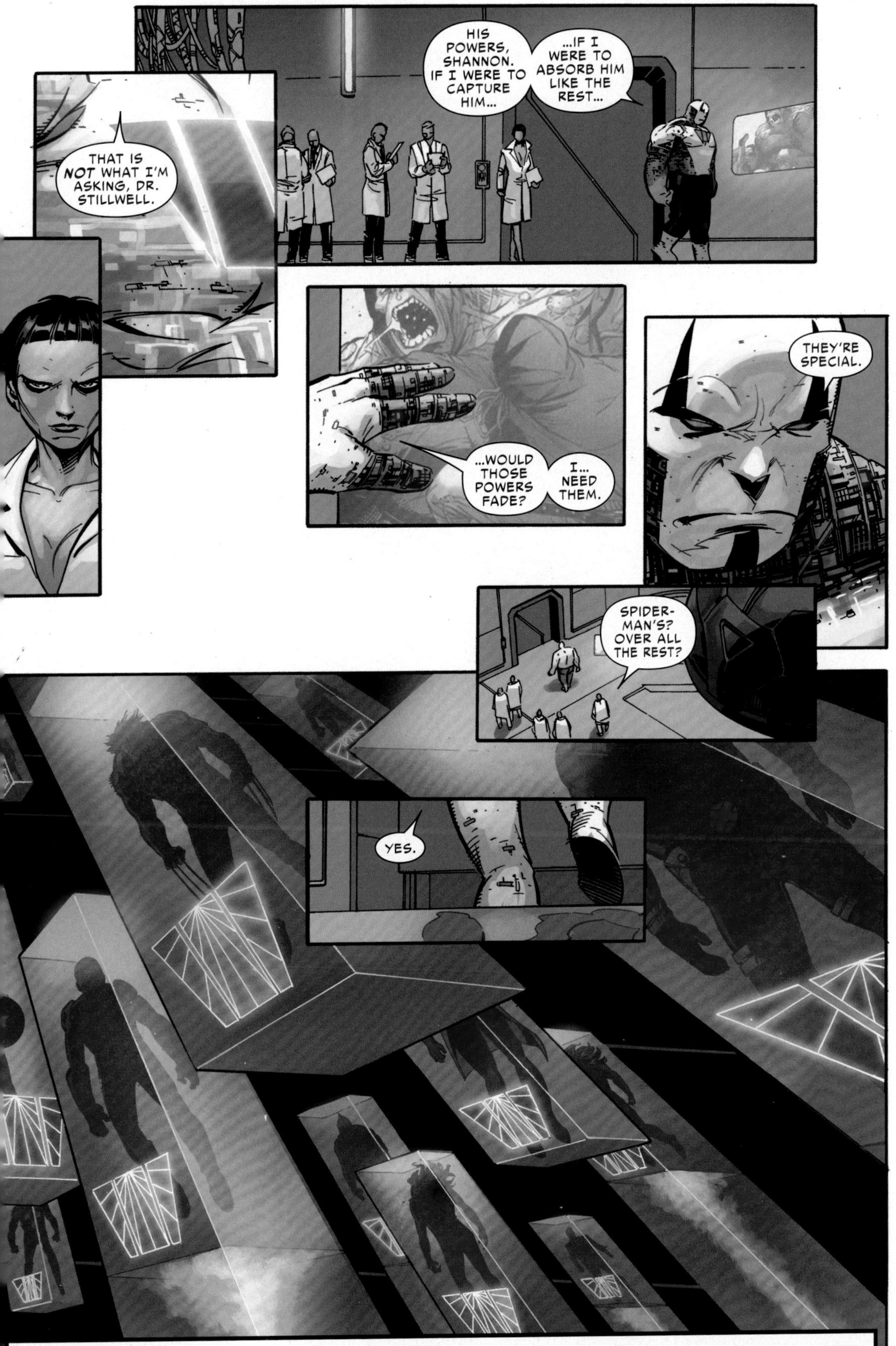
HIS POWERS, SHANNON. IF I WERE TO CAPTURE HIM...
...IF I WERE TO ABSORB HIM LIKE THE REST...
THAT IS NOT WHAT I'M ASKING, DR. STILLWELL.
...WOULD THOSE POWERS FADE?
I... NEED THEM.
THEY'RE SPECIAL.
SPIDER-MAN'S? OVER ALL THE REST?
YES.

"Calling a Family Meeting"

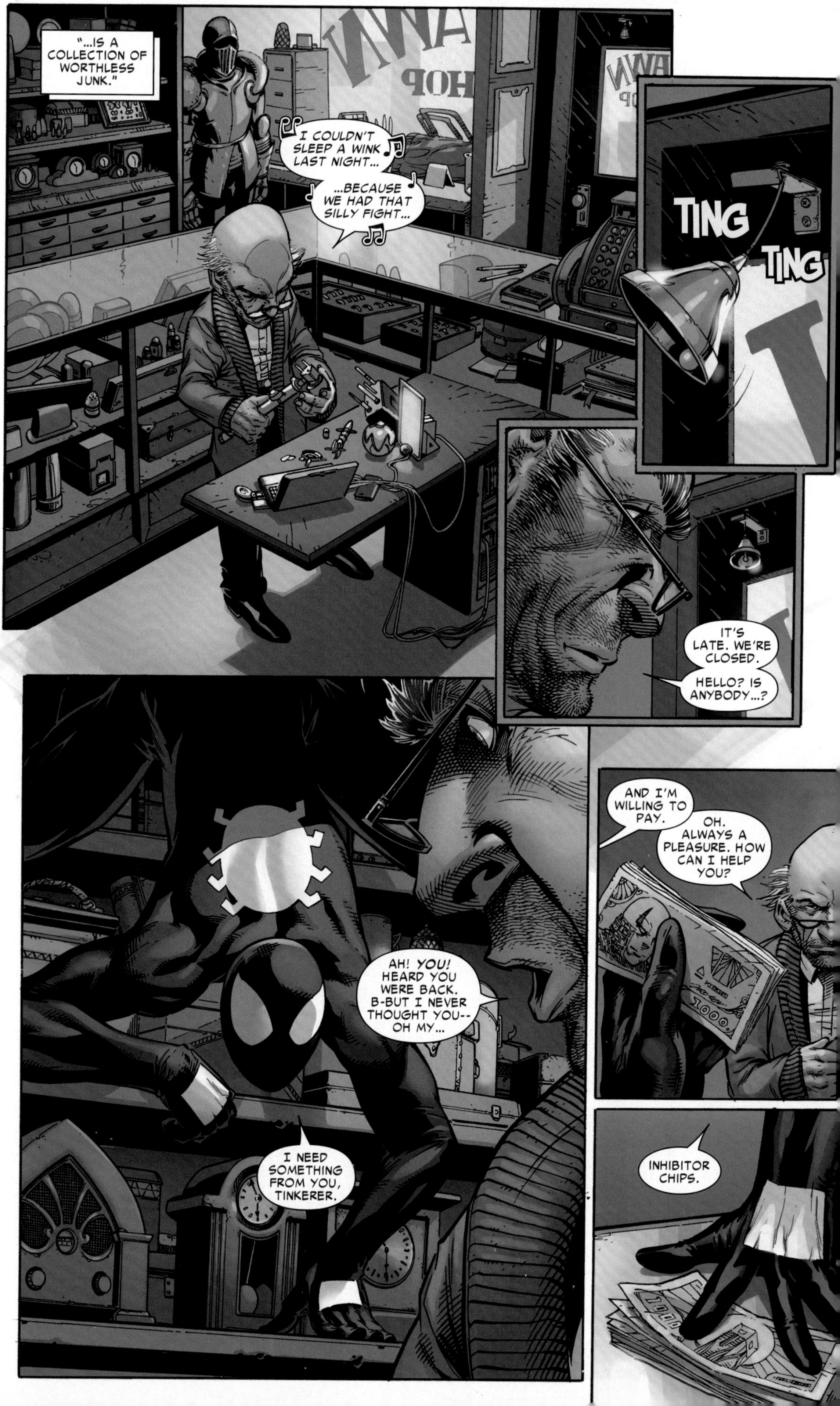
"...IS A COLLECTION OF WORTHLESS JUNK."
I COULDN'T SLEEP A WINK LAST NIGHT...
...BECAUSE WE HAD THAT SILLY FIGHT...
TING
TING
IT'S LATE. WE'RE CLOSED.
HELLO? IS ANYBODY...?
AH! YOU! HEARD YOU WERE BACK. B-BUT I NEVER THOUGHT YOU-- OH MY...
I NEED SOMETHING FROM YOU, TINKERER.
AND I'M WILLING TO PAY.
OH. ALWAYS A PLEASURE. HOW CAN I HELP YOU?
INHIBITOR CHIPS.

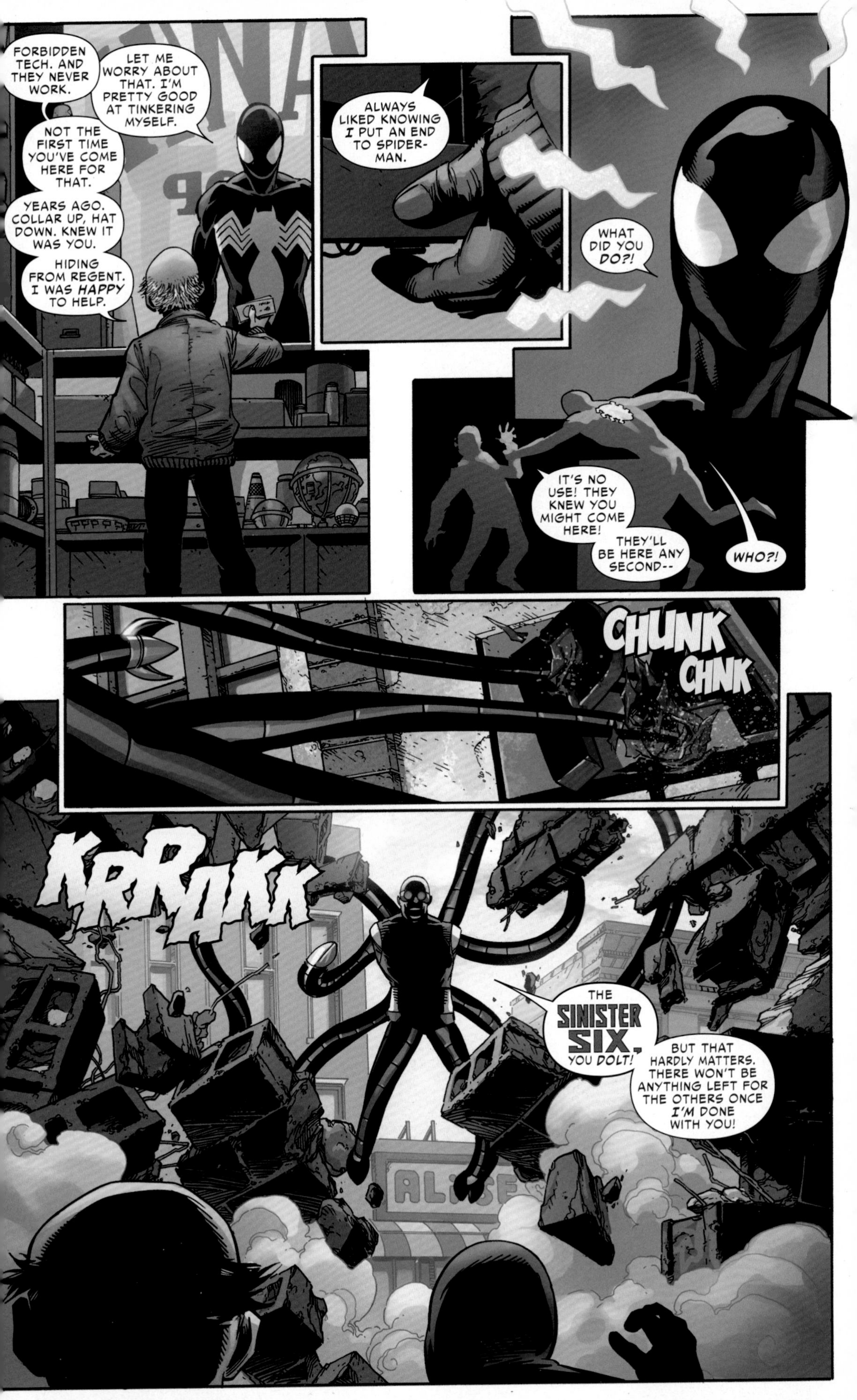

FORBIDDEN TECH. AND THEY NEVER WORK.
LET ME WORRY ABOUT THAT. I'M PRETTY GOOD AT TINKERING MYSELF.
NOT THE FIRST TIME YOU'VE COME HERE FOR THAT.
YEARS AGO. COLLAR UP, HAT DOWN. KNEW IT WAS YOU.
HIDING FROM REGENT. I WAS HAPPY TO HELP.
ALWAYS LIKED KNOWING I PUT AN END TO SPIDER-MAN.
WHAT DID YOU DO?!
IT'S NO USE! THEY KNEW YOU MIGHT COME HERE!
THEY'LL BE HERE ANY SECOND--
WHO?!
CHUNK
CHNK
KRRAKK
THE SINISTER SIX, YOU DOLT!
BUT THAT HARDLY MATTERS. THERE WON'T BE ANYTHING LEFT FOR THE OTHERS ONCE I'M DONE WITH YOU!

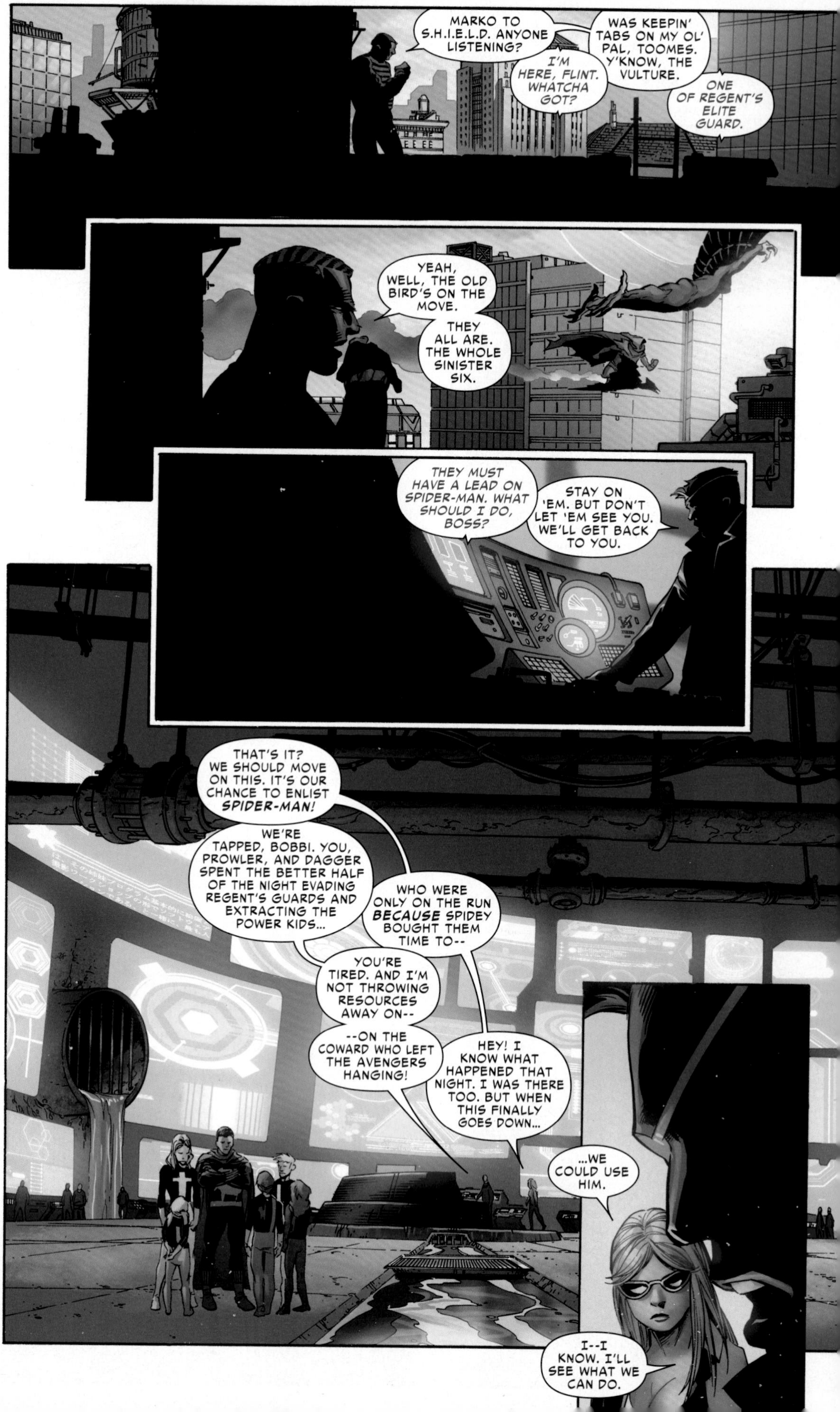
MARKO TO S.H.I.E.L.D. ANYONE LISTENING?
I'M HERE, FLINT. WHATCHA GOT?
WAS KEEPIN' TABS ON MY OL' PAL, TOOMES. Y'KNOW, THE VULTURE.
ONE OF REGENT'S ELITE GUARD.
YEAH, WELL, THE OLD BIRD'S ON THE MOVE.
THEY ALL ARE. THE WHOLE SINISTER SIX.
THEY MUST HAVE A LEAD ON SPIDER-MAN. WHAT SHOULD I DO, BOSS?
STAY ON 'EM. BUT DON'T LET 'EM SEE YOU. WE'LL GET BACK TO YOU.
THAT'S IT? WE SHOULD MOVE ON THIS. IT'S OUR CHANCE TO ENLIST SPIDER-MAN!
WE'RE TAPPED, BOBBI. YOU, PROWLER, AND DAGGER SPENT THE BETTER HALF OF THE NIGHT EVADING REGENT'S GUARDS AND EXTRACTING THE POWER KIDS...
WHO WERE ONLY ON THE RUN BECAUSE SPIDEY BOUGHT THEM TIME TO--
YOU'RE TIRED. AND I'M NOT THROWING RESOURCES AWAY ON--
--ON THE COWARD WHO LEFT THE AVENGERS HANGING!
HEY! I KNOW WHAT HAPPENED THAT NIGHT. I WAS THERE TOO. BUT WHEN THIS FINALLY GOES DOWN...
...WE COULD USE HIM.
I--I KNOW. I'LL SEE WHAT WE CAN DO.

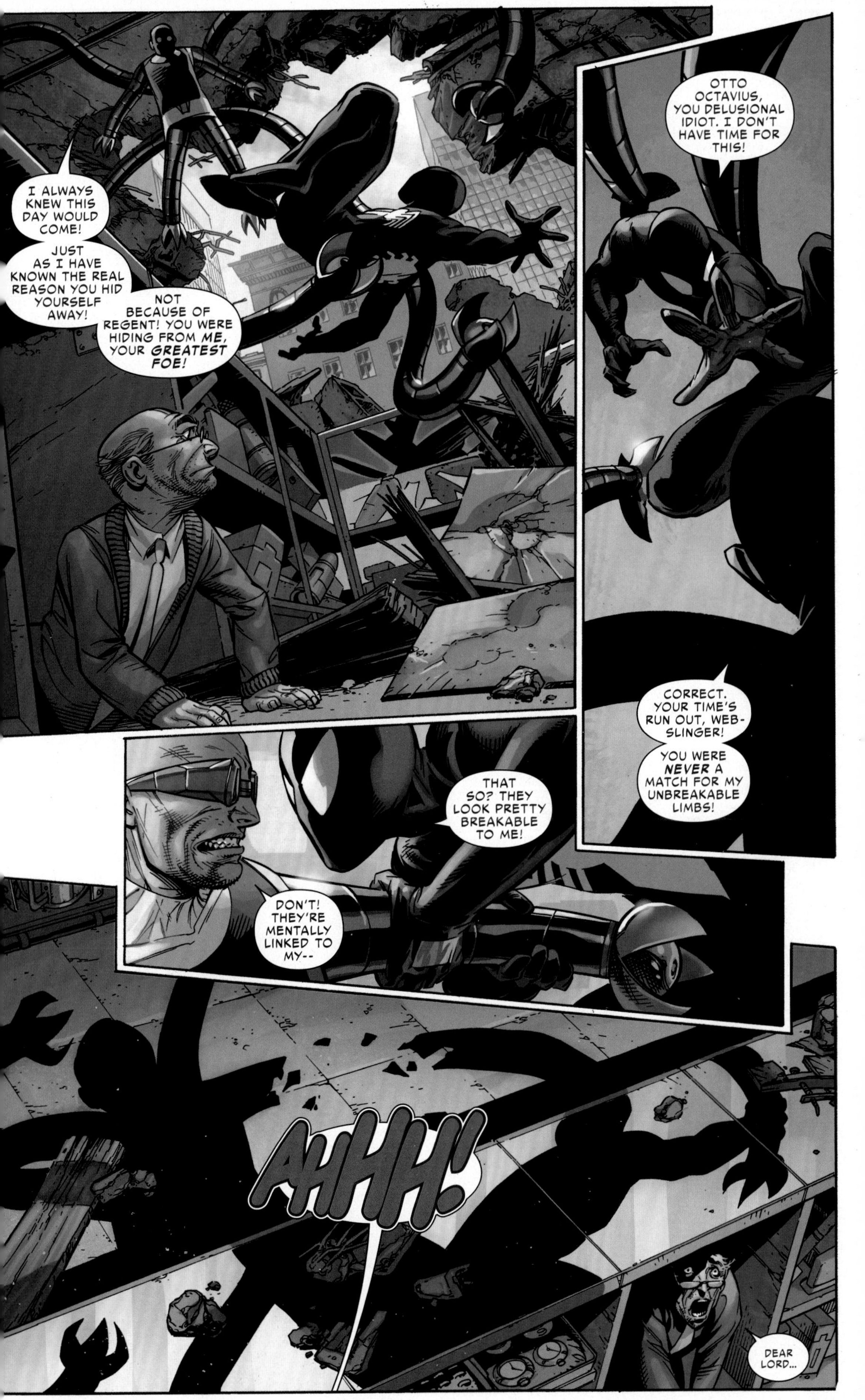
I ALWAYS KNEW THIS DAY WOULD COME!
JUST AS I HAVE KNOWN THE REAL REASON YOU HID YOURSELF AWAY!
NOT BECAUSE OF REGENT! YOU WERE HIDING FROM ME, YOUR GREATEST FOE!
OTTO OCTAVIUS, YOU DELUSIONAL IDIOT. I DON'T HAVE TIME FOR THIS!
CORRECT. YOUR TIME'S RUN OUT, WEB-SLINGER!
YOU WERE NEVER A MATCH FOR MY UNBREAKABLE LIMBS!
THAT SO? THEY LOOK PRETTY BREAKABLE TO ME!
DON'T! THEY'RE MENTALLY LINKED TO MY--
AHHH!
DEAR LORD...

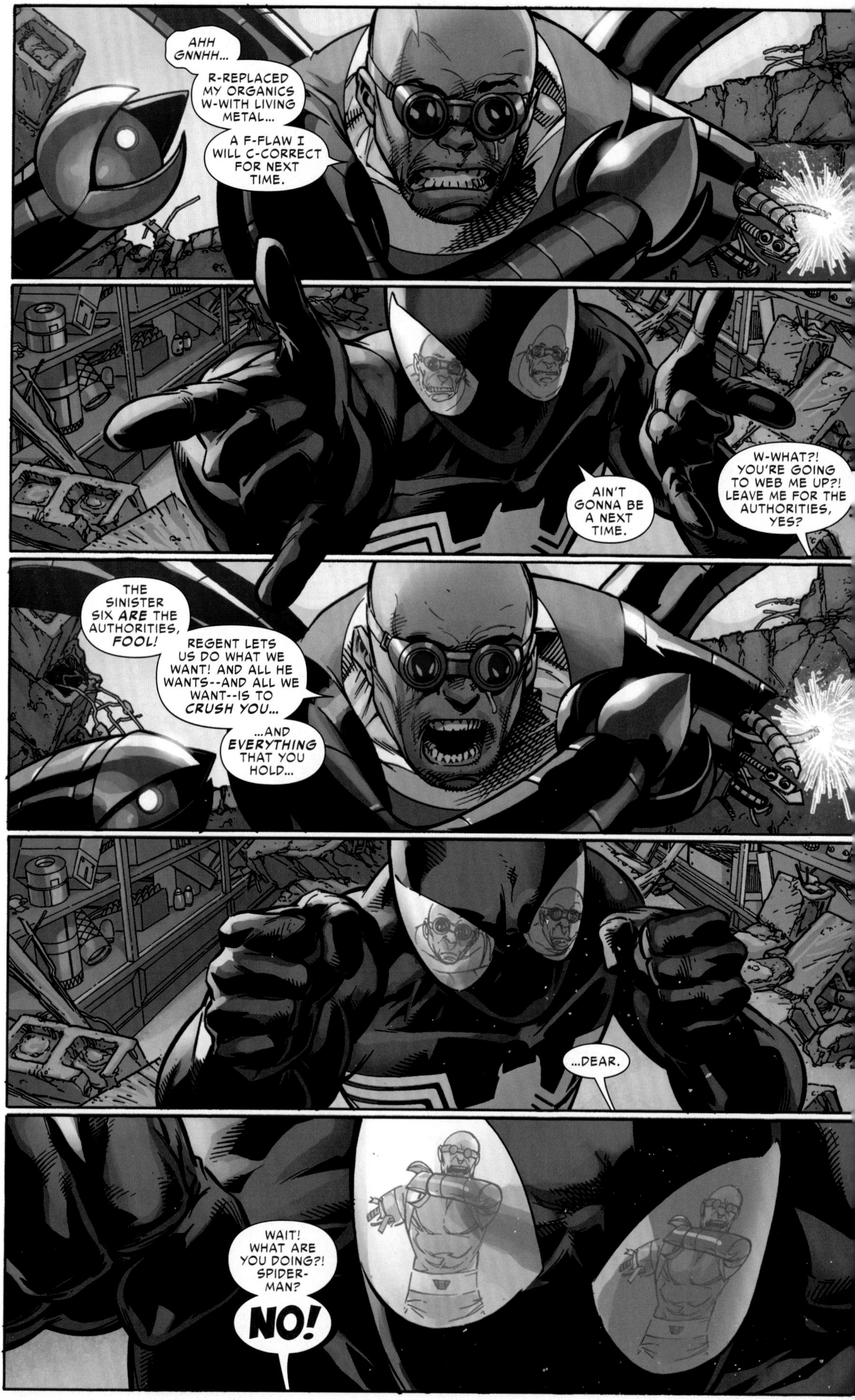
AHH GNNHH...
R-REPLACED MY ORGANICS W-WITH LIVING METAL...
A F-FLAW I WILL C-CORRECT FOR NEXT TIME.
AIN'T GONNA BE A NEXT TIME.
W-WHAT?! YOU'RE GOING TO WEB ME UP?! LEAVE ME FOR THE AUTHORITIES, YES?
THE SINISTER SIX ARE THE AUTHORITIES, FOOL!
REGENT LETS US DO WHAT WE WANT! AND ALL HE WANTS--AND ALL WE WANT--IS TO CRUSH YOU...
...AND EVERYTHING THAT YOU HOLD...
...DEAR.
WAIT! WHAT ARE YOU DOING?! SPIDER-MAN?
NO!

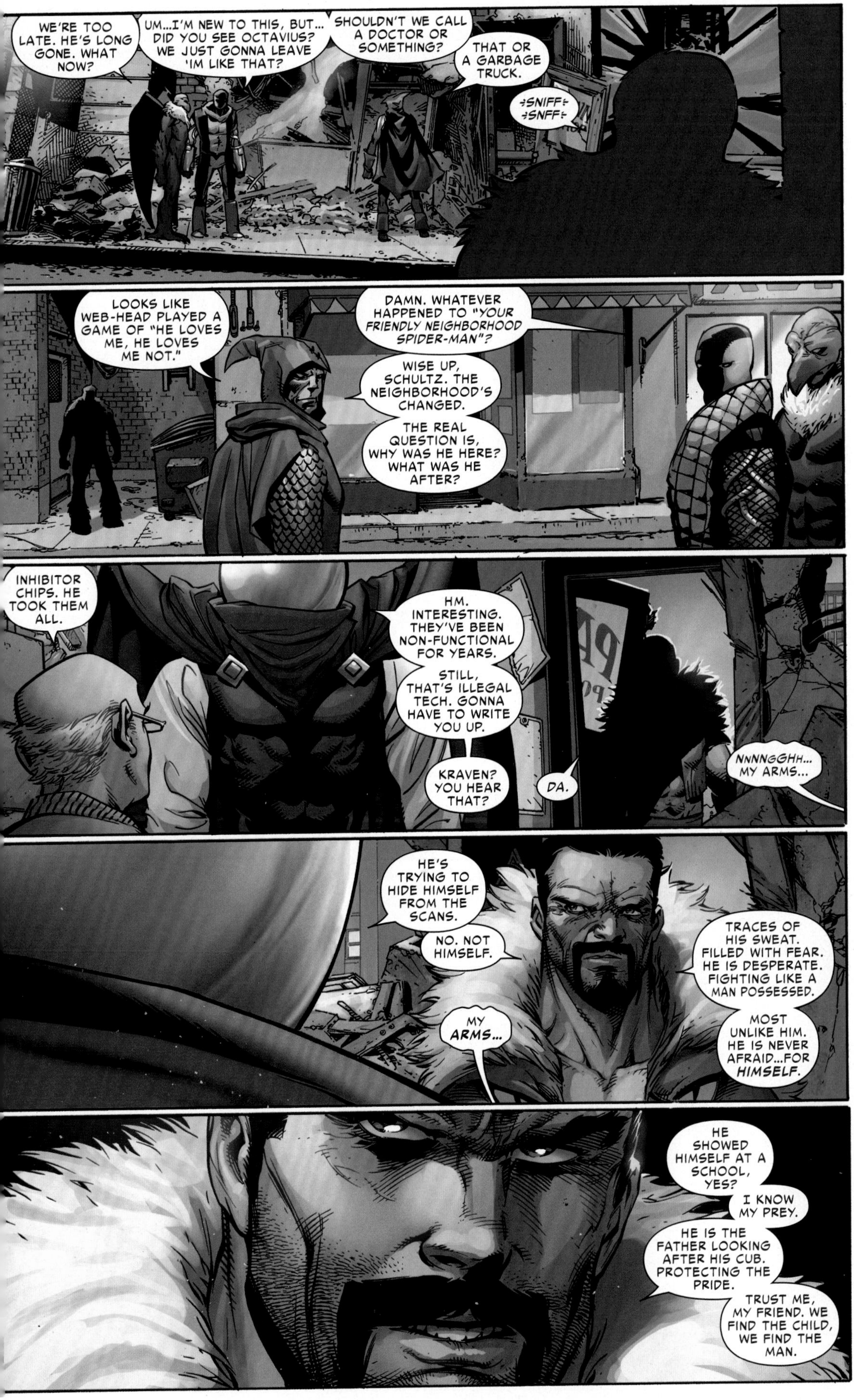

WE'RE TOO LATE. HE'S LONG GONE. WHAT NOW?
UM...I'M NEW TO THIS, BUT... DID YOU SEE OCTAVIUS? WE JUST GONNA LEAVE 'IM LIKE THAT?
SHOULDN'T WE CALL A DOCTOR OR SOMETHING?
THAT OR A GARBAGE TRUCK.
SNIFF SNFF
LOOKS LIKE WEB-HEAD PLAYED A GAME OF "HE LOVES ME, HE LOVES ME NOT."
DAMN. WHATEVER HAPPENED TO "YOUR FRIENDLY NEIGHBORHOOD SPIDER-MAN"?
WISE UP, SCHULTZ. THE NEIGHBORHOOD'S CHANGED.
THE REAL QUESTION IS, WHY WAS HE HERE? WHAT WAS HE AFTER?
INHIBITOR CHIPS. HE TOOK THEM ALL.
HM. INTERESTING. THEY'VE BEEN NON-FUNCTIONAL FOR YEARS.
STILL, THAT'S ILLEGAL TECH. GONNA HAVE TO WRITE YOU UP.
KRAVEN? YOU HEAR THAT?
DA.
NNNNGGHH... MY ARMS...
HE'S TRYING TO HIDE HIMSELF FROM THE SCANS.
NO. NOT HIMSELF.
TRACES OF HIS SWEAT. FILLED WITH FEAR. HE IS DESPERATE. FIGHTING LIKE A MAN POSSESSED.
MY ARMS...
MOST UNLIKE HIM. HE IS NEVER AFRAID...FOR HIMSELF.
HE SHOWED HIMSELF AT A SCHOOL, YES?
I KNOW MY PREY.
HE IS THE FATHER LOOKING AFTER HIS CUB. PROTECTING THE PRIDE.
TRUST ME, MY FRIEND. WE FIND THE CHILD, WE FIND THE MAN.

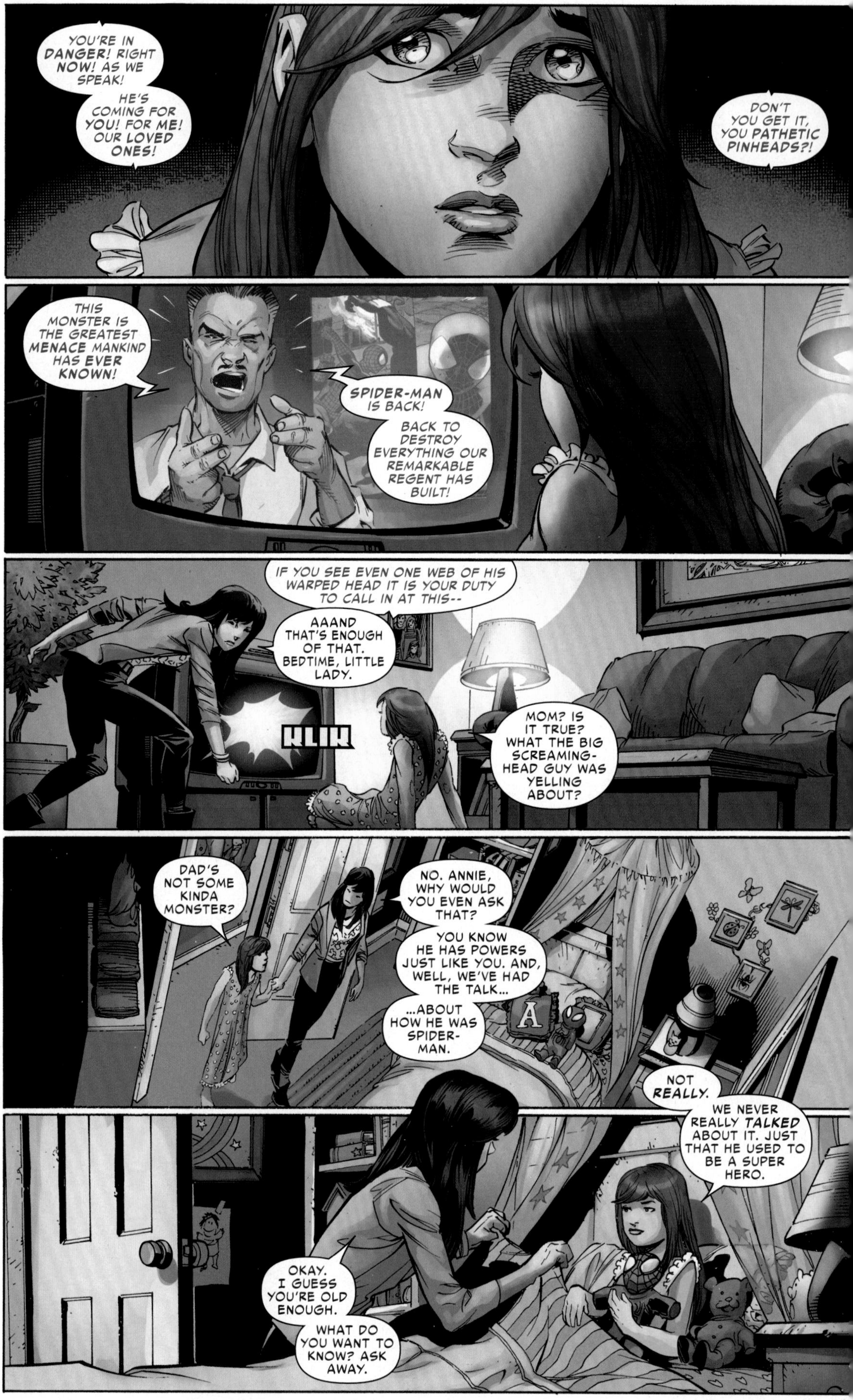

YOU'RE IN DANGER! RIGHT NOW! AS WE SPEAK!
HE'S COMING FOR YOU! FOR ME! OUR LOVED ONES!
DON'T YOU GET IT, YOU PATHETIC PINHEADS?!
THIS MONSTER IS THE GREATEST MENACE MANKIND HAS EVER KNOWN!
SPIDER-MAN IS BACK!
BACK TO DESTROY EVERYTHING OUR REMARKABLE REGENT HAS BUILT!
IF YOU SEE EVEN ONE WEB OF HIS WARPED HEAD IT IS YOUR DUTY TO CALL IN AT THIS--
AAAND THAT'S ENOUGH OF THAT. BEDTIME, LITTLE LADY.
KLIK
MOM? IS IT TRUE? WHAT THE BIG SCREAMING-HEAD GUY WAS YELLING ABOUT?
DAD'S NOT SOME KINDA MONSTER?
NO. ANNIE, WHY WOULD YOU EVEN ASK THAT?
YOU KNOW HE HAS POWERS JUST LIKE YOU. AND, WELL, WE'VE HAD THE TALK...
...ABOUT HOW HE WAS SPIDER-MAN.
NOT REALLY.
WE NEVER REALLY TALKED ABOUT IT. JUST THAT HE USED TO BE A SUPER HERO.
OKAY. I GUESS YOU'RE OLD ENOUGH.
WHAT DO YOU WANT TO KNOW? ASK AWAY.

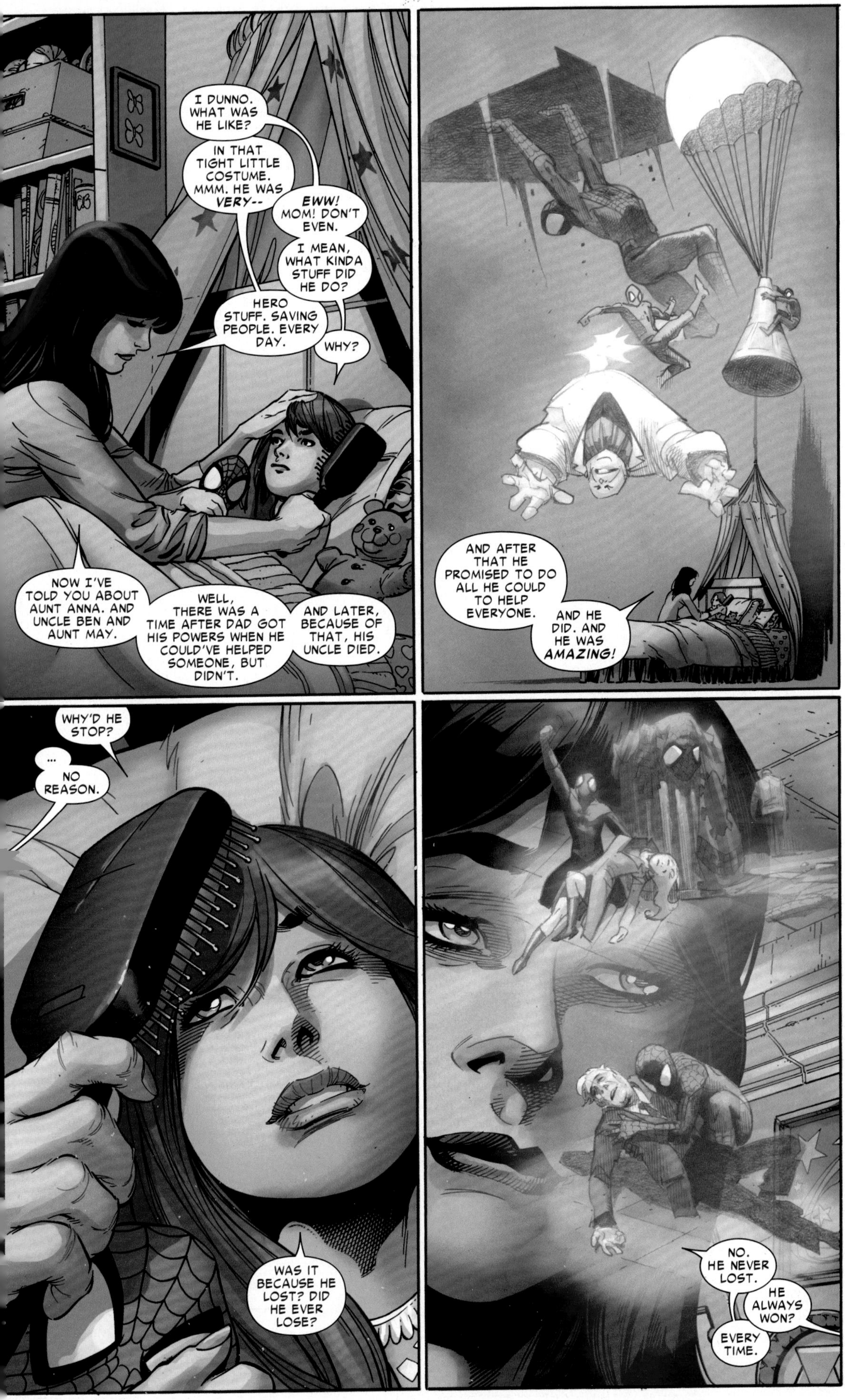
I DUNNO. WHAT WAS HE LIKE?
IN THAT TIGHT LITTLE COSTUME. MMM. HE WAS *VERY*--
EWW! MOM! DON'T EVEN.
I MEAN, WHAT KINDA STUFF DID HE DO?
HERO STUFF. SAVING PEOPLE. EVERY DAY.
WHY?
NOW I'VE TOLD YOU ABOUT AUNT ANNA. AND UNCLE BEN AND AUNT MAY.
WELL, THERE WAS A TIME AFTER DAD GOT HIS POWERS WHEN HE COULD'VE HELPED SOMEONE, BUT DIDN'T.
AND LATER, BECAUSE OF THAT, HIS UNCLE DIED.
AND AFTER THAT HE PROMISED TO DO ALL HE COULD TO HELP EVERYONE.
AND HE DID. AND HE WAS *AMAZING!*
WHY'D HE STOP?
... NO REASON.
WAS IT BECAUSE HE LOST? DID HE EVER LOSE?
NO. HE NEVER LOST.
HE ALWAYS WON?
EVERY TIME.

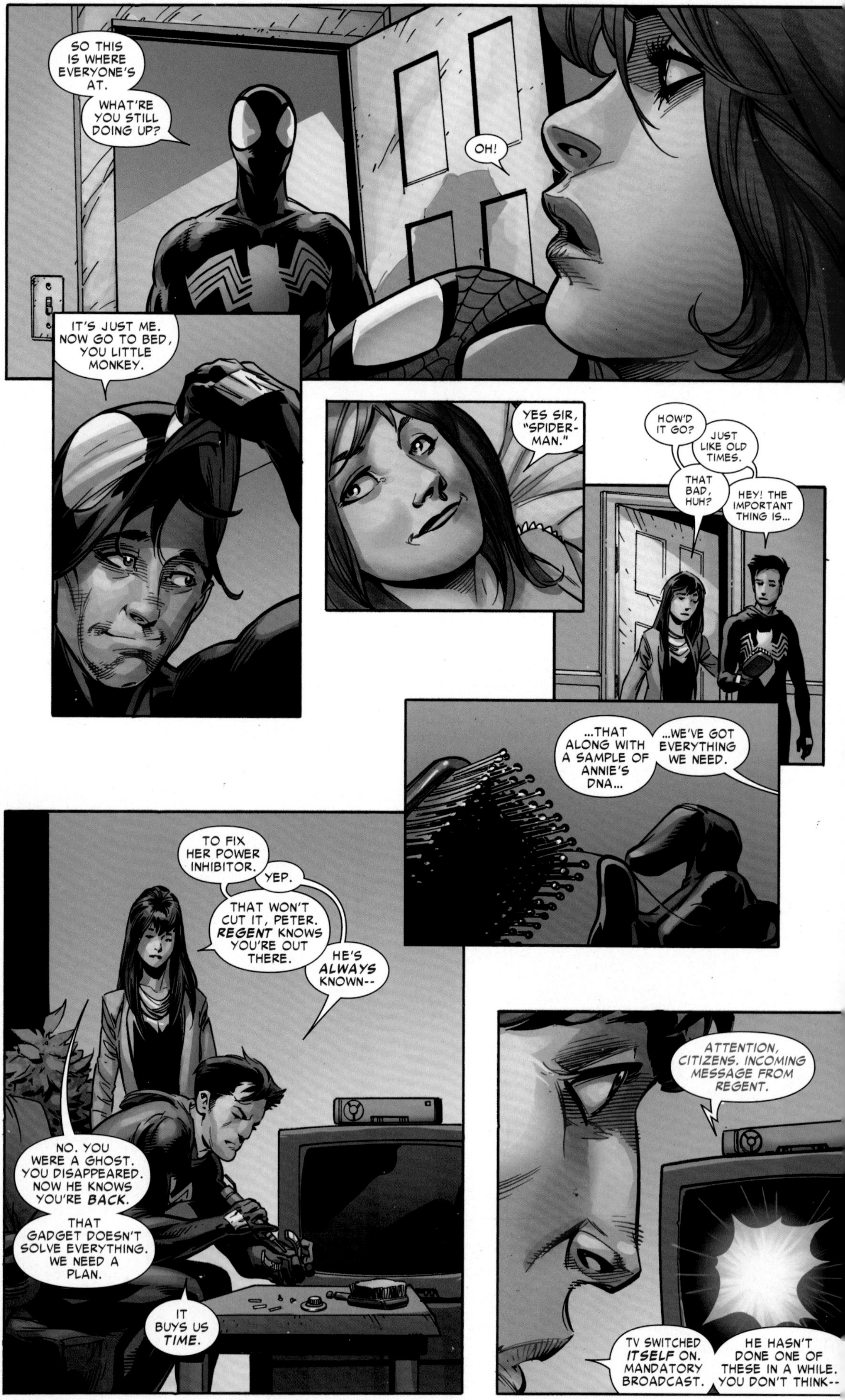
SO THIS IS WHERE EVERYONE'S AT.
WHAT'RE YOU STILL DOING UP?
OH!
IT'S JUST ME. NOW GO TO BED, YOU LITTLE MONKEY.
YES SIR, "SPIDER-MAN."
HOW'D IT GO?
JUST LIKE OLD TIMES.
THAT BAD, HUH?
HEY! THE IMPORTANT THING IS...
...THAT ALONG WITH A SAMPLE OF ANNIE'S DNA...
...WE'VE GOT EVERYTHING WE NEED.
TO FIX HER POWER INHIBITOR.
YEP.
THAT WON'T CUT IT, PETER. REGENT KNOWS YOU'RE OUT THERE.
HE'S ALWAYS KNOWN--
NO. YOU WERE A GHOST. YOU DISAPPEARED. NOW HE KNOWS YOU'RE BACK.
THAT GADGET DOESN'T SOLVE EVERYTHING. WE NEED A PLAN.
IT BUYS US TIME.
ATTENTION, CITIZENS. INCOMING MESSAGE FROM REGENT.
TV SWITCHED ITSELF ON. MANDATORY BROADCAST.
HE HASN'T DONE ONE OF THESE IN A WHILE. YOU DON'T THINK--

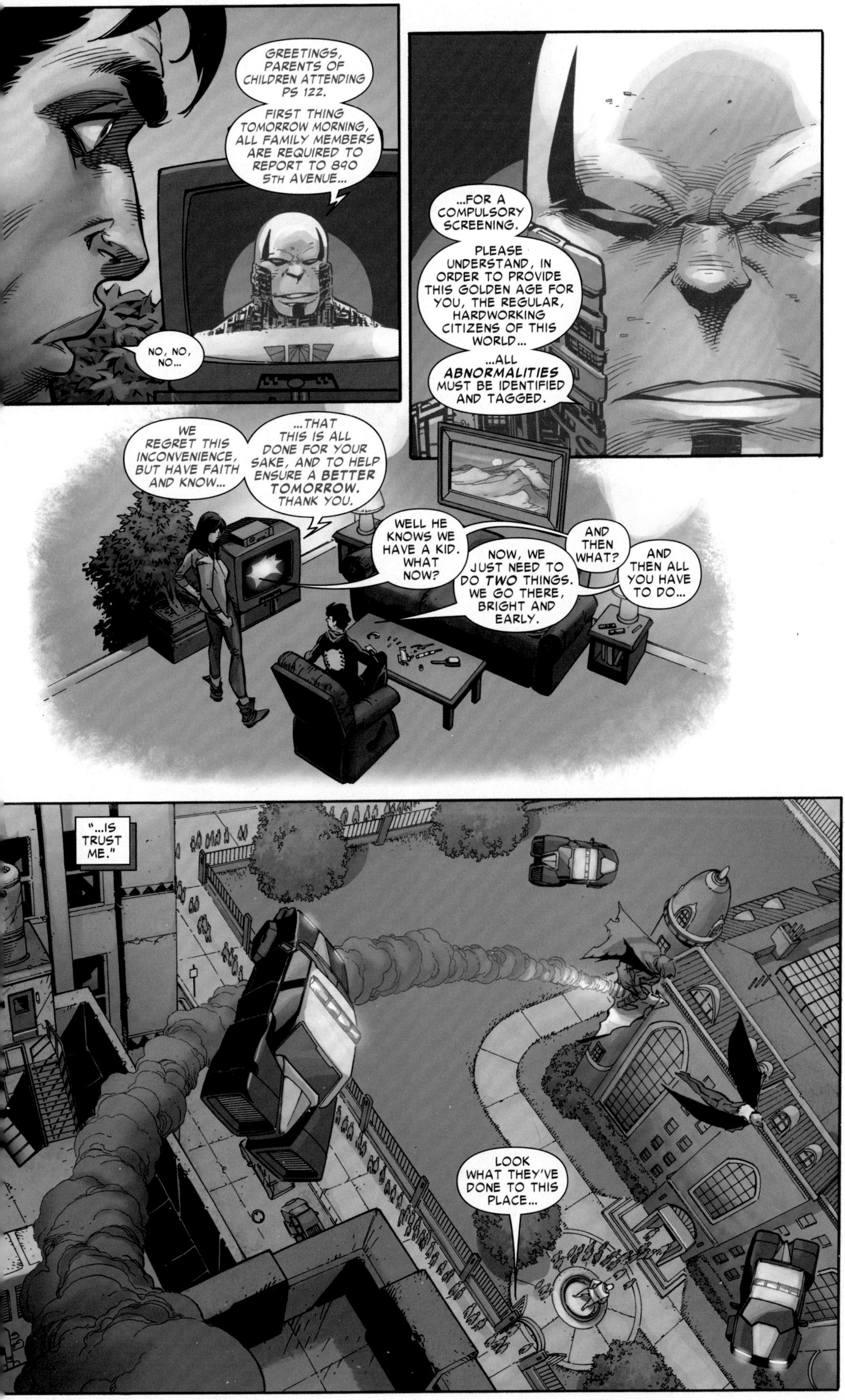
GREETINGS, PARENTS OF CHILDREN ATTENDING PS 122.
FIRST THING TOMORROW MORNING, ALL FAMILY MEMBERS ARE REQUIRED TO REPORT TO 890 5TH AVENUE...
NO, NO, NO...
...FOR A COMPULSORY SCREENING.
PLEASE UNDERSTAND, IN ORDER TO PROVIDE THIS GOLDEN AGE FOR YOU, THE REGULAR, HARDWORKING CITIZENS OF THIS WORLD...
...ALL ABNORMALITIES MUST BE IDENTIFIED AND TAGGED.
WE REGRET THIS INCONVENIENCE, BUT HAVE FAITH AND KNOW...
...THAT THIS IS ALL DONE FOR YOUR SAKE, AND TO HELP ENSURE A BETTER TOMORROW. THANK YOU.
WELL HE KNOWS WE HAVE A KID. WHAT NOW?
NOW, WE JUST NEED TO DO TWO THINGS. WE GO THERE, BRIGHT AND EARLY.
AND THEN WHAT?
AND THEN ALL YOU HAVE TO DO...
"...IS TRUST ME."
LOOK WHAT THEY'VE DONE TO THIS PLACE...

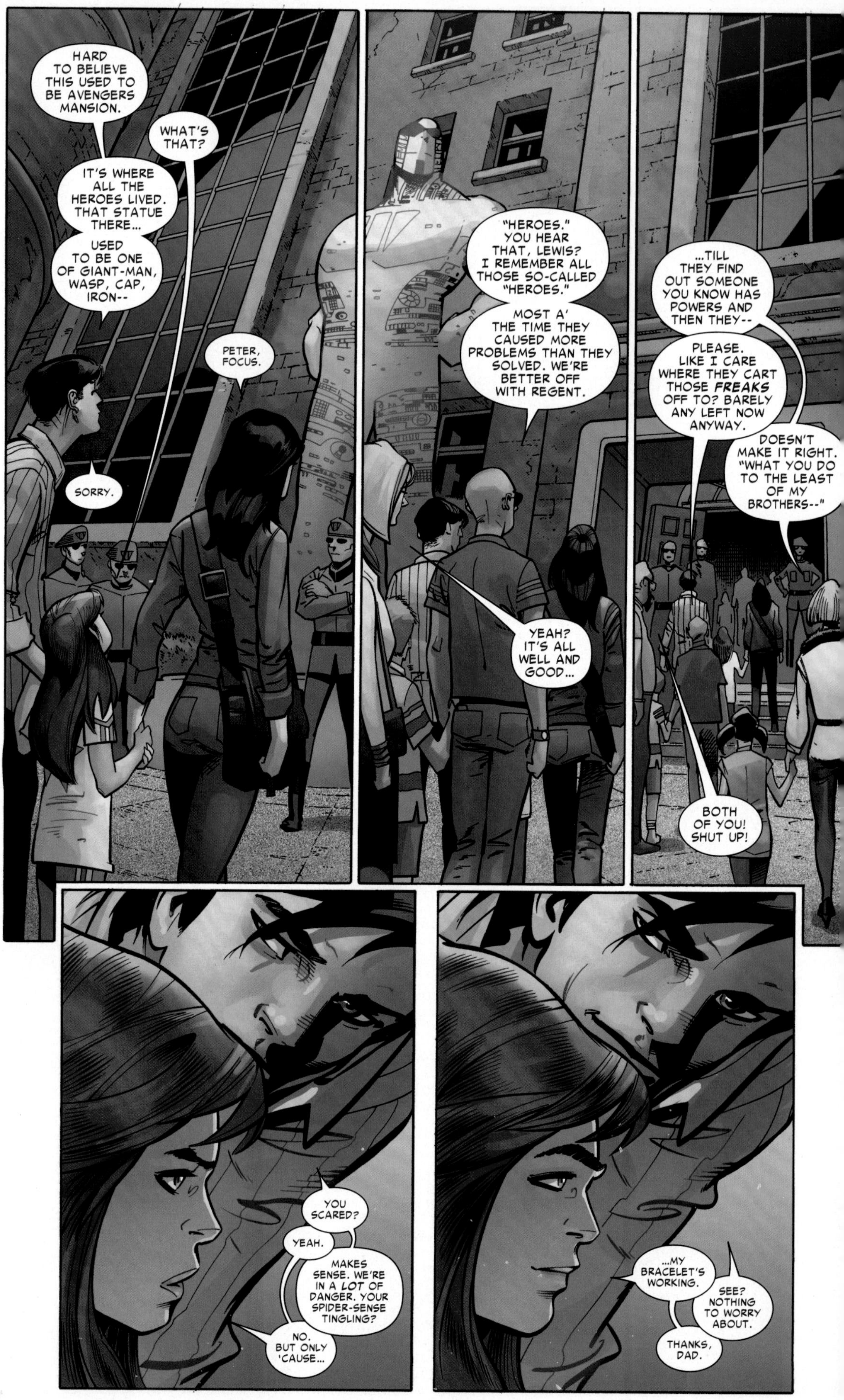
HARD TO BELIEVE THIS USED TO BE AVENGERS MANSION.
WHAT'S THAT?
IT'S WHERE ALL THE HEROES LIVED. THAT STATUE THERE...
USED TO BE ONE OF GIANT-MAN, WASP, CAP, IRON--
PETER, FOCUS.
SORRY.
"HEROES." YOU HEAR THAT, LEWIS? I REMEMBER ALL THOSE SO-CALLED "HEROES."
MOST A' THE TIME THEY CAUSED MORE PROBLEMS THAN THEY SOLVED. WE'RE BETTER OFF WITH REGENT.
YEAH? IT'S ALL WELL AND GOOD...
...TILL THEY FIND OUT SOMEONE YOU KNOW HAS POWERS AND THEN THEY--
PLEASE. LIKE I CARE WHERE THEY CART THOSE FREAKS OFF TO? BARELY ANY LEFT NOW ANYWAY.
DOESN'T MAKE IT RIGHT. "WHAT YOU DO TO THE LEAST OF MY BROTHERS--"
BOTH OF YOU! SHUT UP!
YOU SCARED?
YEAH.
MAKES SENSE. WE'RE IN A LOT OF DANGER. YOUR SPIDER-SENSE TINGLING?
NO. BUT ONLY 'CAUSE...
...MY BRACELET'S WORKING.
SEE? NOTHING TO WORRY ABOUT.
THANKS, DAD.

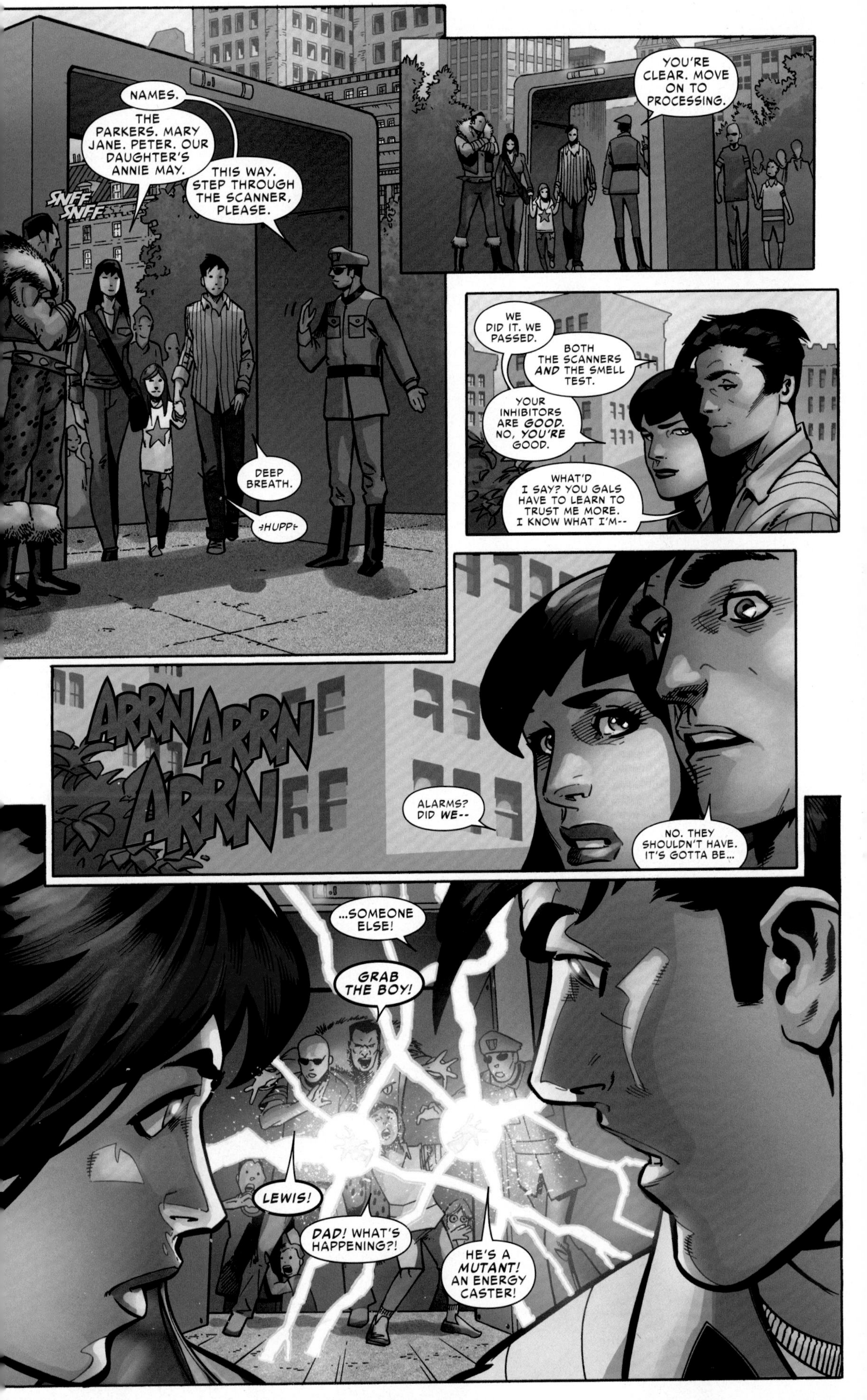
NAMES.
THE PARKERS. MARY JANE. PETER. OUR DAUGHTER'S ANNIE MAY.
THIS WAY. STEP THROUGH THE SCANNER, PLEASE.
SNFF SNFF
DEEP BREATH.
HUPP
YOU'RE CLEAR. MOVE ON TO PROCESSING.
WE DID IT. WE PASSED.
BOTH THE SCANNERS AND THE SMELL TEST.
YOUR INHIBITORS ARE GOOD. NO, YOU'RE GOOD.
WHAT'D I SAY? YOU GALS HAVE TO LEARN TO TRUST ME MORE. I KNOW WHAT I'M--
ARRN ARRN ARRN
ALARMS? DID WE--
NO. THEY SHOULDN'T HAVE. IT'S GOTTA BE...
...SOMEONE ELSE!
GRAB THE BOY!
LEWIS!
DAD! WHAT'S HAPPENING?!
HE'S A MUTANT! AN ENERGY CASTER!

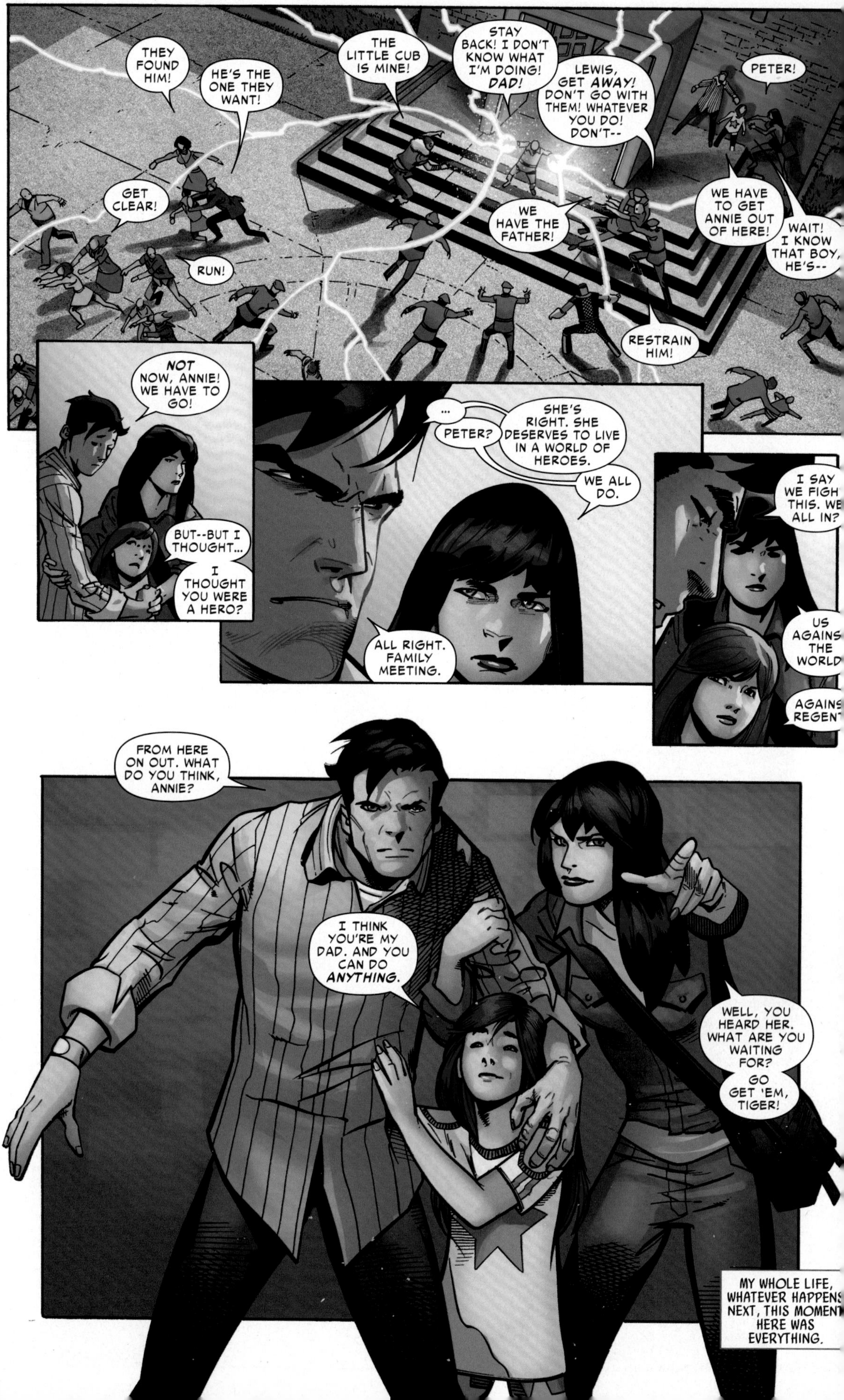

THEY FOUND HIM!
HE'S THE ONE THEY WANT!
THE LITTLE CUB IS MINE!
STAY BACK! I DON'T KNOW WHAT I'M DOING! DAD!
LEWIS, GET AWAY! DON'T GO WITH THEM! WHATEVER YOU DO! DON'T--
PETER!
GET CLEAR!
WE HAVE THE FATHER!
WE HAVE TO GET ANNIE OUT OF HERE!
WAIT! I KNOW THAT BOY, HE'S--
RUN!
RESTRAIN HIM!
NOT NOW, ANNIE! WE HAVE TO GO!
BUT--BUT I THOUGHT...
I THOUGHT YOU WERE A HERO?
...
PETER?
SHE'S RIGHT. SHE DESERVES TO LIVE IN A WORLD OF HEROES.
WE ALL DO.
ALL RIGHT. FAMILY MEETING.
FROM HERE ON OUT. WHAT DO YOU THINK, ANNIE?
I THINK YOU'RE MY DAD. AND YOU CAN DO ANYTHING.
WELL, YOU HEARD HER. WHAT ARE YOU WAITING FOR?
GO GET 'EM, TIGER!

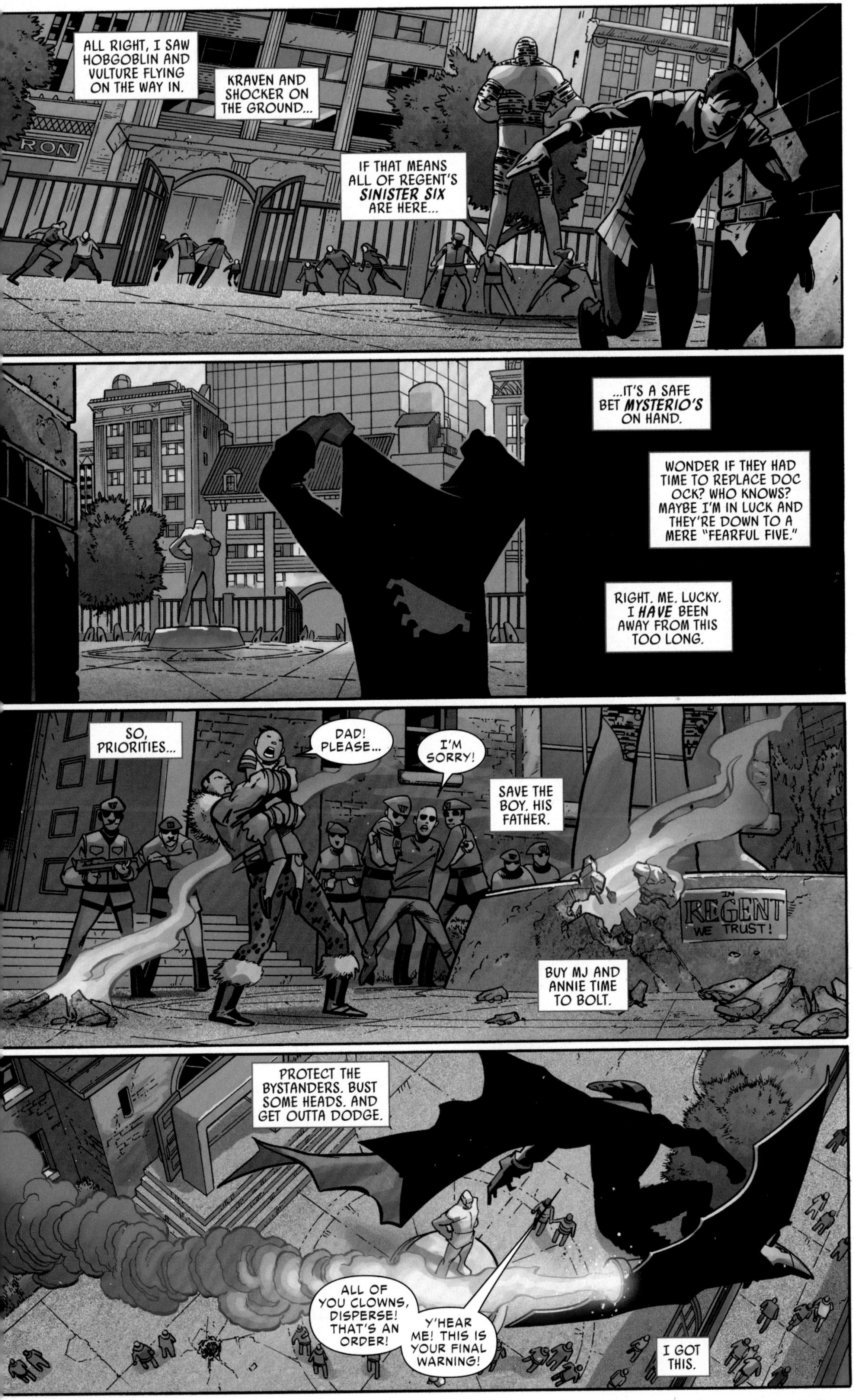

RON
ALL RIGHT, I SAW HOBGOBLIN AND VULTURE FLYING ON THE WAY IN.
KRAVEN AND SHOCKER ON THE GROUND...
IF THAT MEANS ALL OF REGENT'S **SINISTER SIX** ARE HERE...
...IT'S A SAFE BET **MYSTERIO'S** ON HAND.
WONDER IF THEY HAD TIME TO REPLACE DOC OCK? WHO KNOWS? MAYBE I'M IN LUCK AND THEY'RE DOWN TO A MERE "FEARFUL FIVE."
RIGHT. ME. LUCKY. I **HAVE** BEEN AWAY FROM THIS TOO LONG.
SO, PRIORITIES...
DAD! PLEASE...
I'M SORRY!
SAVE THE BOY. HIS FATHER.
IN REGENT WE TRUST!
BUY MJ AND ANNIE TIME TO BOLT.
PROTECT THE BYSTANDERS. BUST SOME HEADS. AND GET OUTTA DODGE.
ALL OF YOU CLOWNS, DISPERSE! THAT'S AN ORDER!
Y'HEAR ME! THIS IS YOUR FINAL WARNING!
I GOT THIS.

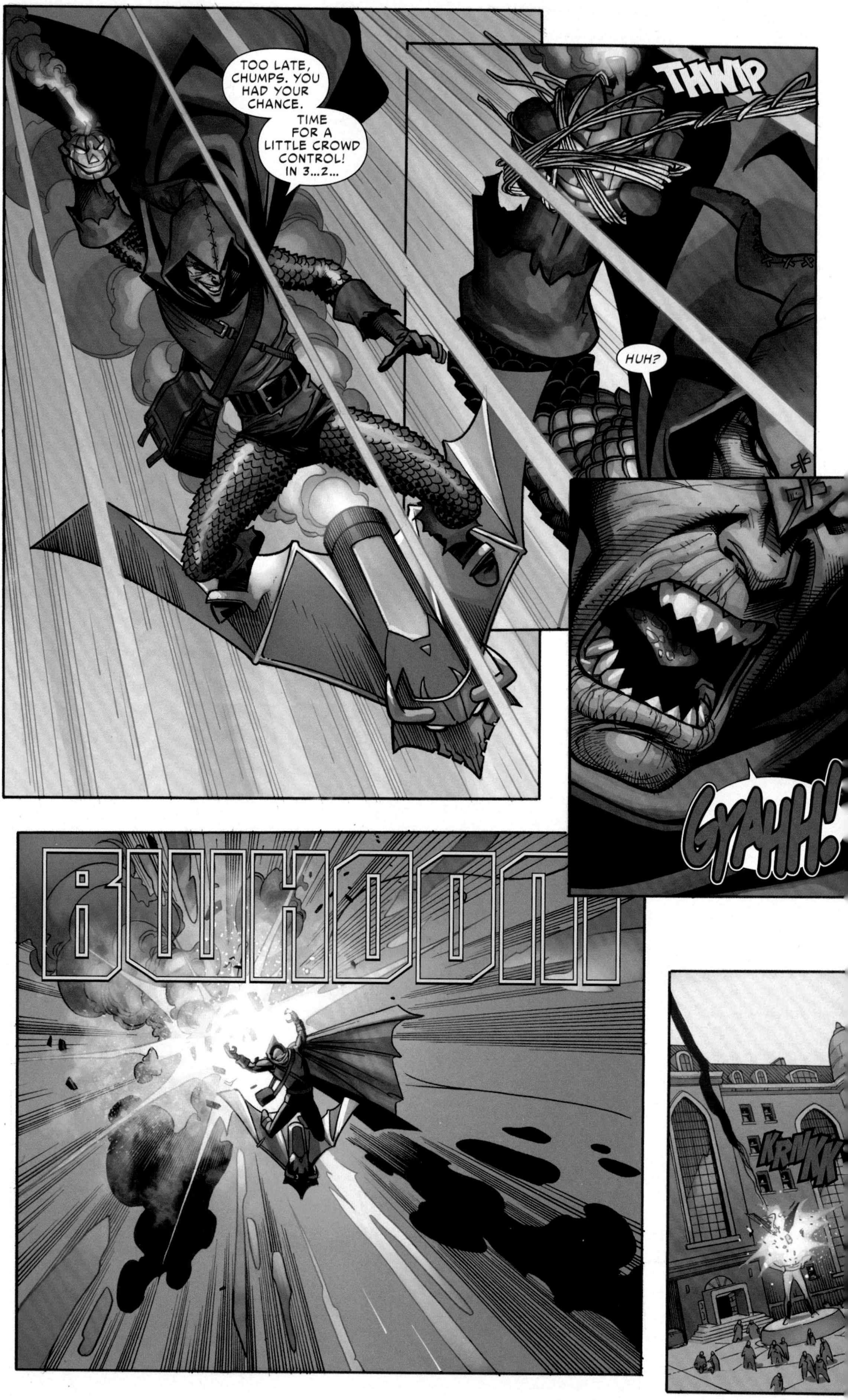
TOO LATE, CHUMPS. YOU HAD YOUR CHANCE.
TIME FOR A LITTLE CROWD CONTROL! IN 3...2...
THWIP
HUH?
GYAHH!
BUHOOM
KRNKK

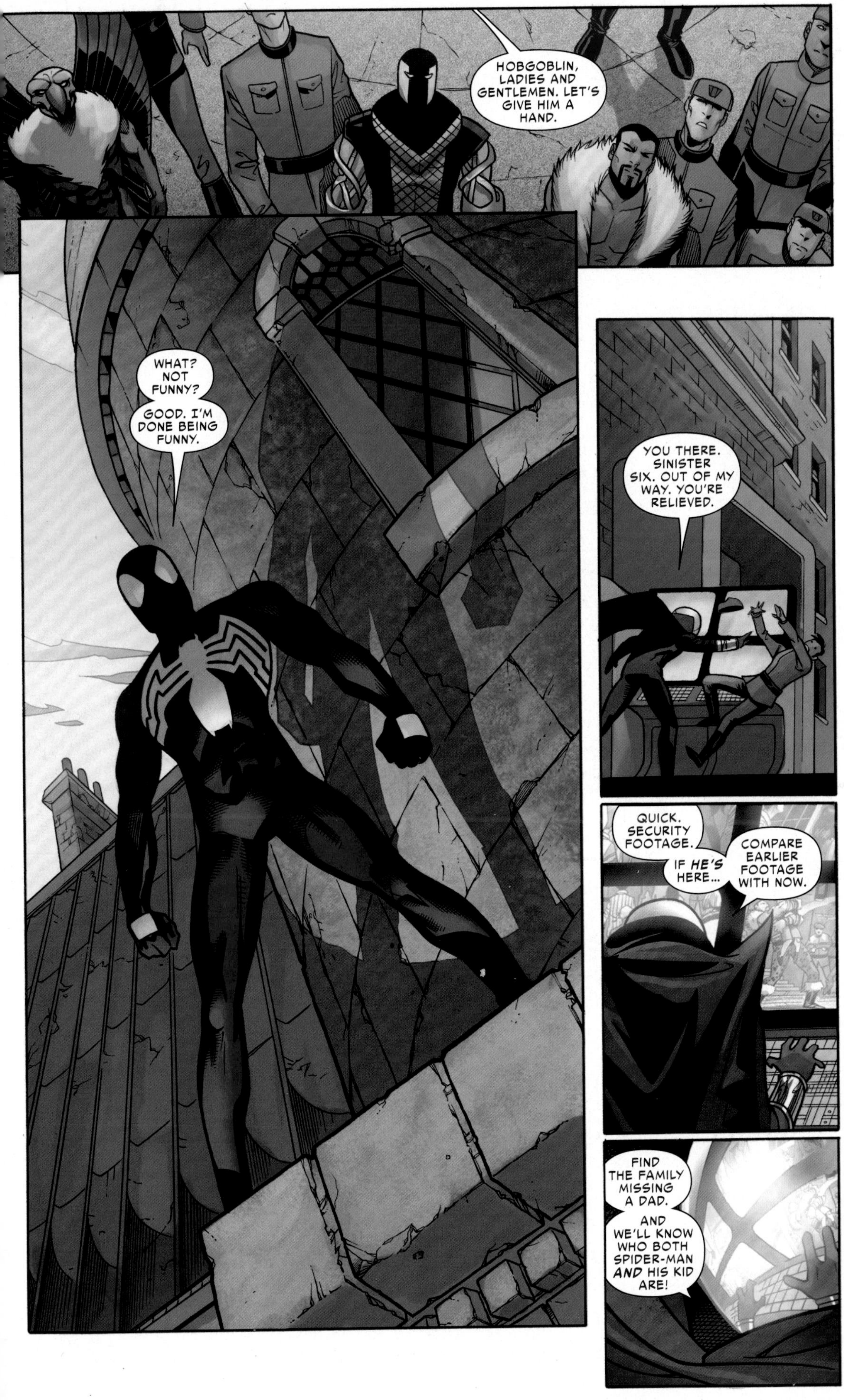
HOBGOBLIN, LADIES AND GENTLEMEN. LET'S GIVE HIM A HAND.
WHAT? NOT FUNNY?
GOOD. I'M DONE BEING FUNNY.
YOU THERE. SINISTER SIX. OUT OF MY WAY. YOU'RE RELIEVED.
QUICK. SECURITY FOOTAGE.
IF ***HE'S*** HERE...
COMPARE EARLIER FOOTAGE WITH NOW.
FIND THE FAMILY MISSING A DAD.
AND WE'LL KNOW WHO BOTH SPIDER-MAN ***AND*** HIS KID ARE!

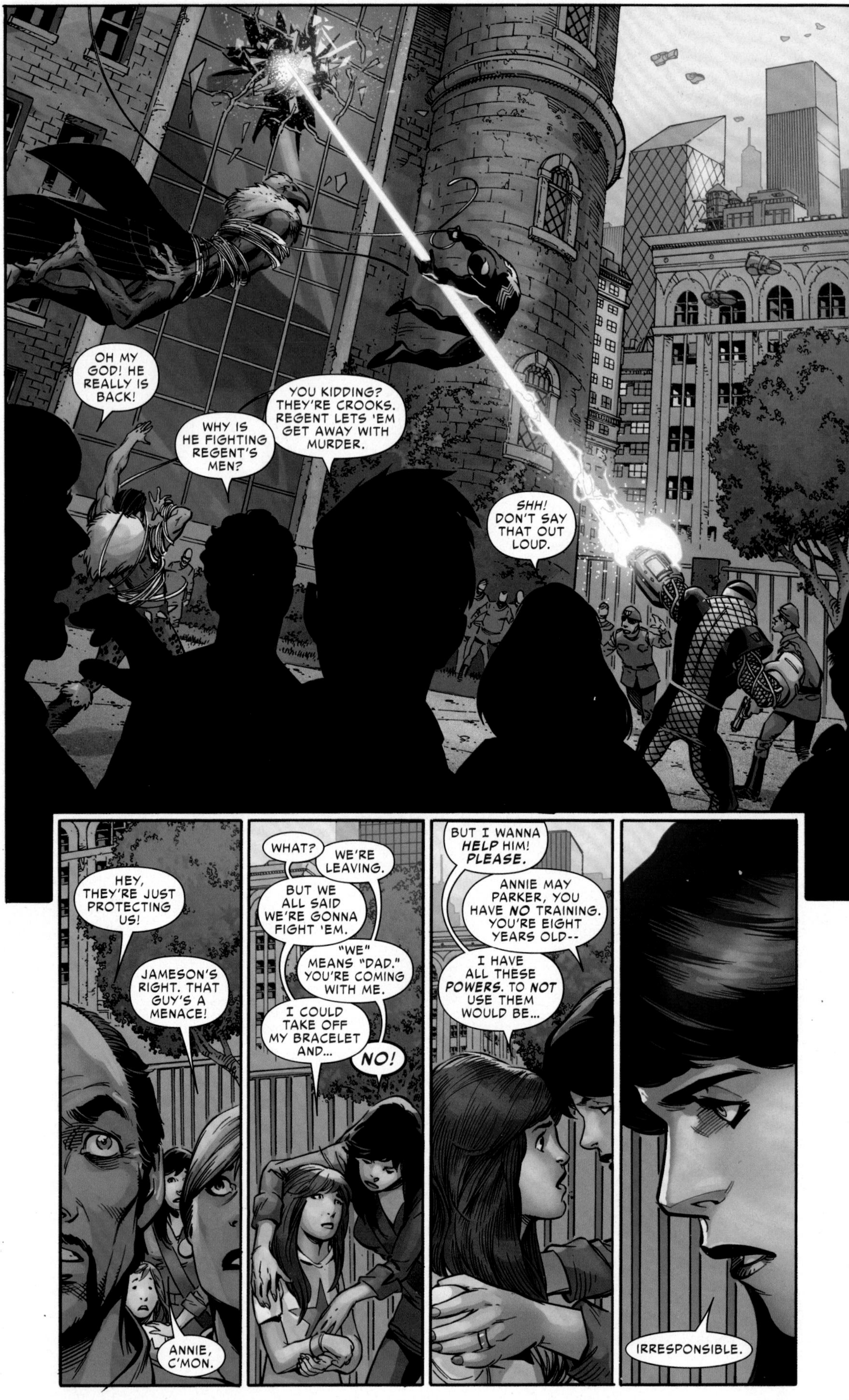
OH MY GOD! HE REALLY IS BACK!
WHY IS HE FIGHTING REGENT'S MEN?
YOU KIDDING? THEY'RE CROOKS. REGENT LETS 'EM GET AWAY WITH MURDER.
SHH! DON'T SAY THAT OUT LOUD.
HEY, THEY'RE JUST PROTECTING US!
JAMESON'S RIGHT. THAT GUY'S A MENACE!
ANNIE, C'MON.
WHAT?
WE'RE LEAVING.
BUT WE ALL SAID WE'RE GONNA FIGHT 'EM.
"WE" MEANS "DAD." YOU'RE COMING WITH ME.
I COULD TAKE OFF MY BRACELET AND...
NO!
BUT I WANNA HELP HIM! PLEASE.
ANNIE MAY PARKER, YOU HAVE NO TRAINING. YOU'RE EIGHT YEARS OLD--
I HAVE ALL THESE POWERS. TO NOT USE THEM WOULD BE...
IRRESPONSIBLE.

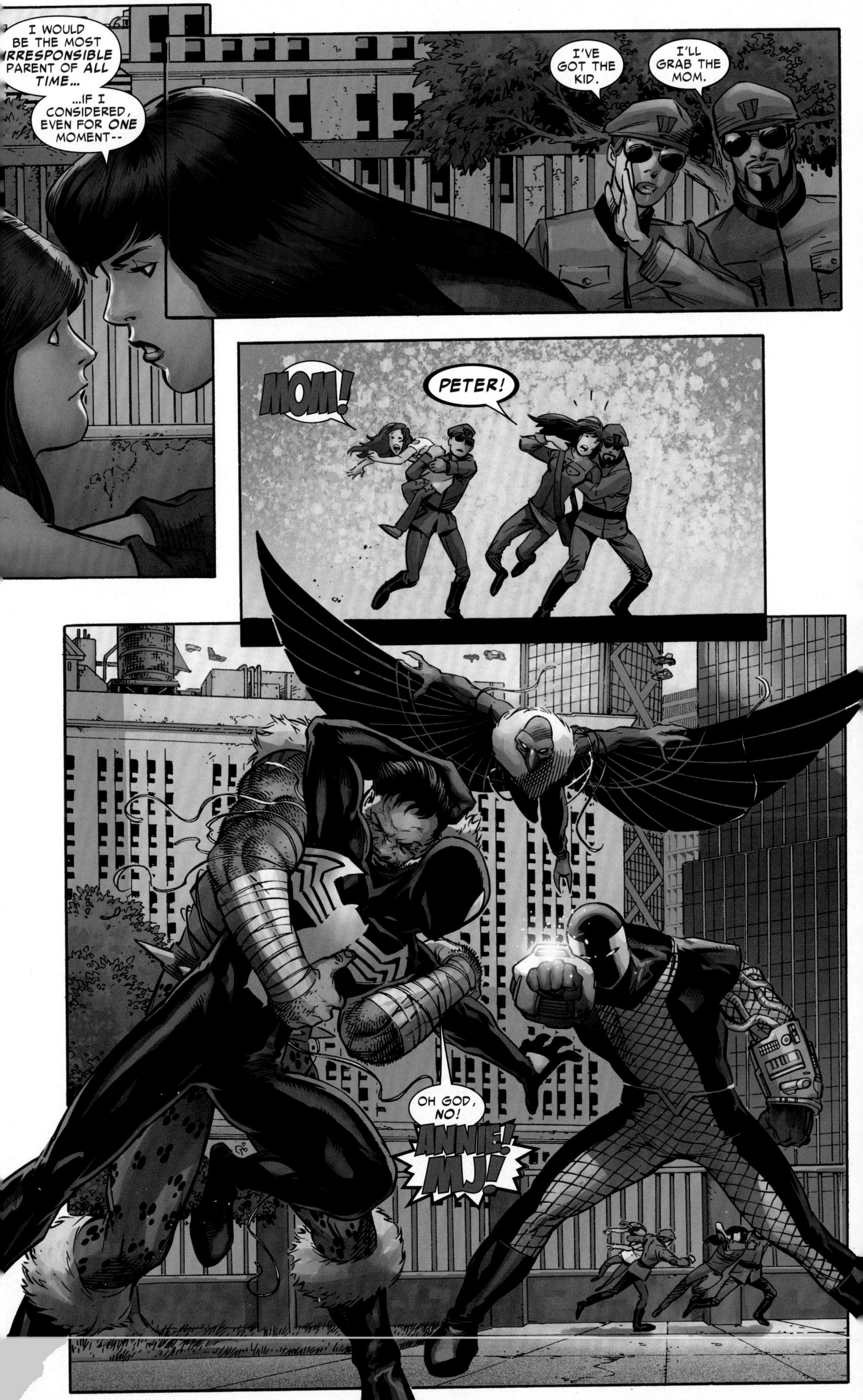
I WOULD BE THE MOST IRRESPONSIBLE PARENT OF ALL TIME...
...IF I CONSIDERED, EVEN FOR ONE MOMENT--
I'VE GOT THE KID.
I'LL GRAB THE MOM.
MOM!
PETER!
OH GOD, NO!
ANNIE! MJ!

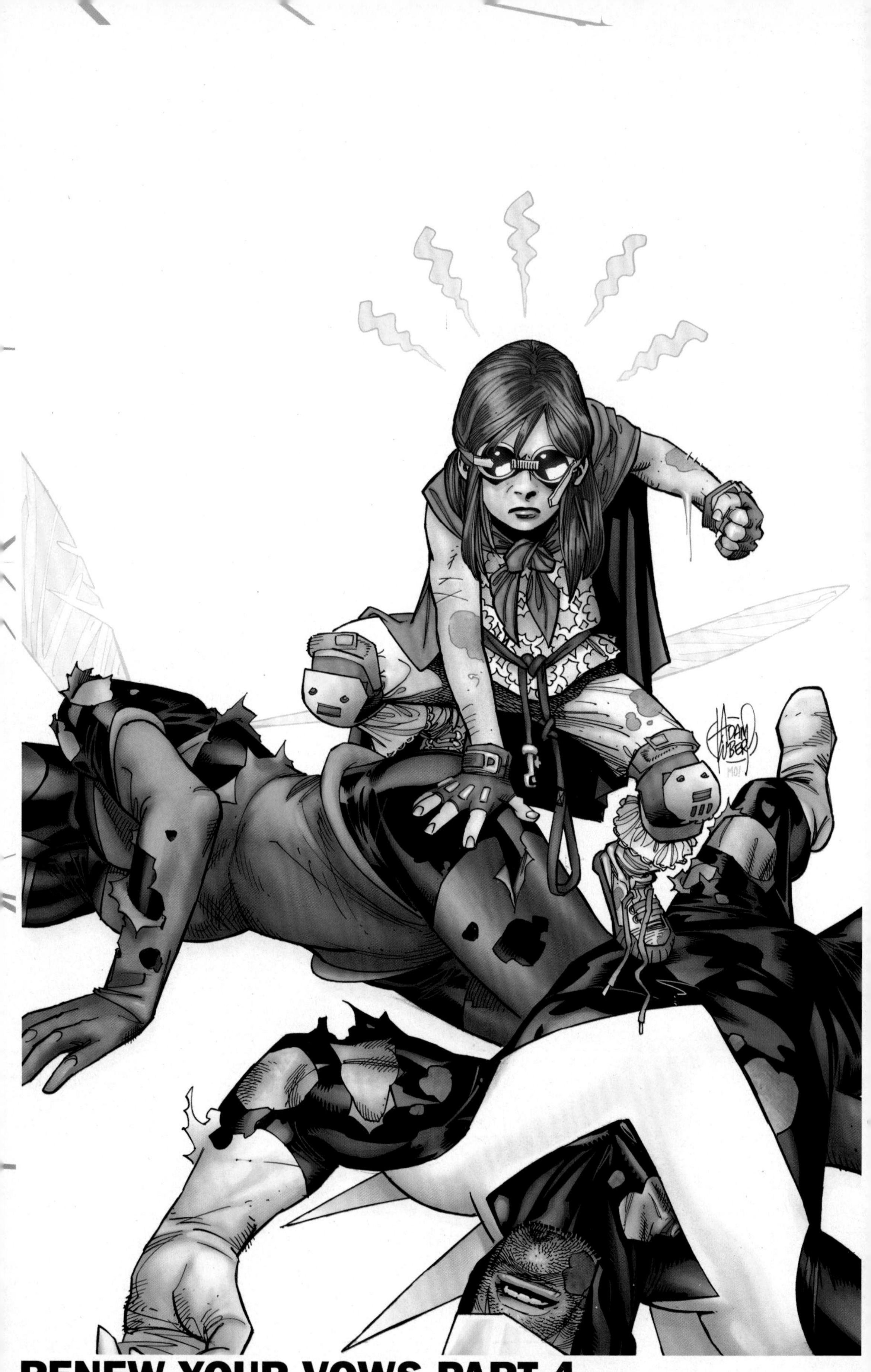

RENEW YOUR VOWS PART 4
"DADDY HAS TO GO AWAY FOR AWHILE"

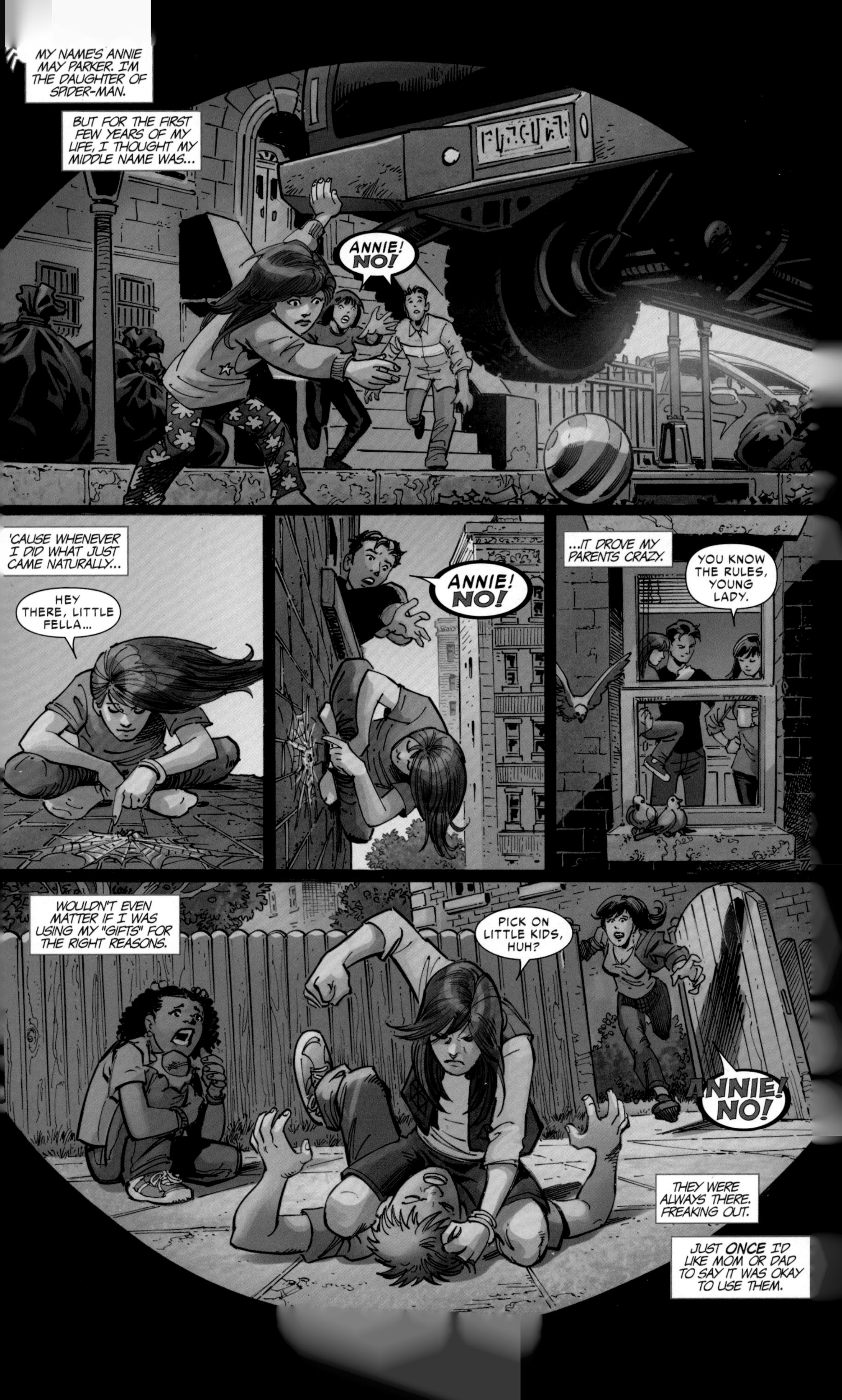
MY NAME'S ANNIE MAY PARKER. I'M THE DAUGHTER OF SPIDER-MAN.
BUT FOR THE FIRST FEW YEARS OF MY LIFE, I THOUGHT MY MIDDLE NAME WAS...
ANNIE! NO!
'CAUSE WHENEVER I DID WHAT JUST CAME NATURALLY...
HEY THERE, LITTLE FELLA...
ANNIE! NO!
...IT DROVE MY PARENTS CRAZY.
YOU KNOW THE RULES, YOUNG LADY.
WOULDN'T EVEN MATTER IF I WAS USING MY "GIFTS" FOR THE RIGHT REASONS.
PICK ON LITTLE KIDS, HUH?
ANNIE! NO!
THEY WERE ALWAYS THERE. FREAKING OUT.
JUST ONCE I'D LIKE MOM OR DAD TO SAY IT WAS OKAY TO USE THEM.

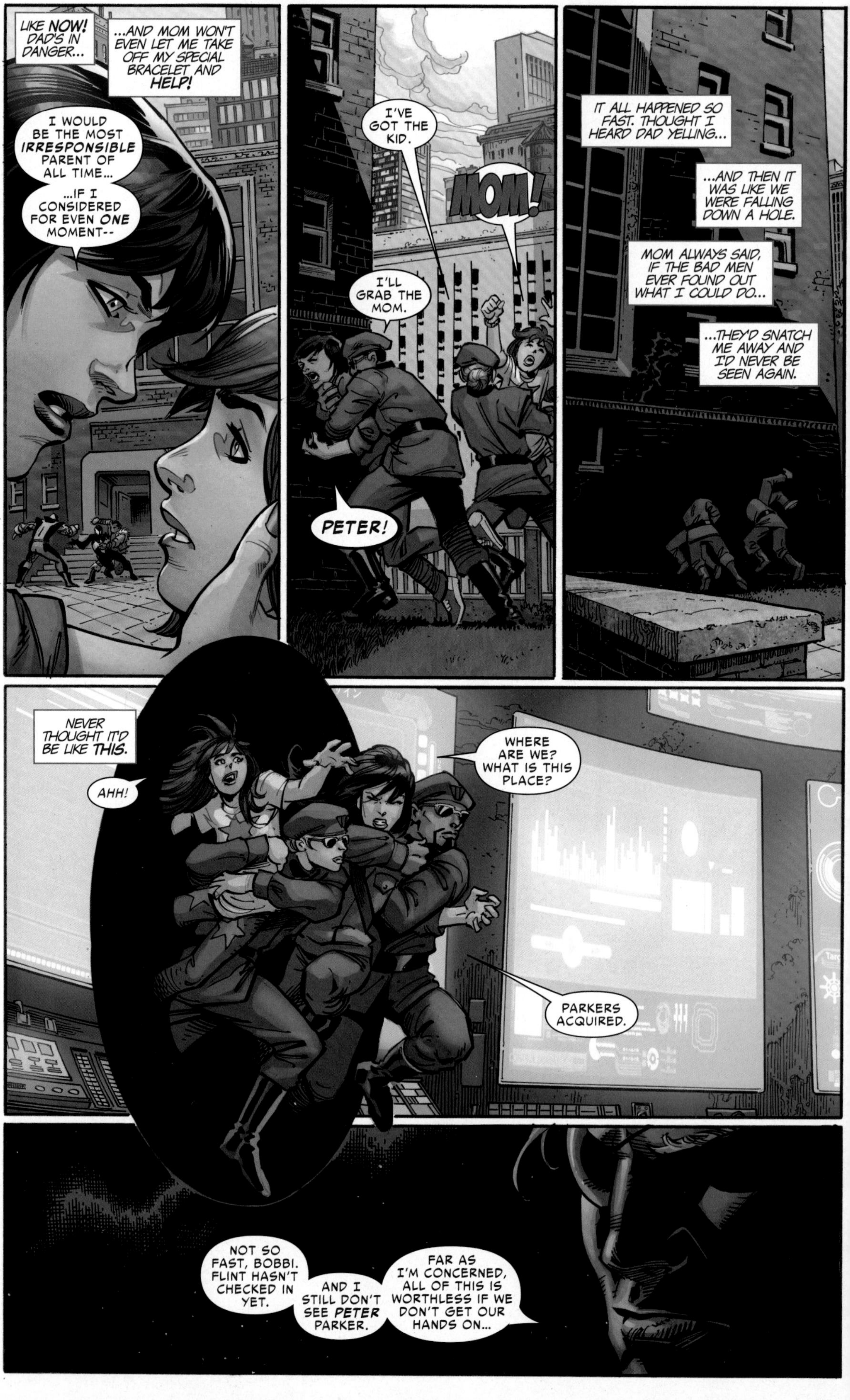

LIKE NOW! DAD'S IN DANGER...
...AND MOM WON'T EVEN LET ME TAKE OFF MY SPECIAL BRACELET AND HELP!
I WOULD BE THE MOST IRRESPONSIBLE PARENT OF ALL TIME...
...IF I CONSIDERED FOR EVEN ONE MOMENT--
I'VE GOT THE KID.
MOM!
I'LL GRAB THE MOM.
PETER!
IT ALL HAPPENED SO FAST. THOUGHT I HEARD DAD YELLING...
...AND THEN IT WAS LIKE WE WERE FALLING DOWN A HOLE.
MOM ALWAYS SAID, IF THE BAD MEN EVER FOUND OUT WHAT I COULD DO...
...THEY'D SNATCH ME AWAY AND I'D NEVER BE SEEN AGAIN.
NEVER THOUGHT IT'D BE LIKE THIS.
AHH!
WHERE ARE WE? WHAT IS THIS PLACE?
PARKERS ACQUIRED.
NOT SO FAST, BOBBI. FLINT HASN'T CHECKED IN YET.
AND I STILL DON'T SEE PETER PARKER.
FAR AS I'M CONCERNED, ALL OF THIS IS WORTHLESS IF WE DON'T GET OUR HANDS ON...

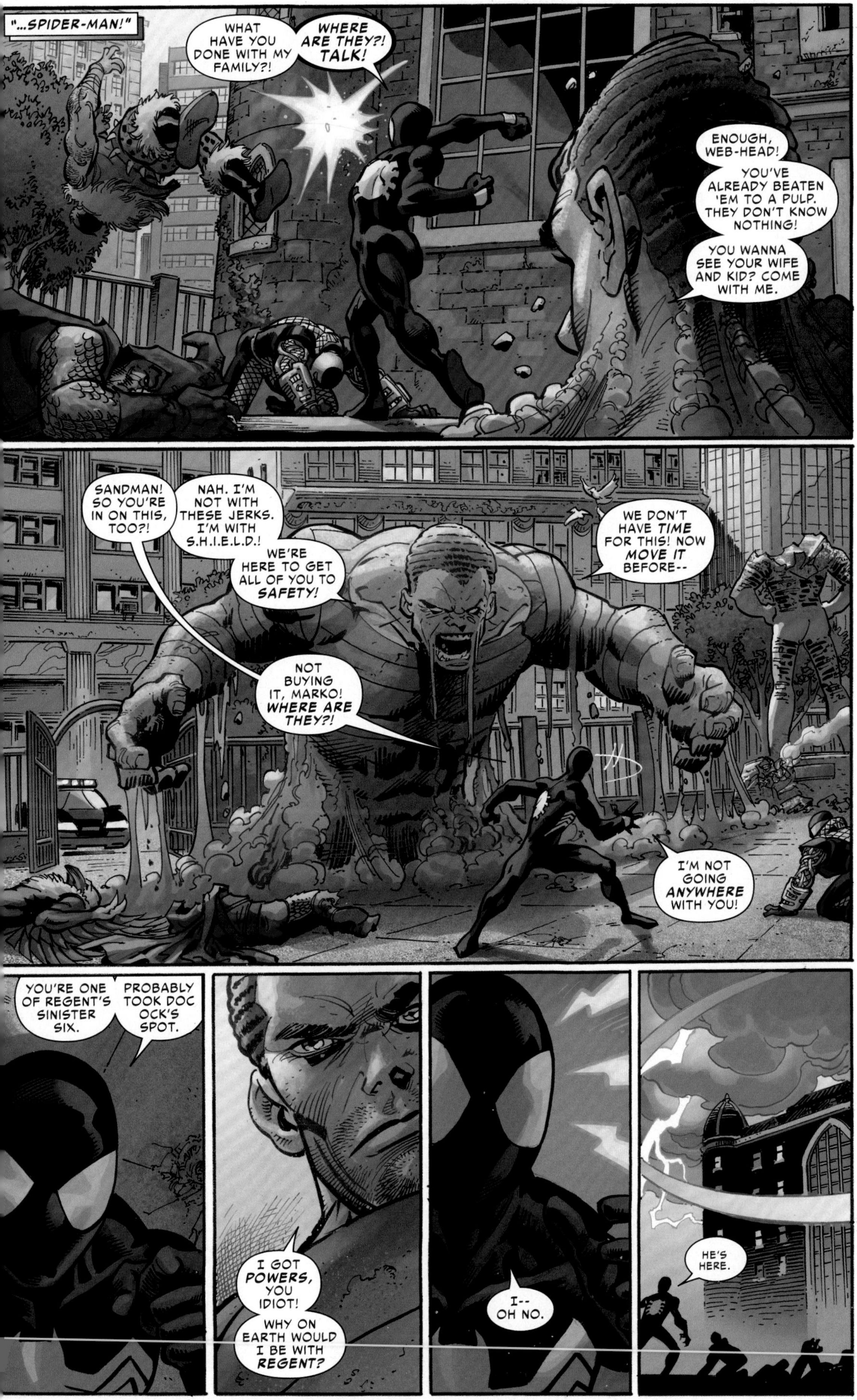
"...SPIDER-MAN!"
WHAT HAVE YOU DONE WITH MY FAMILY?!
WHERE ARE THEY?! TALK!
ENOUGH, WEB-HEAD!
YOU'VE ALREADY BEATEN 'EM TO A PULP. THEY DON'T KNOW NOTHING!
YOU WANNA SEE YOUR WIFE AND KID? COME WITH ME.
SANDMAN! SO YOU'RE IN ON THIS, TOO?!
NAH. I'M NOT WITH THESE JERKS. I'M WITH S.H.I.E.L.D.!
WE'RE HERE TO GET ALL OF YOU TO SAFETY!
WE DON'T HAVE TIME FOR THIS! NOW MOVE IT BEFORE--
NOT BUYING IT, MARKO! WHERE ARE THEY?!
I'M NOT GOING ANYWHERE WITH YOU!
YOU'RE ONE OF REGENT'S SINISTER SIX.
PROBABLY TOOK DOC OCK'S SPOT.
I GOT POWERS, YOU IDIOT!
WHY ON EARTH WOULD I BE WITH REGENT?
I-- OH NO.
HE'S HERE.

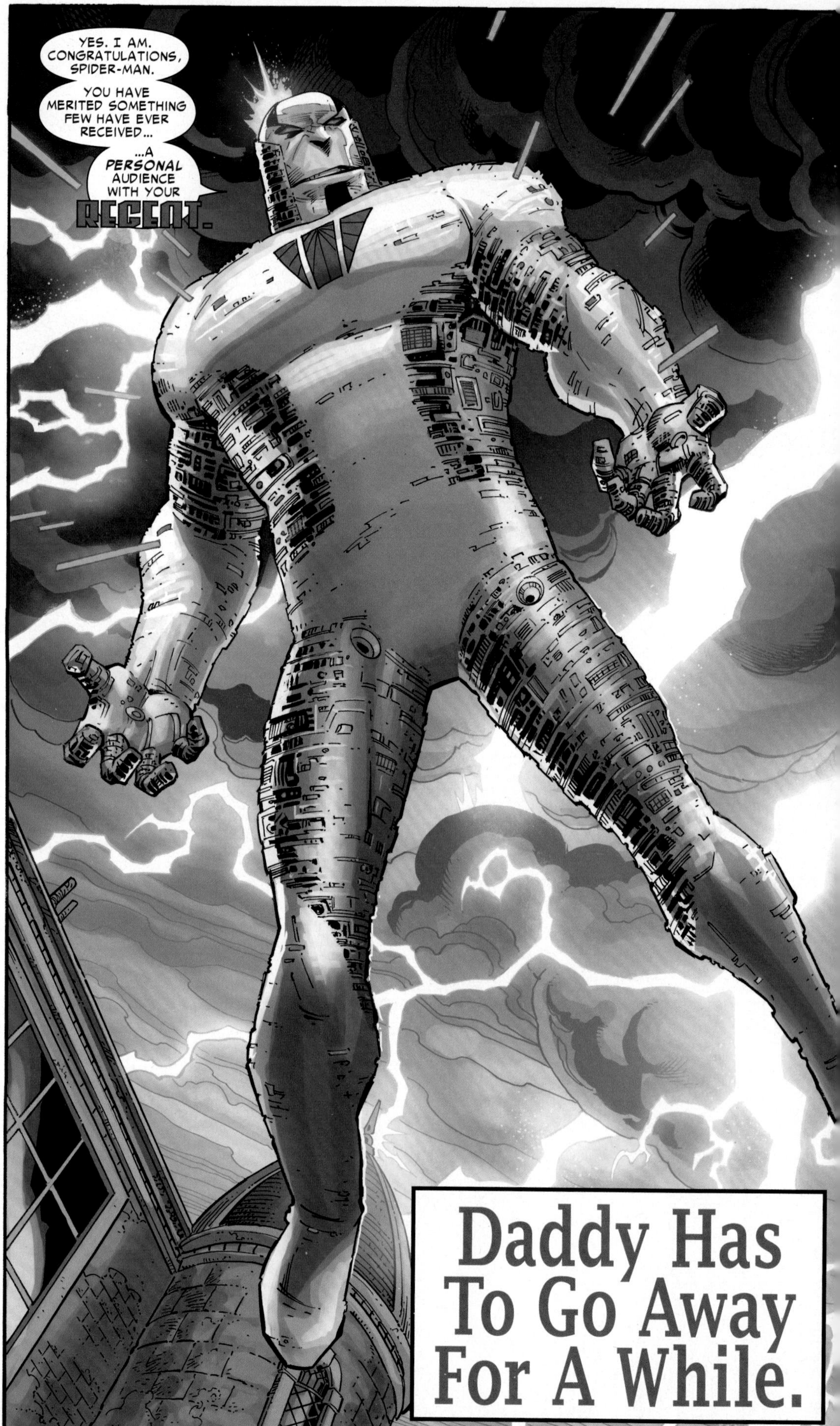
YES. I AM. CONGRATULATIONS, SPIDER-MAN.
YOU HAVE MERITED SOMETHING FEW HAVE EVER RECEIVED...
...A PERSONAL AUDIENCE WITH YOUR REGENT.
Daddy Has To Go Away For A While.

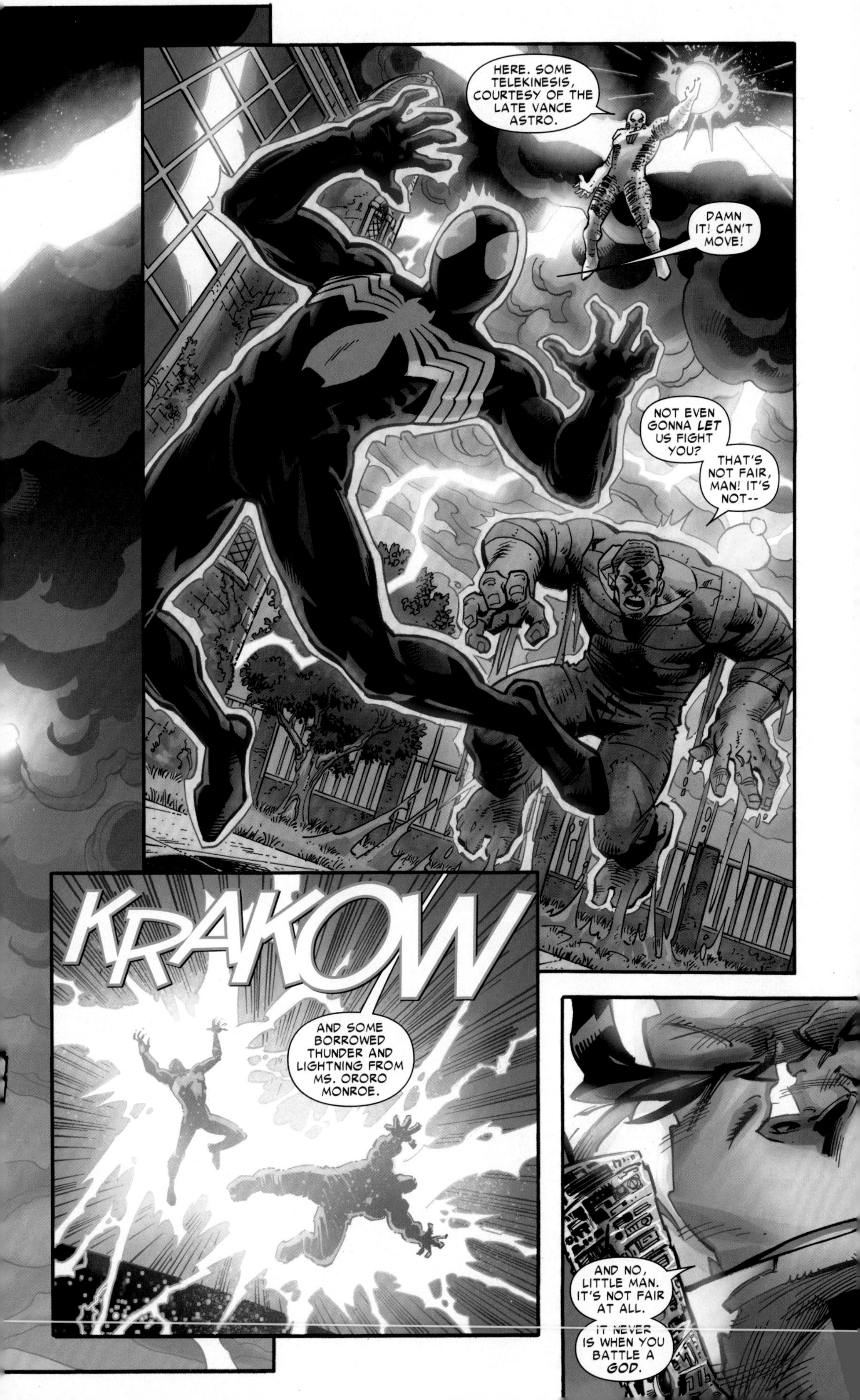
HERE. SOME TELEKINESIS, COURTESY OF THE LATE VANCE ASTRO.
DAMN IT! CAN'T MOVE!
NOT EVEN GONNA LET US FIGHT YOU?
THAT'S NOT FAIR, MAN! IT'S NOT--
KRAKOW
AND SOME BORROWED THUNDER AND LIGHTNING FROM MS. ORORO MONROE.
AND NO, LITTLE MAN. IT'S NOT FAIR AT ALL.
IT NEVER IS WHEN YOU BATTLE A GOD.

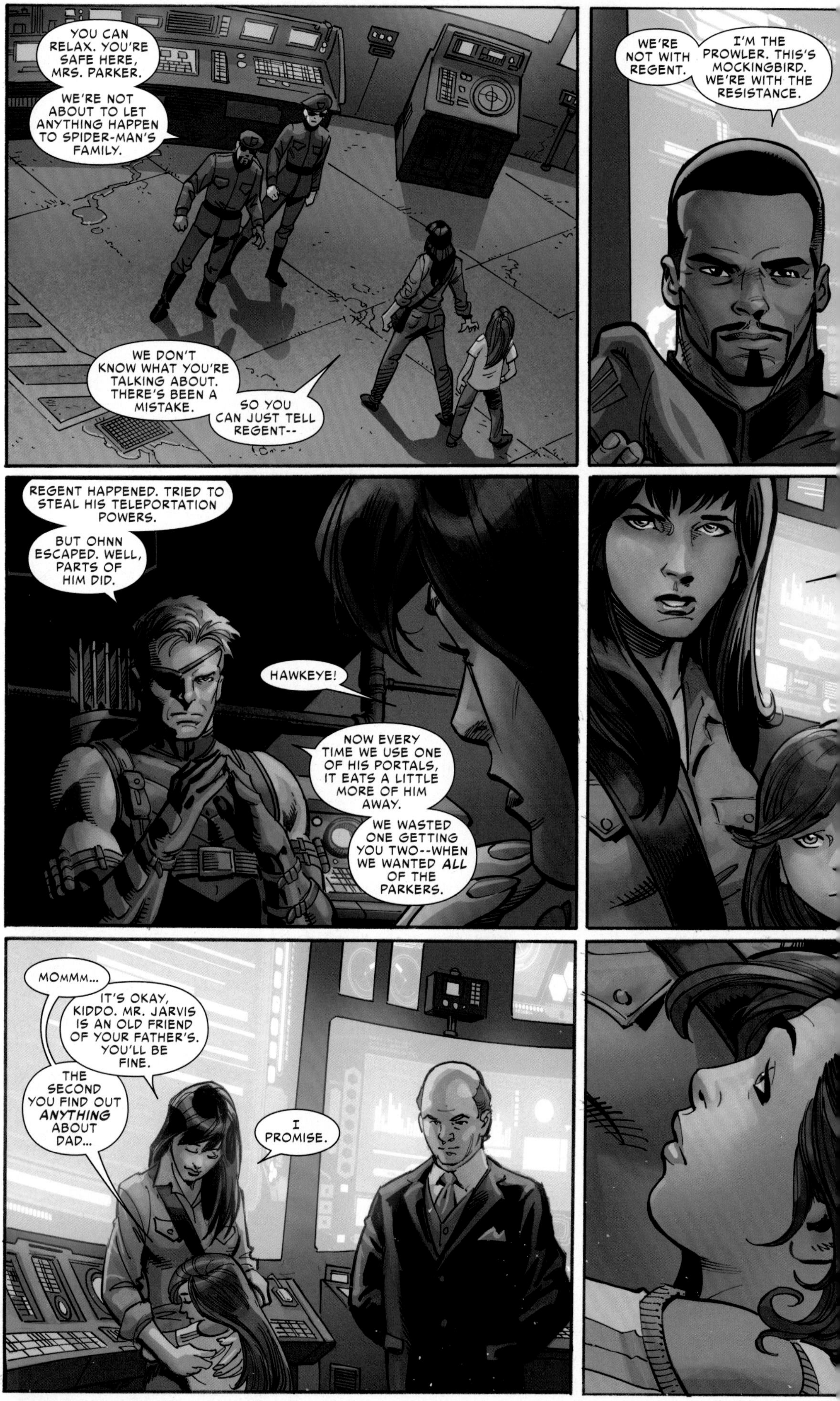
YOU CAN RELAX. YOU'RE SAFE HERE, MRS. PARKER.
WE'RE NOT ABOUT TO LET ANYTHING HAPPEN TO SPIDER-MAN'S FAMILY.
WE DON'T KNOW WHAT YOU'RE TALKING ABOUT. THERE'S BEEN A MISTAKE.
SO YOU CAN JUST TELL REGENT--
WE'RE NOT WITH REGENT.
I'M THE PROWLER. THIS'S MOCKINGBIRD. WE'RE WITH THE RESISTANCE.
REGENT HAPPENED. TRIED TO STEAL HIS TELEPORTATION POWERS.
BUT OHNN ESCAPED. WELL, PARTS OF HIM DID.
HAWKEYE!
NOW EVERY TIME WE USE ONE OF HIS PORTALS, IT EATS A LITTLE MORE OF HIM AWAY.
WE WASTED ONE GETTING YOU TWO--WHEN WE WANTED *ALL* OF THE PARKERS.
MOMMM...
IT'S OKAY, KIDDO. MR. JARVIS IS AN OLD FRIEND OF YOUR FATHER'S. YOU'LL BE FINE.
THE SECOND YOU FIND OUT *ANYTHING* ABOUT DAD...
I PROMISE.

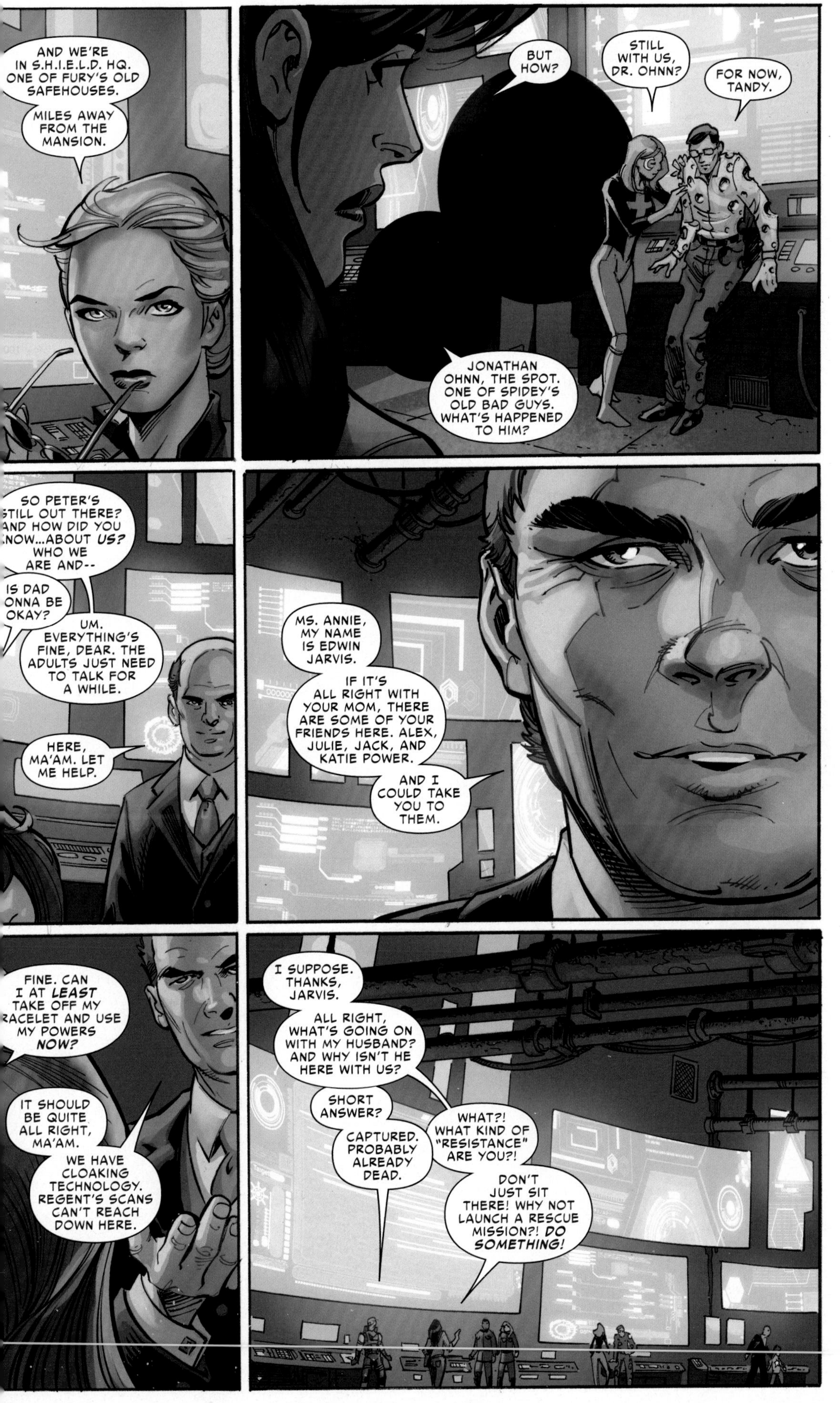
AND WE'RE IN S.H.I.E.L.D. HQ. ONE OF FURY'S OLD SAFEHOUSES.
MILES AWAY FROM THE MANSION.
BUT HOW?
STILL WITH US, DR. OHNN?
FOR NOW, TANDY.
JONATHAN OHNN, THE SPOT. ONE OF SPIDEY'S OLD BAD GUYS. WHAT'S HAPPENED TO HIM?
SO PETER'S STILL OUT THERE? AND HOW DID YOU NOW...ABOUT US? WHO WE ARE AND--
IS DAD ONNA BE OKAY?
UM. EVERYTHING'S FINE, DEAR. THE ADULTS JUST NEED TO TALK FOR A WHILE.
HERE, MA'AM. LET ME HELP.
MS. ANNIE, MY NAME IS EDWIN JARVIS.
IF IT'S ALL RIGHT WITH YOUR MOM, THERE ARE SOME OF YOUR FRIENDS HERE. ALEX, JULIE, JACK, AND KATIE POWER.
AND I COULD TAKE YOU TO THEM.
FINE. CAN I AT LEAST TAKE OFF MY RACELET AND USE MY POWERS NOW?
IT SHOULD BE QUITE ALL RIGHT, MA'AM.
WE HAVE CLOAKING TECHNOLOGY. REGENT'S SCANS CAN'T REACH DOWN HERE.
I SUPPOSE. THANKS, JARVIS.
ALL RIGHT, WHAT'S GOING ON WITH MY HUSBAND? AND WHY ISN'T HE HERE WITH US?
SHORT ANSWER?
CAPTURED. PROBABLY ALREADY DEAD.
WHAT?! WHAT KIND OF "RESISTANCE" ARE YOU?!
DON'T JUST SIT THERE! WHY NOT LAUNCH A RESCUE MISSION?! DO SOMETHING!

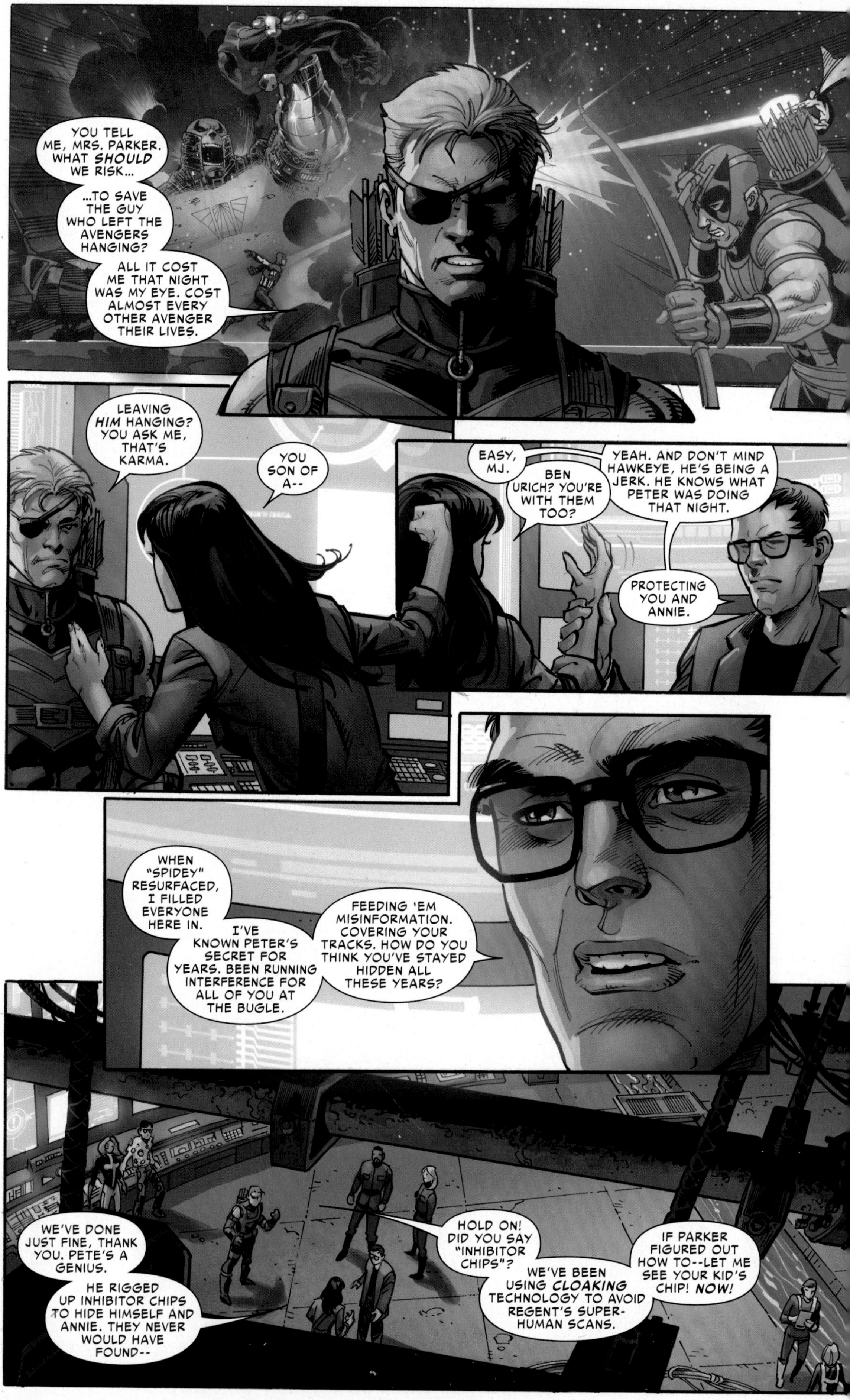
YOU TELL ME, MRS. PARKER. WHAT SHOULD WE RISK...
...TO SAVE THE GUY WHO LEFT THE AVENGERS HANGING?
ALL IT COST ME THAT NIGHT WAS MY EYE. COST ALMOST EVERY OTHER AVENGER THEIR LIVES.
LEAVING HIM HANGING? YOU ASK ME, THAT'S KARMA.
YOU SON OF A--
EASY, MJ.
BEN URICH? YOU'RE WITH THEM TOO?
YEAH. AND DON'T MIND HAWKEYE, HE'S BEING A JERK. HE KNOWS WHAT PETER WAS DOING THAT NIGHT.
PROTECTING YOU AND ANNIE.
WHEN "SPIDEY" RESURFACED, I FILLED EVERYONE HERE IN.
I'VE KNOWN PETER'S SECRET FOR YEARS. BEEN RUNNING INTERFERENCE FOR ALL OF YOU AT THE BUGLE.
FEEDING 'EM MISINFORMATION. COVERING YOUR TRACKS. HOW DO YOU THINK YOU'VE STAYED HIDDEN ALL THESE YEARS?
WE'VE DONE JUST FINE, THANK YOU. PETE'S A GENIUS.
HE RIGGED UP INHIBITOR CHIPS TO HIDE HIMSELF AND ANNIE. THEY NEVER WOULD HAVE FOUND--
HOLD ON! DID YOU SAY "INHIBITOR CHIPS"?
WE'VE BEEN USING CLOAKING TECHNOLOGY TO AVOID REGENT'S SUPER-HUMAN SCANS.
IF PARKER FIGURED OUT HOW TO--LET ME SEE YOUR KID'S CHIP! NOW!

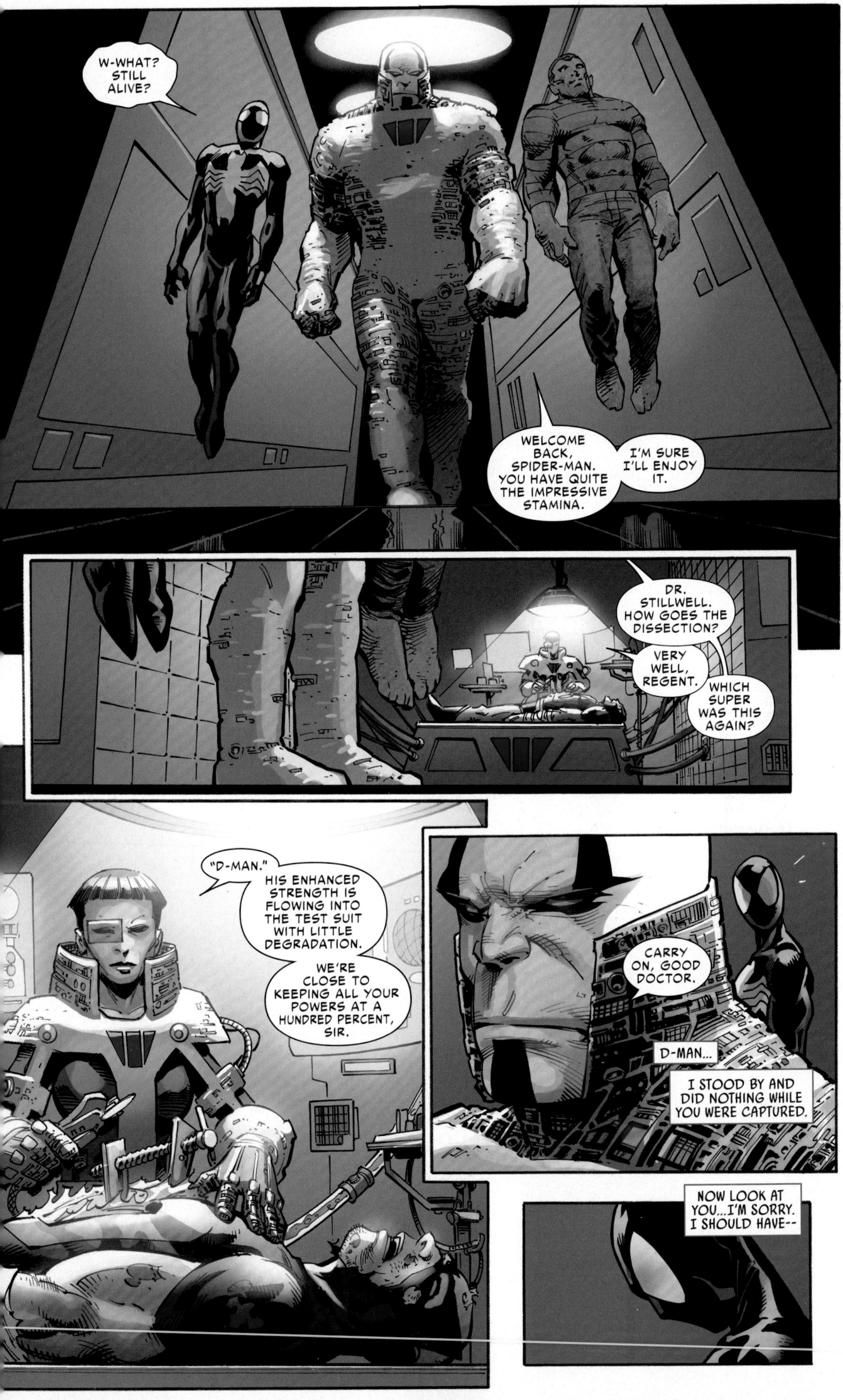

W-WHAT? STILL ALIVE?
WELCOME BACK, SPIDER-MAN. YOU HAVE QUITE THE IMPRESSIVE STAMINA.
I'M SURE I'LL ENJOY IT.
DR. STILLWELL. HOW GOES THE DISSECTION?
VERY WELL, REGENT.
WHICH SUPER WAS THIS AGAIN?
"D-MAN."
HIS ENHANCED STRENGTH IS FLOWING INTO THE TEST SUIT WITH LITTLE DEGRADATION.
WE'RE CLOSE TO KEEPING ALL YOUR POWERS AT A HUNDRED PERCENT, SIR.
CARRY ON, GOOD DOCTOR.
D-MAN...
I STOOD BY AND DID NOTHING WHILE YOU WERE CAPTURED.
NOW LOOK AT YOU...I'M SORRY. I SHOULD HAVE--

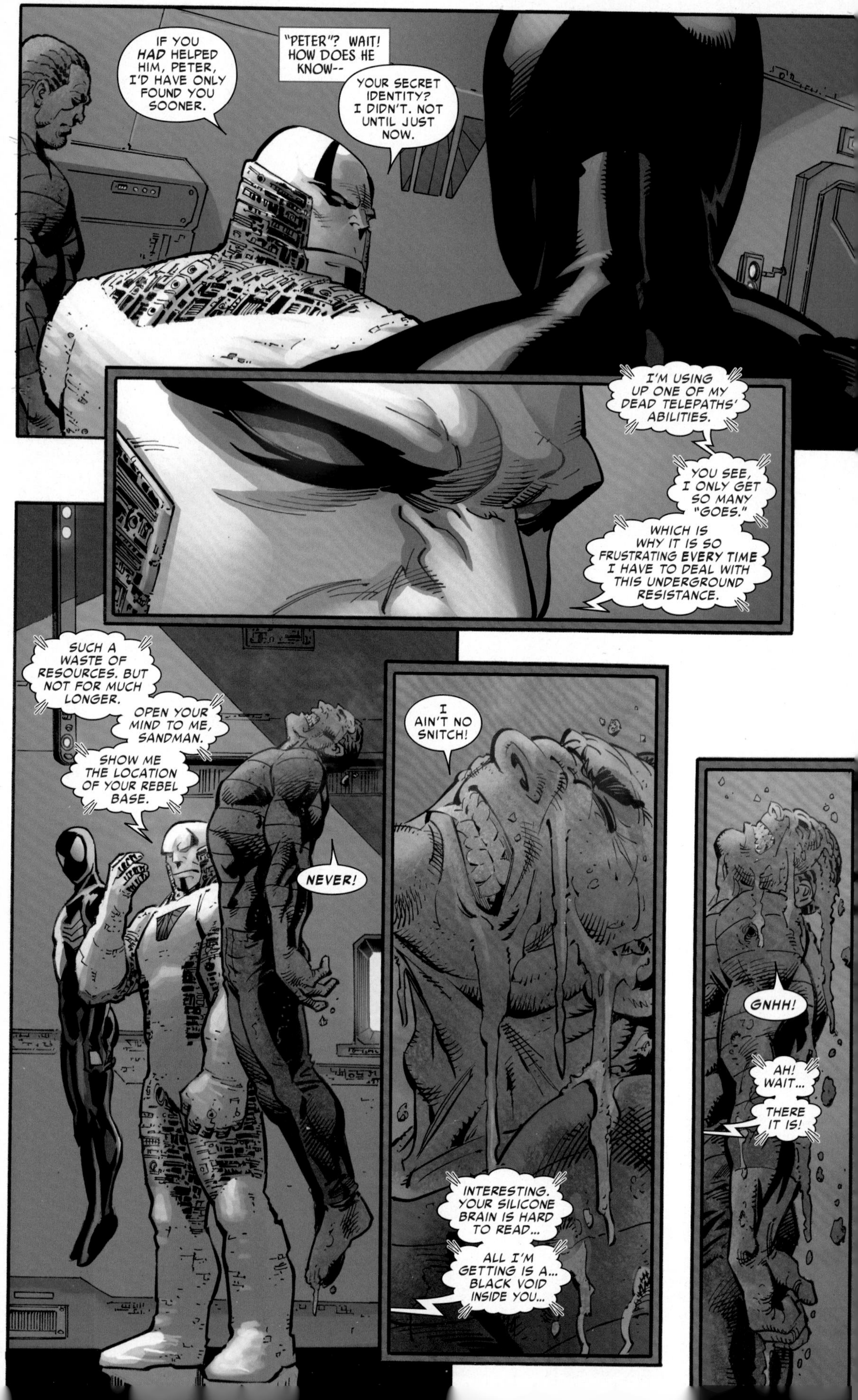

IF YOU HAD HELPED HIM, PETER, I'D HAVE ONLY FOUND YOU SOONER.
"PETER"? WAIT! HOW DOES HE KNOW--
YOUR SECRET IDENTITY? I DIDN'T. NOT UNTIL JUST NOW.
I'M USING UP ONE OF MY DEAD TELEPATHS' ABILITIES.
YOU SEE, I ONLY GET SO MANY "GOES."
WHICH IS WHY IT IS SO FRUSTRATING EVERY TIME I HAVE TO DEAL WITH THIS UNDERGROUND RESISTANCE.
SUCH A WASTE OF RESOURCES. BUT NOT FOR MUCH LONGER.
OPEN YOUR MIND TO ME, SANDMAN.
SHOW ME THE LOCATION OF YOUR REBEL BASE.
NEVER!
I AIN'T NO SNITCH!
INTERESTING. YOUR SILICONE BRAIN IS HARD TO READ...
ALL I'M GETTING IS A... BLACK VOID INSIDE YOU...
GNHH!
AH! WAIT...
THERE IT IS!

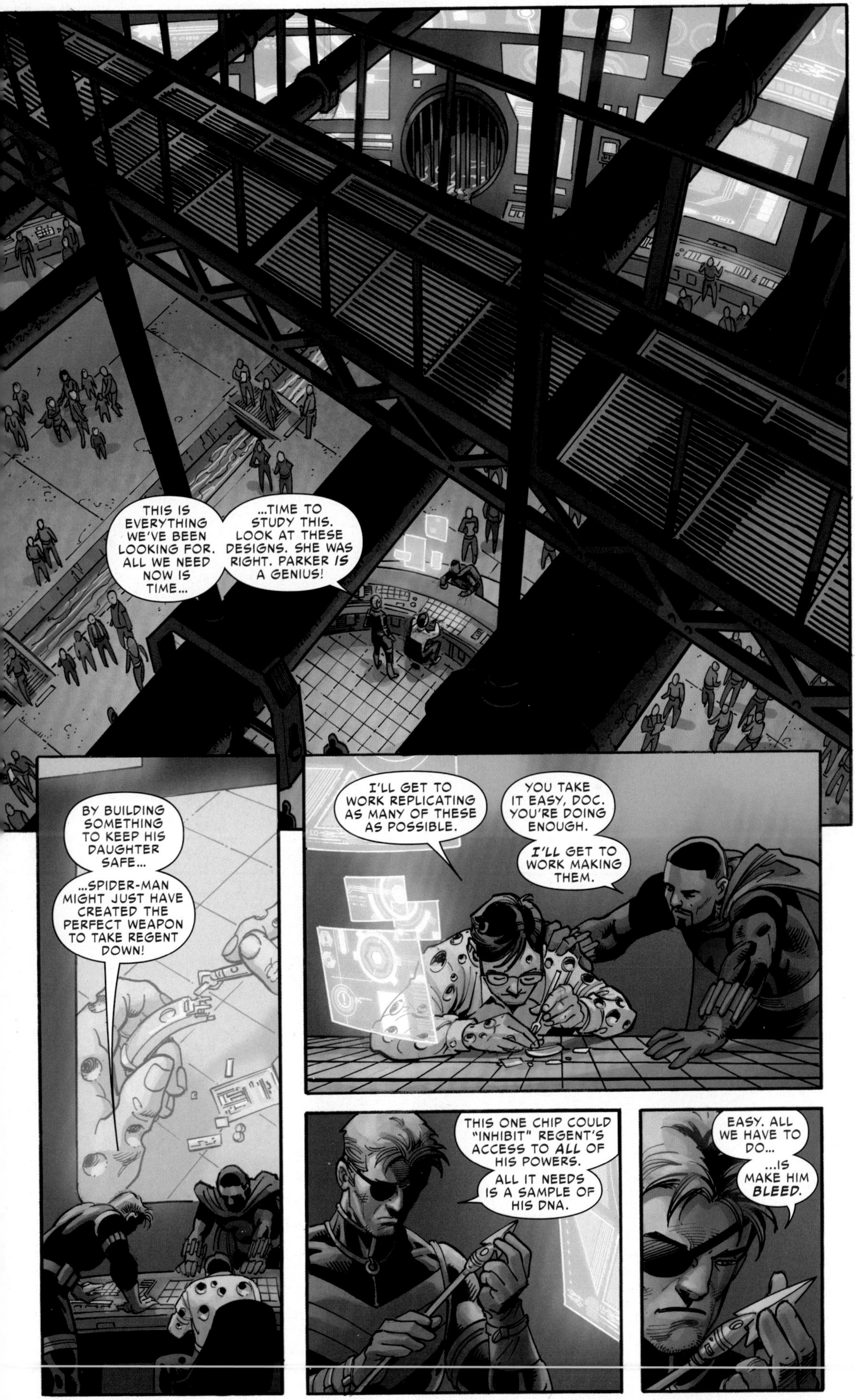

THIS IS EVERYTHING WE'VE BEEN LOOKING FOR. ALL WE NEED NOW IS TIME...
...TIME TO STUDY THIS. LOOK AT THESE DESIGNS. SHE WAS RIGHT. PARKER *IS* A GENIUS!
BY BUILDING SOMETHING TO KEEP HIS DAUGHTER SAFE...
...SPIDER-MAN MIGHT JUST HAVE CREATED THE PERFECT WEAPON TO TAKE REGENT DOWN!
I'LL GET TO WORK REPLICATING AS MANY OF THESE AS POSSIBLE.
YOU TAKE IT EASY, DOC. YOU'RE DOING ENOUGH.
I'LL GET TO WORK MAKING THEM.
THIS ONE CHIP COULD "INHIBIT" REGENT'S ACCESS TO *ALL* OF HIS POWERS.
ALL IT NEEDS IS A SAMPLE OF HIS DNA.
EASY. ALL WE HAVE TO DO...
...IS MAKE HIM *BLEED*.

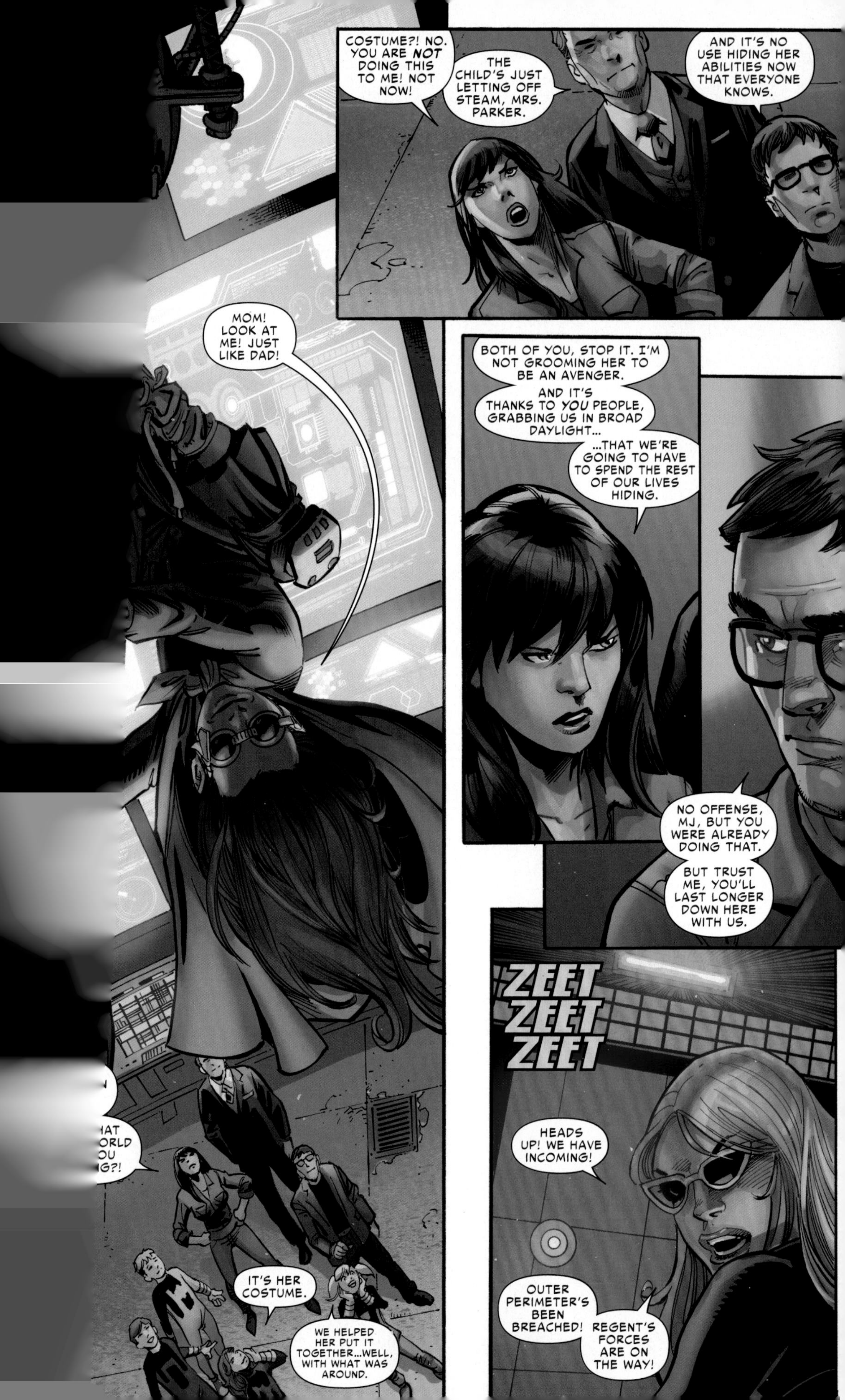
MOM! LOOK AT ME! JUST LIKE DAD!
IT'S HER COSTUME.
WE HELPED HER PUT IT TOGETHER...WELL, WITH WHAT WAS AROUND.
COSTUME?! NO. YOU ARE *NOT* DOING THIS TO ME! NOT NOW!
THE CHILD'S JUST LETTING OFF STEAM, MRS. PARKER.
AND IT'S NO USE HIDING HER ABILITIES NOW THAT EVERYONE KNOWS.
BOTH OF YOU, STOP IT. I'M NOT GROOMING HER TO BE AN AVENGER.
AND IT'S THANKS TO *YOU* PEOPLE, GRABBING US IN BROAD DAYLIGHT...
...THAT WE'RE GOING TO HAVE TO SPEND THE REST OF OUR LIVES HIDING.
NO OFFENSE, MJ, BUT YOU WERE ALREADY DOING THAT.
BUT TRUST ME, YOU'LL LAST LONGER DOWN HERE WITH US.
ZEET ZEET ZEET
HEADS UP! WE HAVE INCOMING!
OUTER PERIMETER'S BEEN BREACHED!
REGENT'S FORCES ARE ON THE WAY!

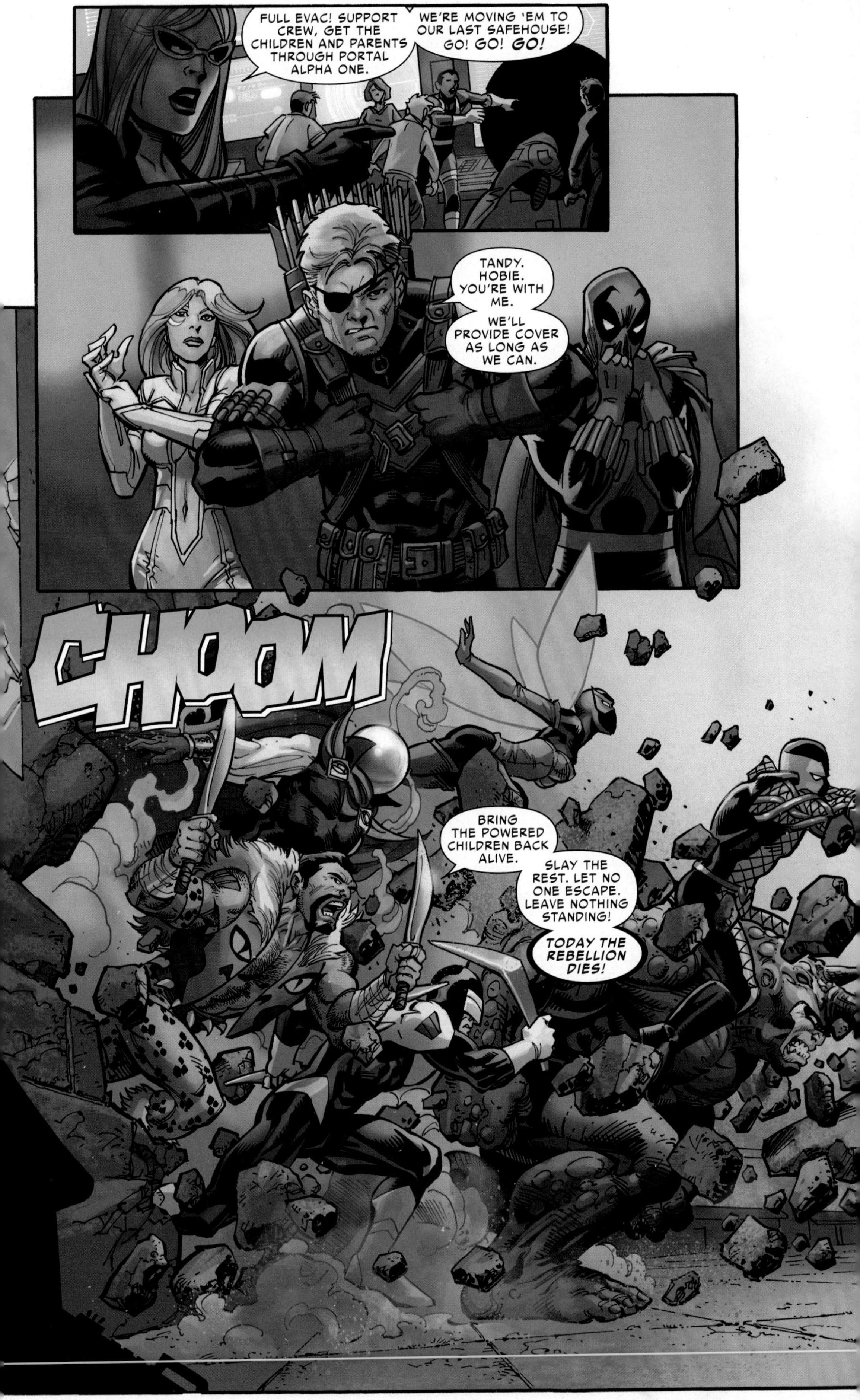
FULL EVAC! SUPPORT CREW, GET THE CHILDREN AND PARENTS THROUGH PORTAL ALPHA ONE.
WE'RE MOVING 'EM TO OUR LAST SAFEHOUSE! GO! GO! GO!
TANDY. HOBIE. YOU'RE WITH ME.
WE'LL PROVIDE COVER AS LONG AS WE CAN.
CHOOM
BRING THE POWERED CHILDREN BACK ALIVE.
SLAY THE REST. LET NO ONE ESCAPE. LEAVE NOTHING STANDING!
TODAY THE REBELLION DIES!

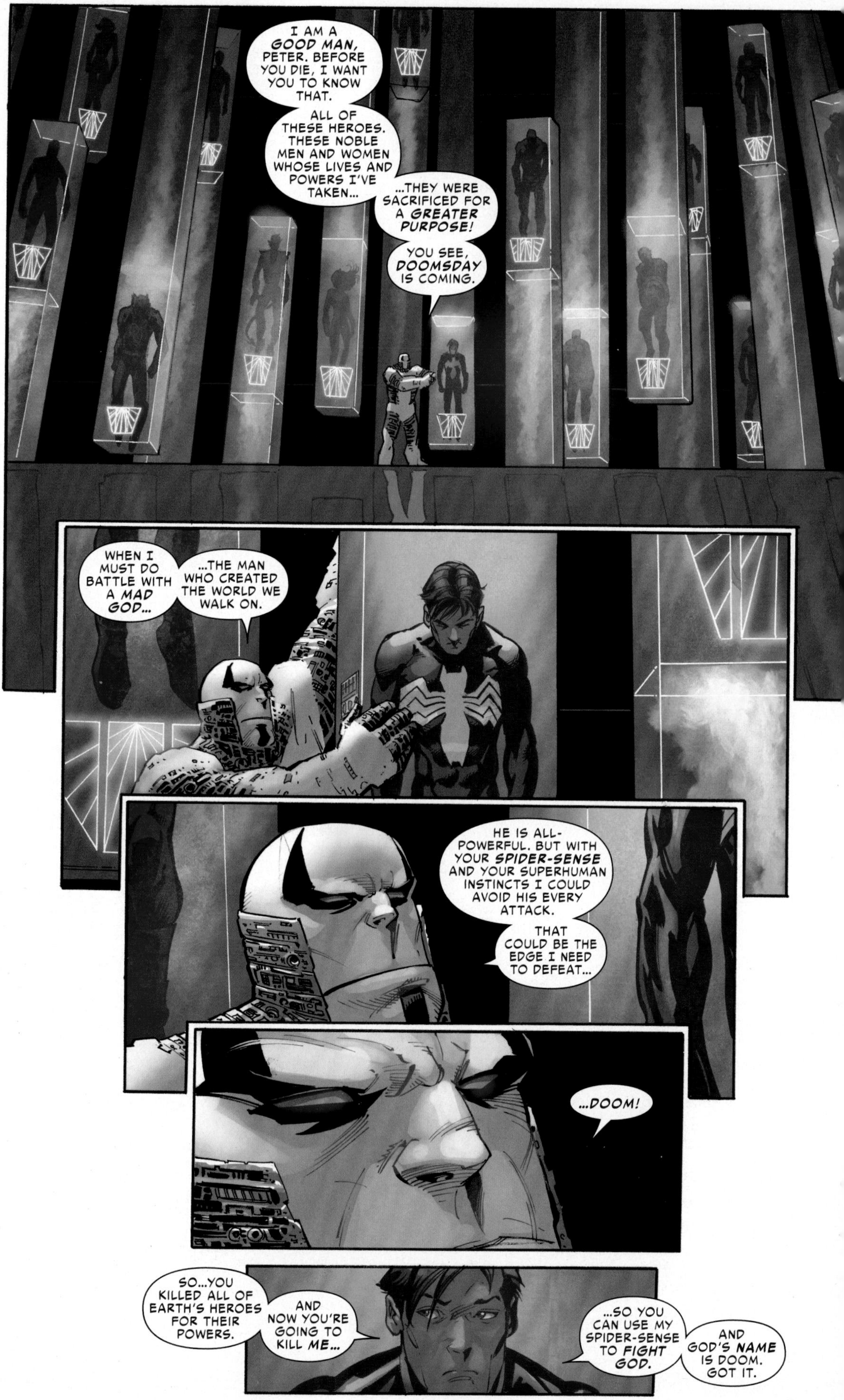
I AM A GOOD MAN, PETER. BEFORE YOU DIE, I WANT YOU TO KNOW THAT.
ALL OF THESE HEROES. THESE NOBLE MEN AND WOMEN WHOSE LIVES AND POWERS I'VE TAKEN...
...THEY WERE SACRIFICED FOR A GREATER PURPOSE!
YOU SEE, DOOMSDAY IS COMING.
WHEN I MUST DO BATTLE WITH A MAD GOD...
...THE MAN WHO CREATED THE WORLD WE WALK ON.
HE IS ALL-POWERFUL. BUT WITH YOUR SPIDER-SENSE AND YOUR SUPERHUMAN INSTINCTS I COULD AVOID HIS EVERY ATTACK.
THAT COULD BE THE EDGE I NEED TO DEFEAT...
...DOOM!
SO...YOU KILLED ALL OF EARTH'S HEROES FOR THEIR POWERS.
AND NOW YOU'RE GOING TO KILL ME...
...SO YOU CAN USE MY SPIDER-SENSE TO FIGHT GOD.
AND GOD'S NAME IS DOOM. GOT IT.

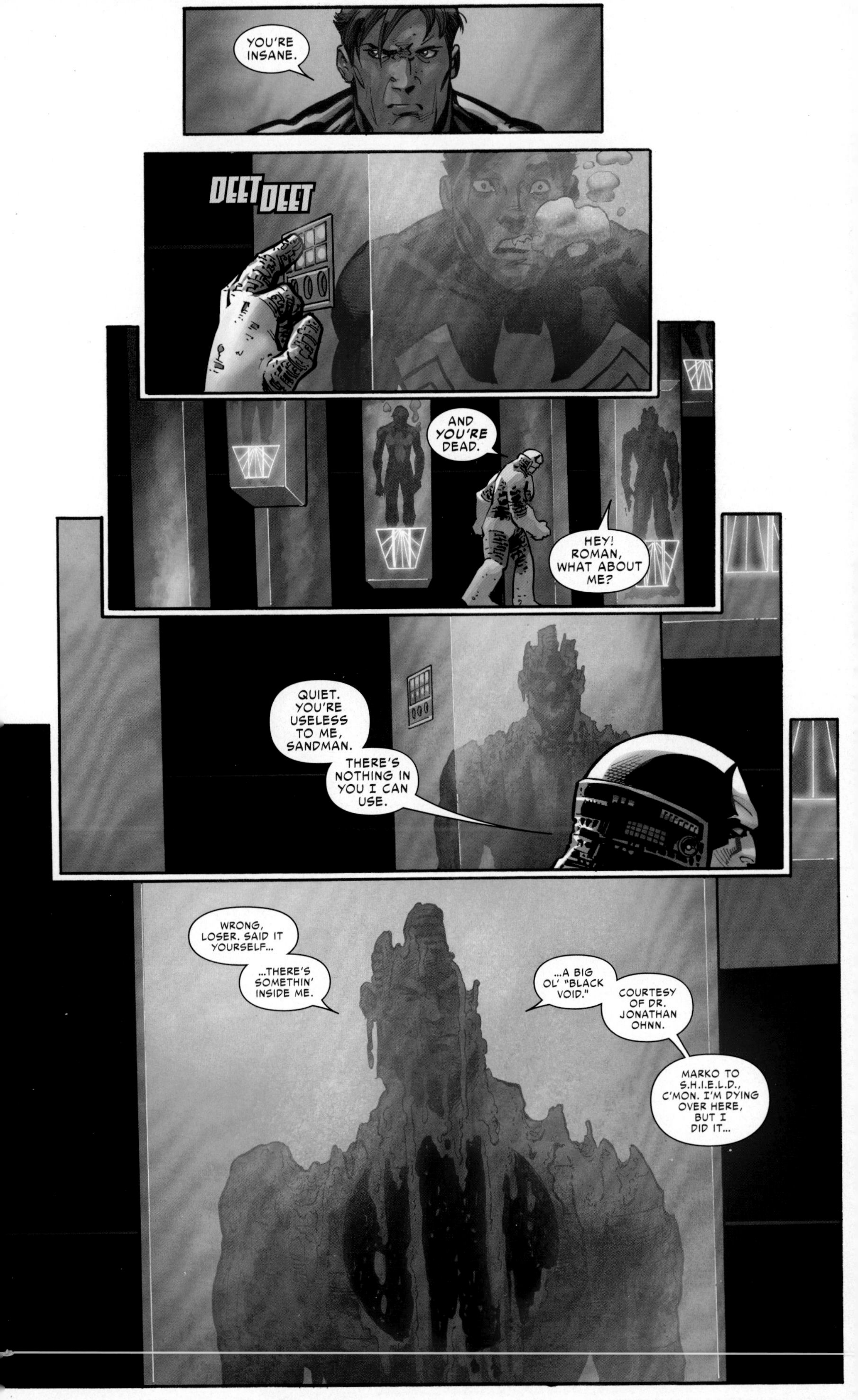
YOU'RE INSANE.
DEET DEET
AND YOU'RE DEAD.
HEY! ROMAN, WHAT ABOUT ME?
QUIET. YOU'RE USELESS TO ME, SANDMAN.
THERE'S NOTHING IN YOU I CAN USE.
WRONG, LOSER. SAID IT YOURSELF...
...THERE'S SOMETHIN' INSIDE ME.
...A BIG OL' "BLACK VOID."
COURTESY OF DR. JONATHAN OHNN.
MARKO TO S.H.I.E.L.D., C'MON. I'M DYING OVER HERE, BUT I DID IT...

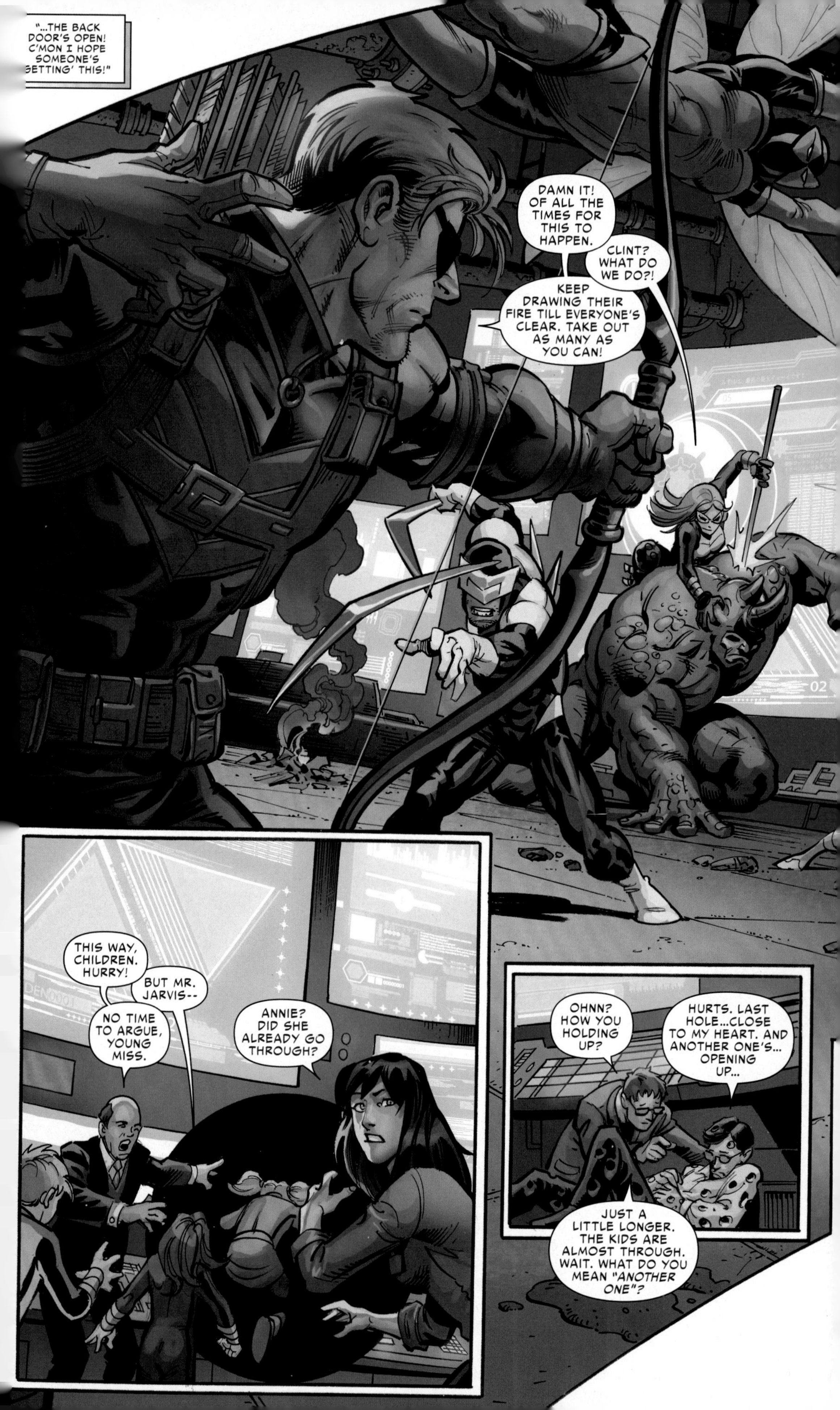
"...THE BACK DOOR'S OPEN! C'MON I HOPE SOMEONE'S GETTING' THIS!"
DAMN IT! OF ALL THE TIMES FOR THIS TO HAPPEN.
CLINT? WHAT DO WE DO?!
KEEP DRAWING THEIR FIRE TILL EVERYONE'S CLEAR. TAKE OUT AS MANY AS YOU CAN!
THIS WAY, CHILDREN. HURRY!
BUT MR. JARVIS--
NO TIME TO ARGUE, YOUNG MISS.
ANNIE? DID SHE ALREADY GO THROUGH?
OHNN? HOW YOU HOLDING UP?
HURTS. LAST HOLE...CLOSE TO MY HEART. AND ANOTHER ONE'S... OPENING UP...
JUST A LITTLE LONGER. THE KIDS ARE ALMOST THROUGH. WAIT. WHAT DO YOU MEAN "ANOTHER ONE"?

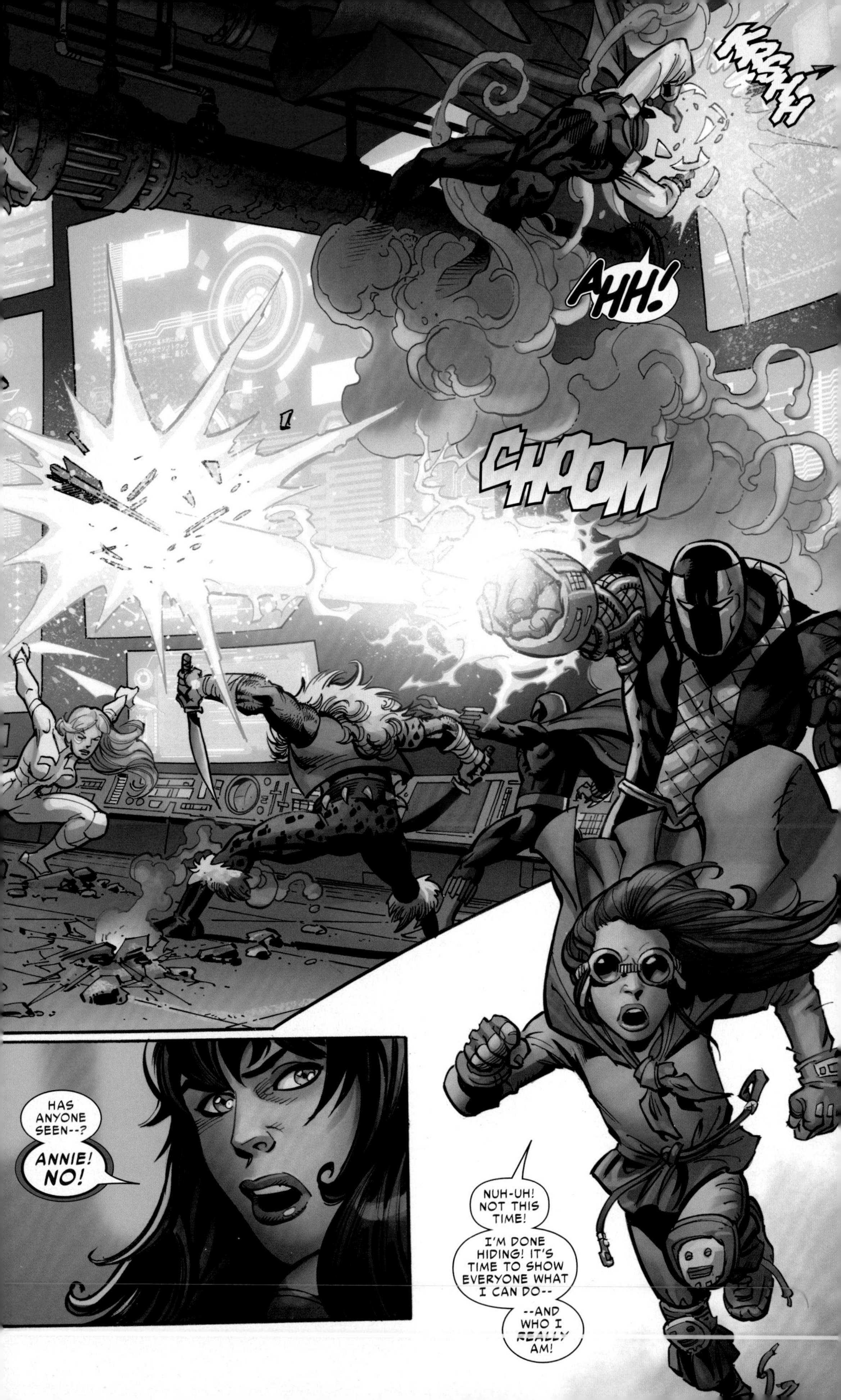

KRSSH!
AHH!
CHOOOM
HAS ANYONE SEEN--?
ANNIE! NO!
NUH-UH! NOT THIS TIME!
I'M DONE HIDING! IT'S TIME TO SHOW EVERYONE WHAT I CAN DO--
--AND WHO I REALLY AM!

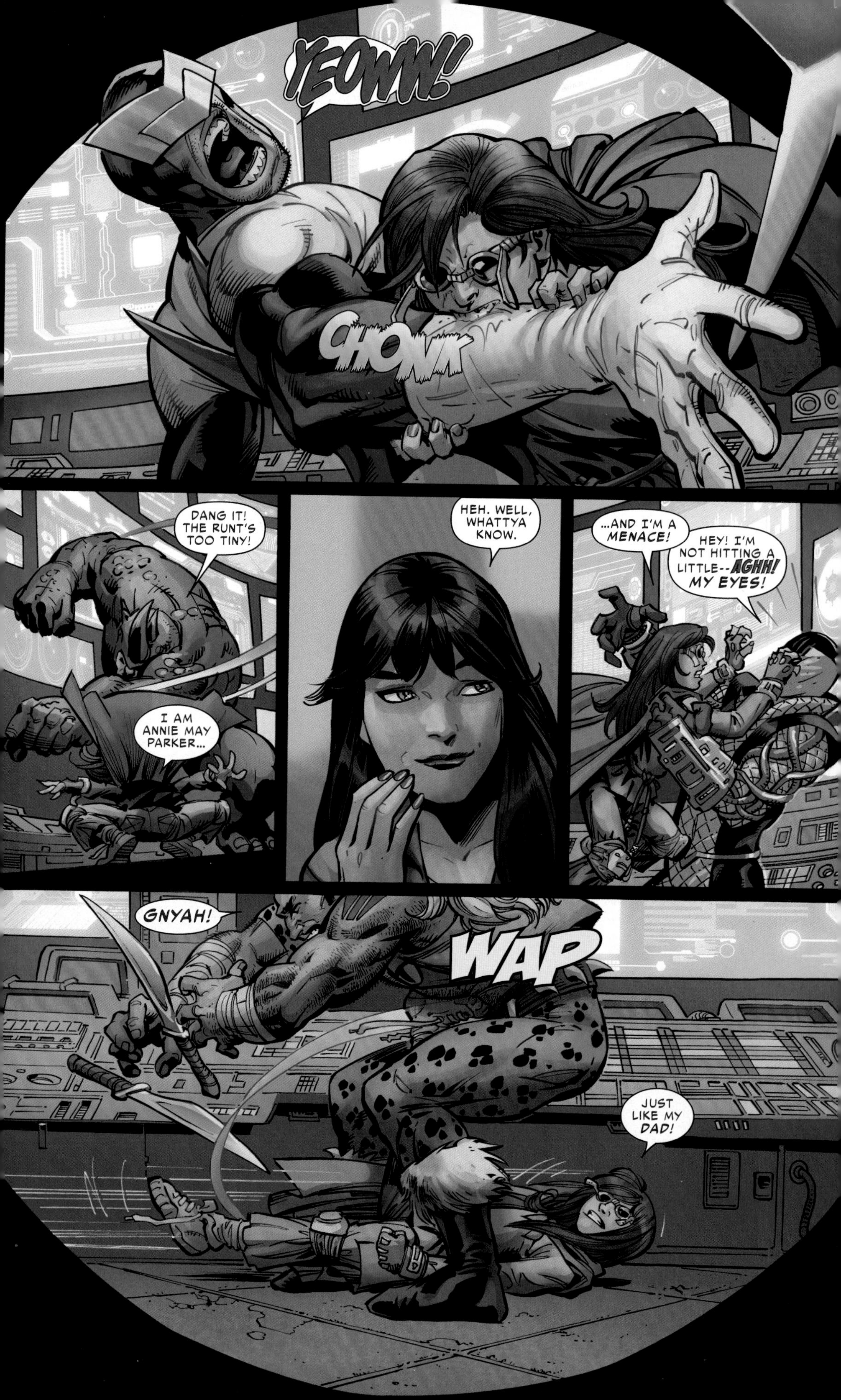
YEOWW!
CHOMP
DANG IT! THE RUNT'S TOO TINY!
I AM ANNIE MAY PARKER...
HEH. WELL, WHATTYA KNOW.
...AND I'M A MENACE!
HEY! I'M NOT HITTING A LITTLE--AGHH! MY EYES!
GNYAH!
WAP
JUST LIKE MY DAD!

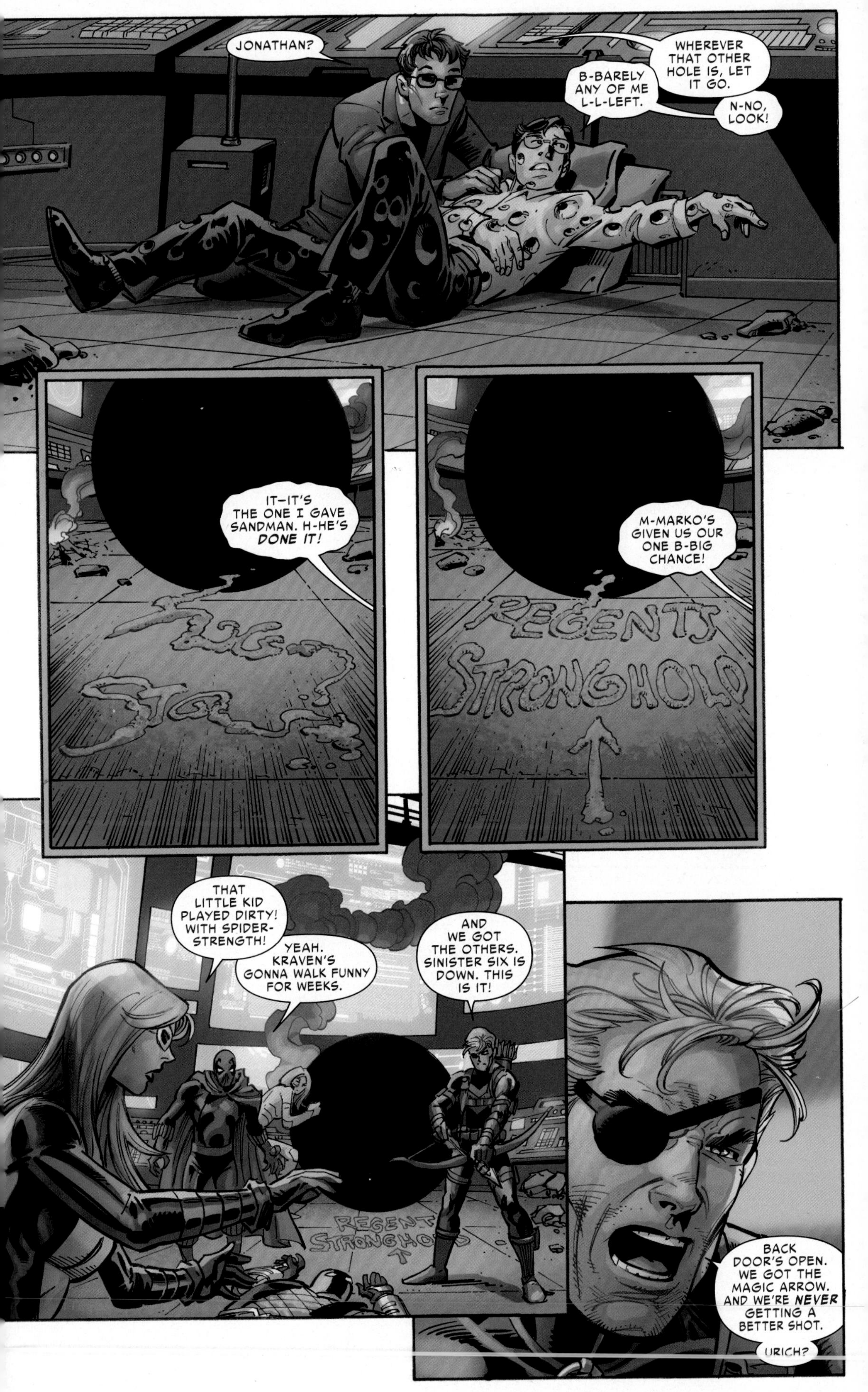
JONATHAN?
WHEREVER THAT OTHER HOLE IS, LET IT GO.
B-BARELY ANY OF ME L-L-LEFT.
N-NO, LOOK!
IT—IT'S THE ONE I GAVE SANDMAN. H-HE'S DONE IT!
M-MARKO'S GIVEN US OUR ONE B-BIG CHANCE!
REGENTS STRONGHOLD
THAT LITTLE KID PLAYED DIRTY! WITH SPIDER-STRENGTH!
YEAH. KRAVEN'S GONNA WALK FUNNY FOR WEEKS.
AND WE GOT THE OTHERS. SINISTER SIX IS DOWN. THIS IS IT!
BACK DOOR'S OPEN. WE GOT THE MAGIC ARROW. AND WE'RE NEVER GETTING A BETTER SHOT.
URICH?

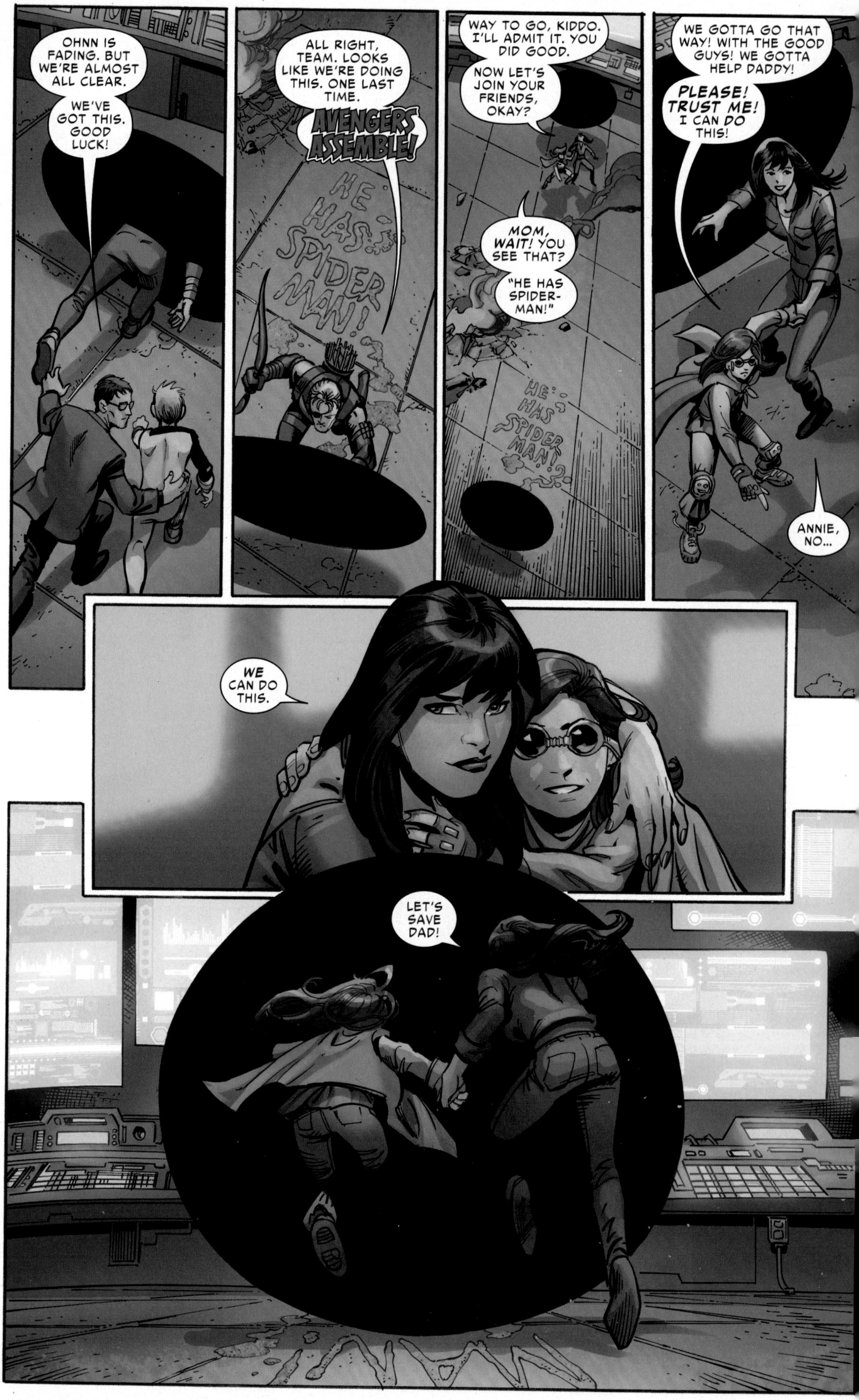

OHNN IS FADING. BUT WE'RE ALMOST ALL CLEAR.
WE'VE GOT THIS. GOOD LUCK!
ALL RIGHT, TEAM. LOOKS LIKE WE'RE DOING THIS. ONE LAST TIME.
AVENGERS ASSEMBLE!
HE HAS SPIDER MAN!
WAY TO GO, KIDDO. I'LL ADMIT IT. YOU DID GOOD.
NOW LET'S JOIN YOUR FRIENDS, OKAY?
MOM, WAIT! YOU SEE THAT?
"HE HAS SPIDER-MAN!"
HE HAS SPIDER MAN!
WE GOTTA GO THAT WAY! WITH THE GOOD GUYS! WE GOTTA HELP DADDY!
PLEASE! TRUST ME! I CAN DO THIS!
ANNIE, NO...
WE CAN DO THIS.
LET'S SAVE DAD!

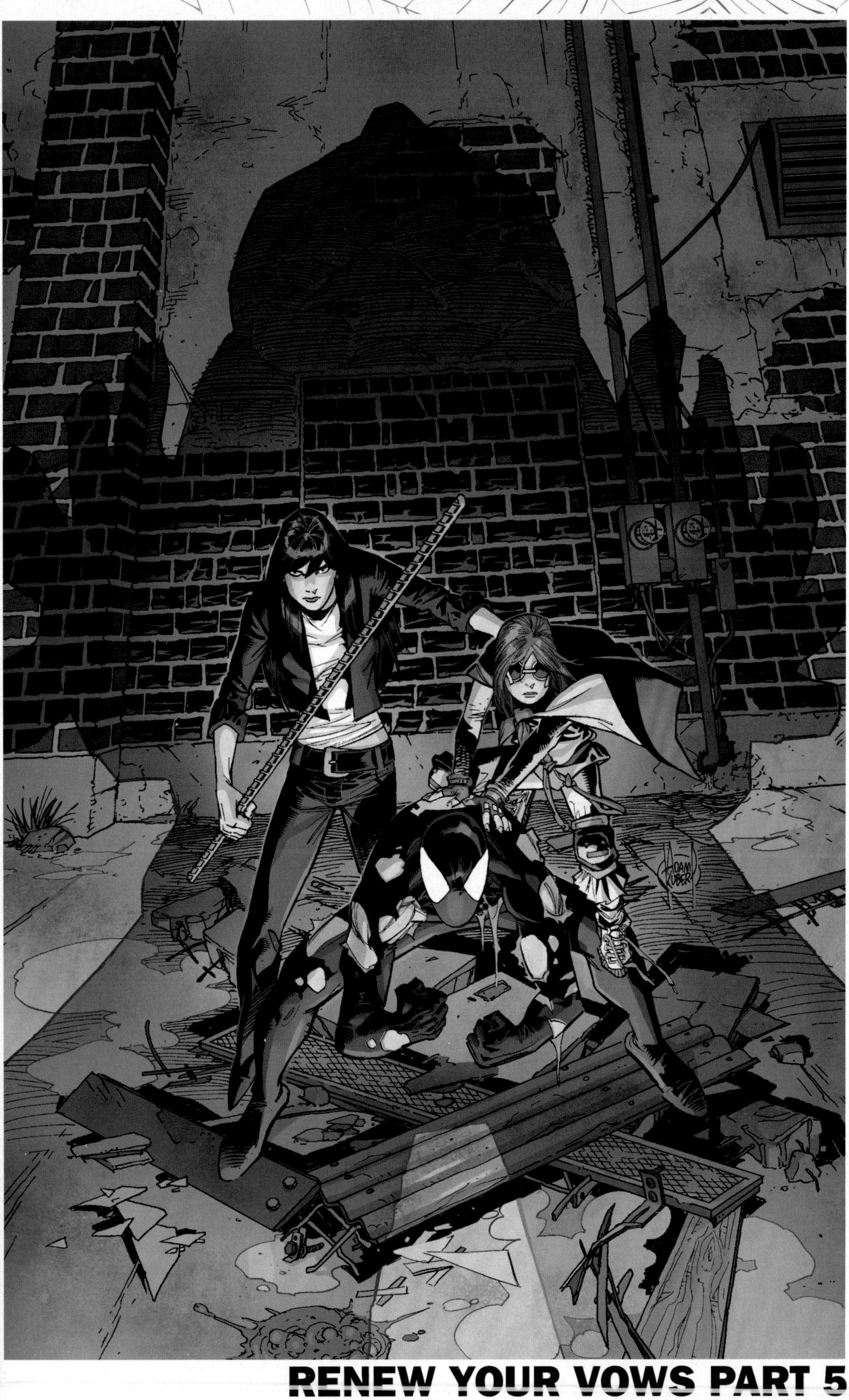
ADAM KUBERT

RENEW YOUR VOWS PART 5

"I'LL ALWAYS BE THERE FOR YOU"

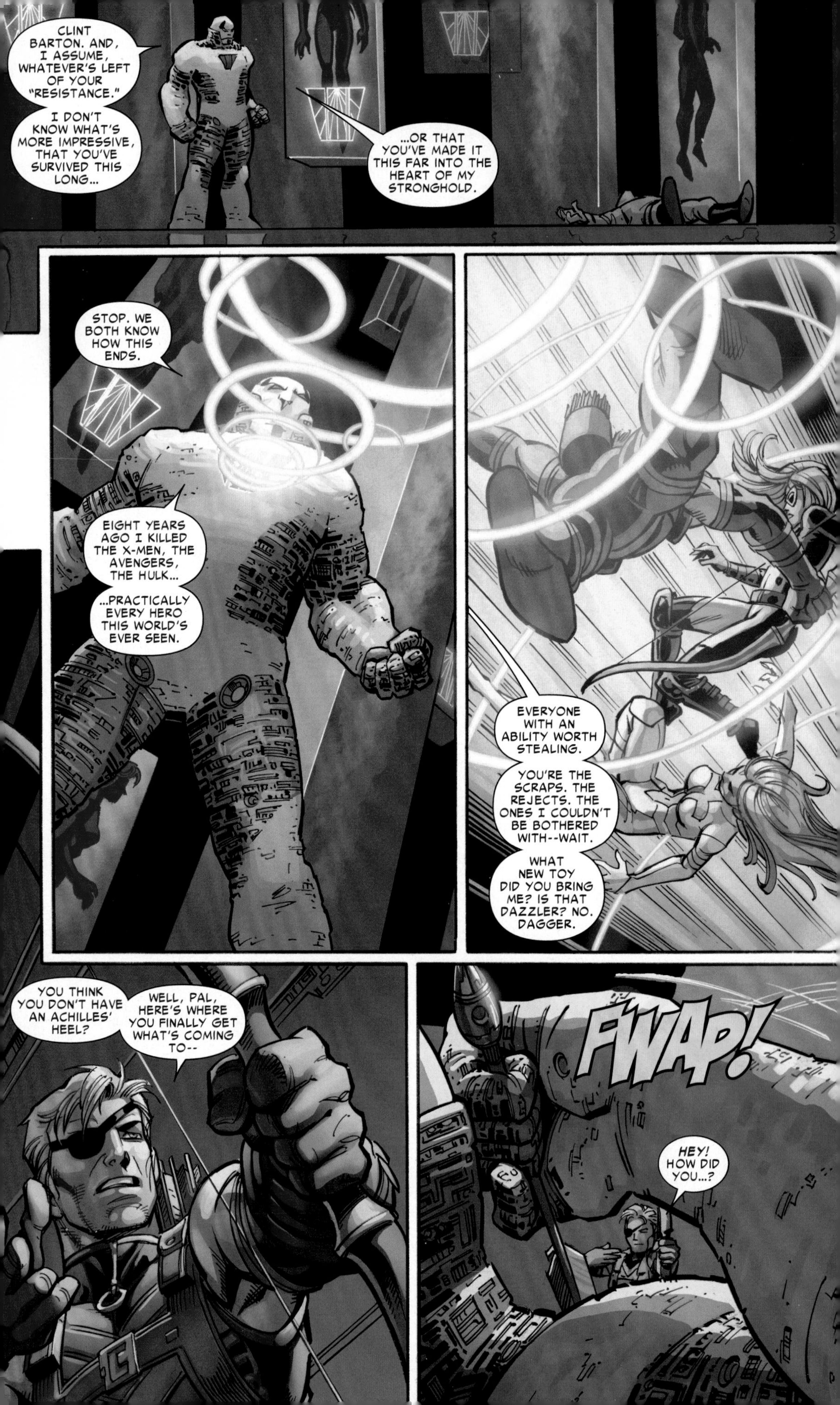
CLINT BARTON. AND, I ASSUME, WHATEVER'S LEFT OF YOUR "RESISTANCE."
I DON'T KNOW WHAT'S MORE IMPRESSIVE, THAT YOU'VE SURVIVED THIS LONG...
...OR THAT YOU'VE MADE IT THIS FAR INTO THE HEART OF MY STRONGHOLD.
STOP. WE BOTH KNOW HOW THIS ENDS.
EIGHT YEARS AGO I KILLED THE X-MEN, THE AVENGERS, THE HULK...
...PRACTICALLY EVERY HERO THIS WORLD'S EVER SEEN.
EVERYONE WITH AN ABILITY WORTH STEALING.
YOU'RE THE SCRAPS. THE REJECTS. THE ONES I COULDN'T BE BOTHERED WITH--WAIT.
WHAT NEW TOY DID YOU BRING ME? IS THAT DAZZLER? NO. DAGGER.
YOU THINK YOU DON'T HAVE AN ACHILLES' HEEL?
WELL, PAL, HERE'S WHERE YOU FINALLY GET WHAT'S COMING TO--
FWAP!
HEY! HOW DID YOU...?

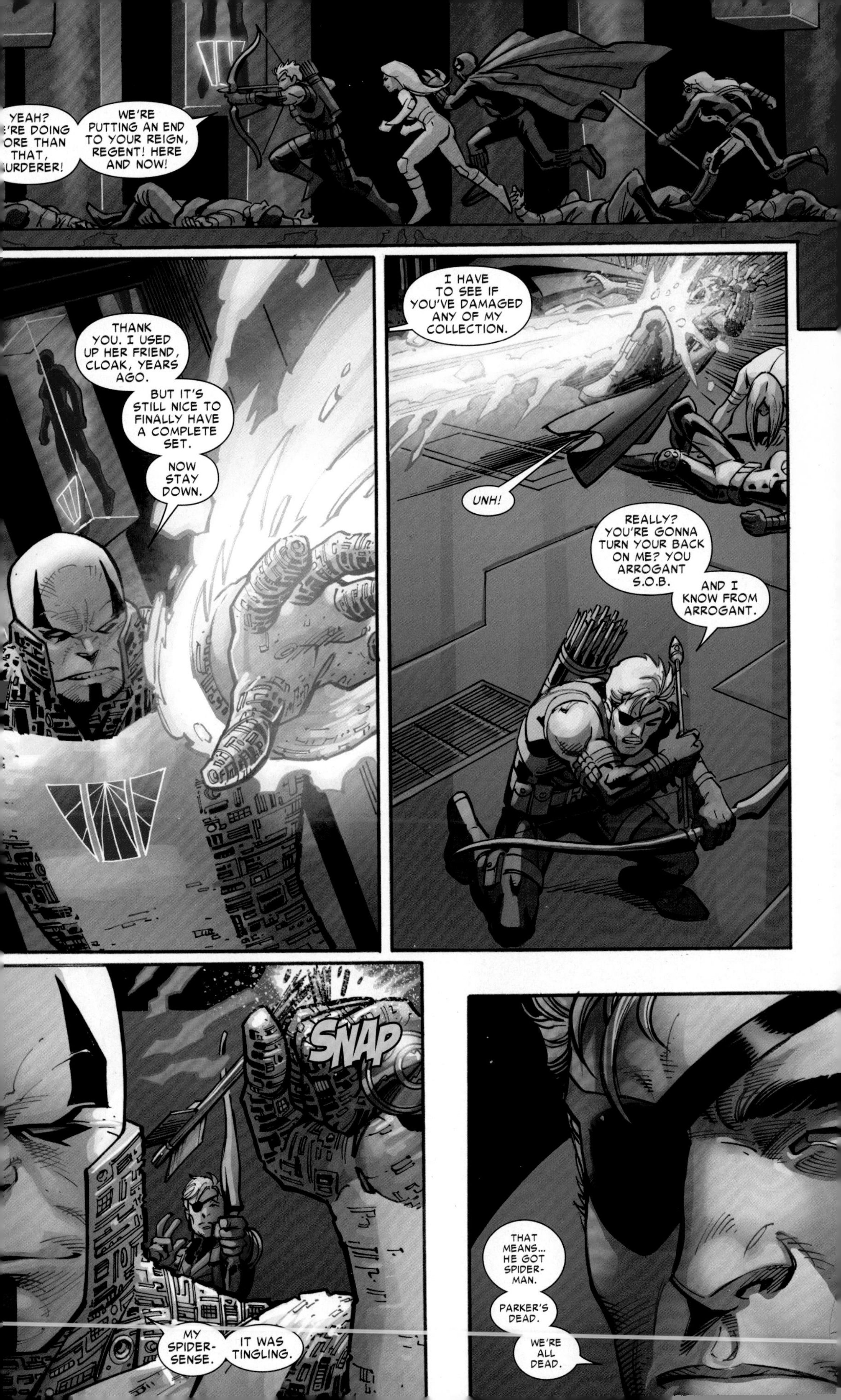

YEAH? 'E'RE DOING ORE THAN THAT, URDERER!
WE'RE PUTTING AN END TO YOUR REIGN, REGENT! HERE AND NOW!
THANK YOU. I USED UP HER FRIEND, CLOAK, YEARS AGO.
BUT IT'S STILL NICE TO FINALLY HAVE A COMPLETE SET.
NOW STAY DOWN.
I HAVE TO SEE IF YOU'VE DAMAGED ANY OF MY COLLECTION.
UNH!
REALLY? YOU'RE GONNA TURN YOUR BACK ON ME? YOU ARROGANT S.O.B.
AND I KNOW FROM ARROGANT.
SNAP
MY SPIDER-SENSE.
IT WAS TINGLING.
THAT MEANS... HE GOT SPIDER-MAN.
PARKER'S DEAD.
WE'RE ALL DEAD.

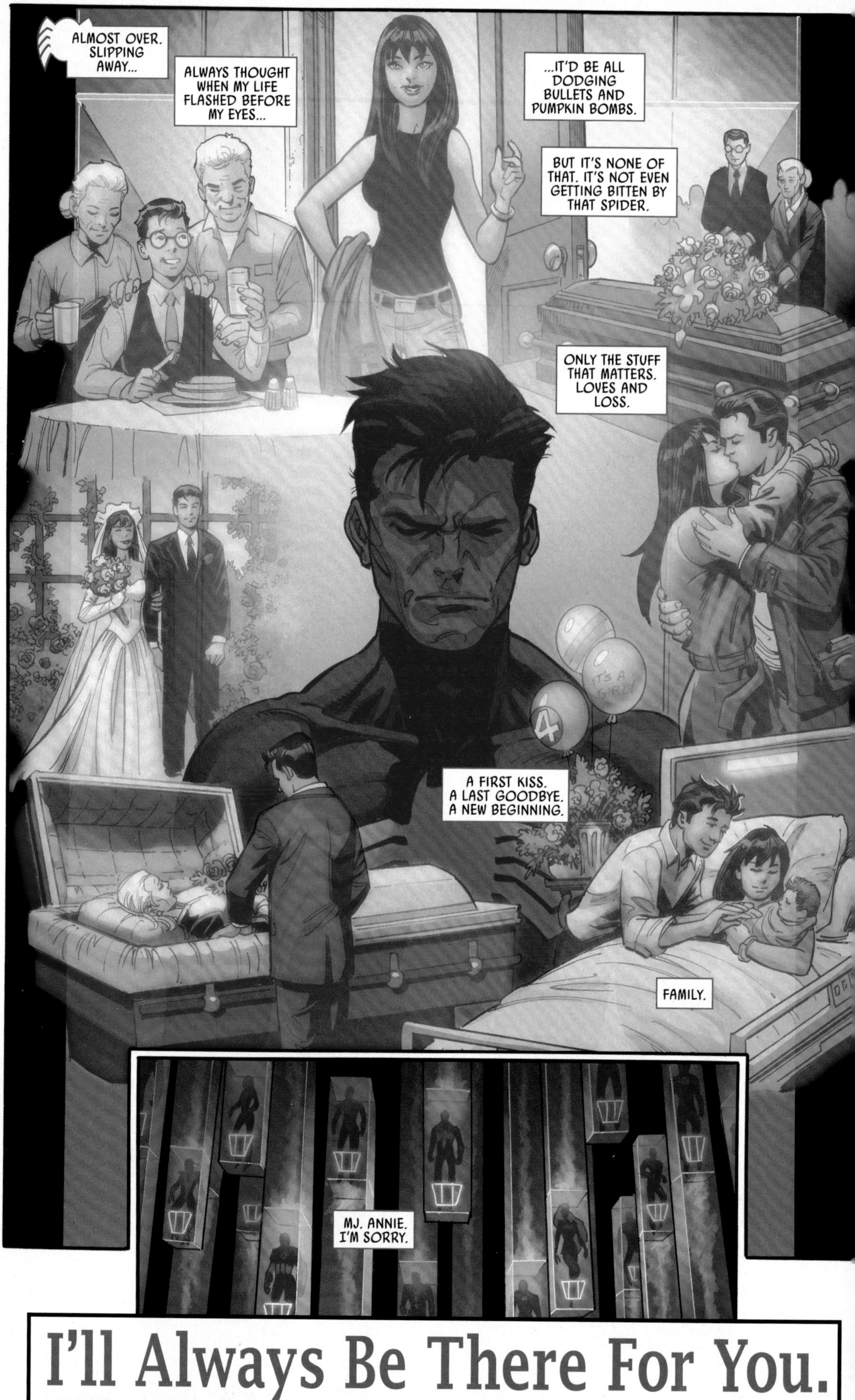
ALMOST OVER. SLIPPING AWAY...
ALWAYS THOUGHT WHEN MY LIFE FLASHED BEFORE MY EYES...
...IT'D BE ALL DODGING BULLETS AND PUMPKIN BOMBS.
BUT IT'S NONE OF THAT. IT'S NOT EVEN GETTING BITTEN BY THAT SPIDER.
ONLY THE STUFF THAT MATTERS. LOVES AND LOSS.
A FIRST KISS. A LAST GOODBYE. A NEW BEGINNING.
FAMILY.
MJ. ANNIE. I'M SORRY.
I'll Always Be There For You.

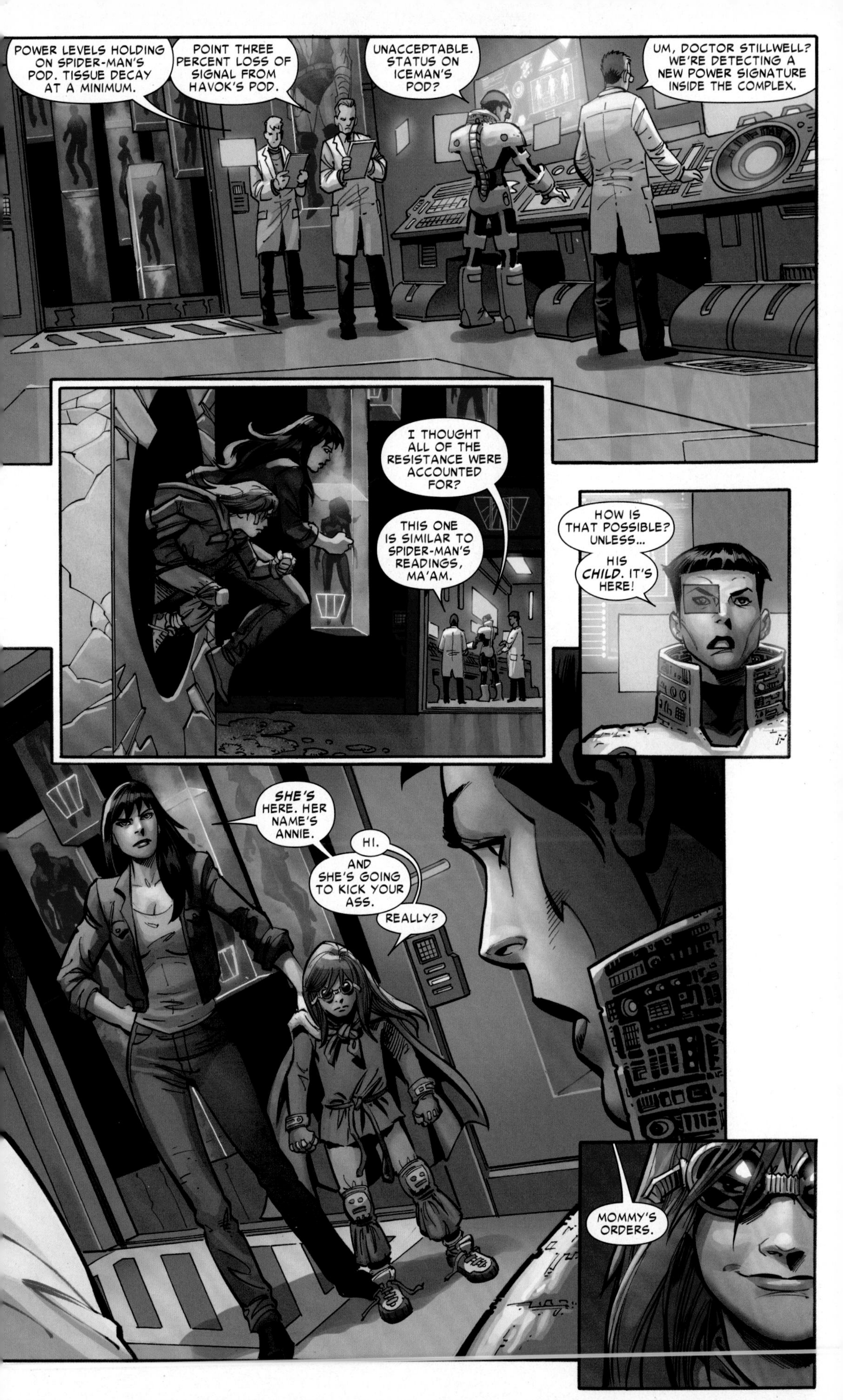
POWER LEVELS HOLDING ON SPIDER-MAN'S POD. TISSUE DECAY AT A MINIMUM.
POINT THREE PERCENT LOSS OF SIGNAL FROM HAVOK'S POD.
UNACCEPTABLE. STATUS ON ICEMAN'S POD?
UM, DOCTOR STILLWELL? WE'RE DETECTING A NEW POWER SIGNATURE INSIDE THE COMPLEX.
I THOUGHT ALL OF THE RESISTANCE WERE ACCOUNTED FOR?
THIS ONE IS SIMILAR TO SPIDER-MAN'S READINGS, MA'AM.
HOW IS THAT POSSIBLE? UNLESS...
HIS CHILD. IT'S HERE!
SHE'S HERE. HER NAME'S ANNIE.
HI.
AND SHE'S GOING TO KICK YOUR ASS.
REALLY?
MOMMY'S ORDERS.

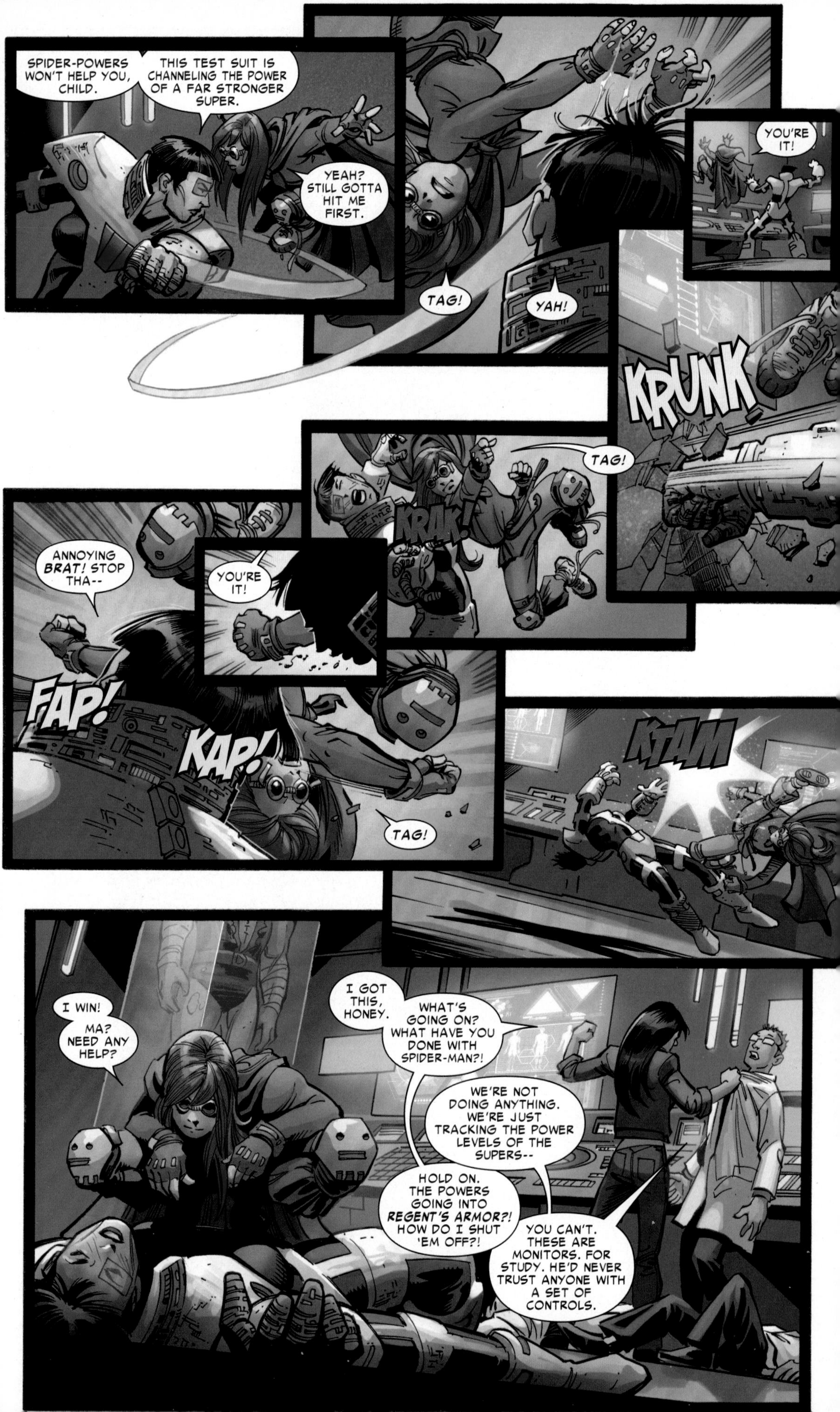

SPIDER-POWERS WON'T HELP YOU, CHILD.
THIS TEST SUIT IS CHANNELING THE POWER OF A FAR STRONGER SUPER.
YEAH? STILL GOTTA HIT ME FIRST.
TAG!
YAH!
YOU'RE IT!
KRUNK
TAG!
KRAK!
ANNOYING BRAT! STOP THA--
YOU'RE IT!
FAP!
KAP!
TAG!
KTAM
I WIN!
MA? NEED ANY HELP?
I GOT THIS, HONEY.
WHAT'S GOING ON? WHAT HAVE YOU DONE WITH SPIDER-MAN?!
WE'RE NOT DOING ANYTHING. WE'RE JUST TRACKING THE POWER LEVELS OF THE SUPERS--
HOLD ON. THE POWERS GOING INTO REGENT'S ARMOR?! HOW DO I SHUT 'EM OFF?!
YOU CAN'T. THESE ARE MONITORS. FOR STUDY. HE'D NEVER TRUST ANYONE WITH A SET OF CONTROLS.

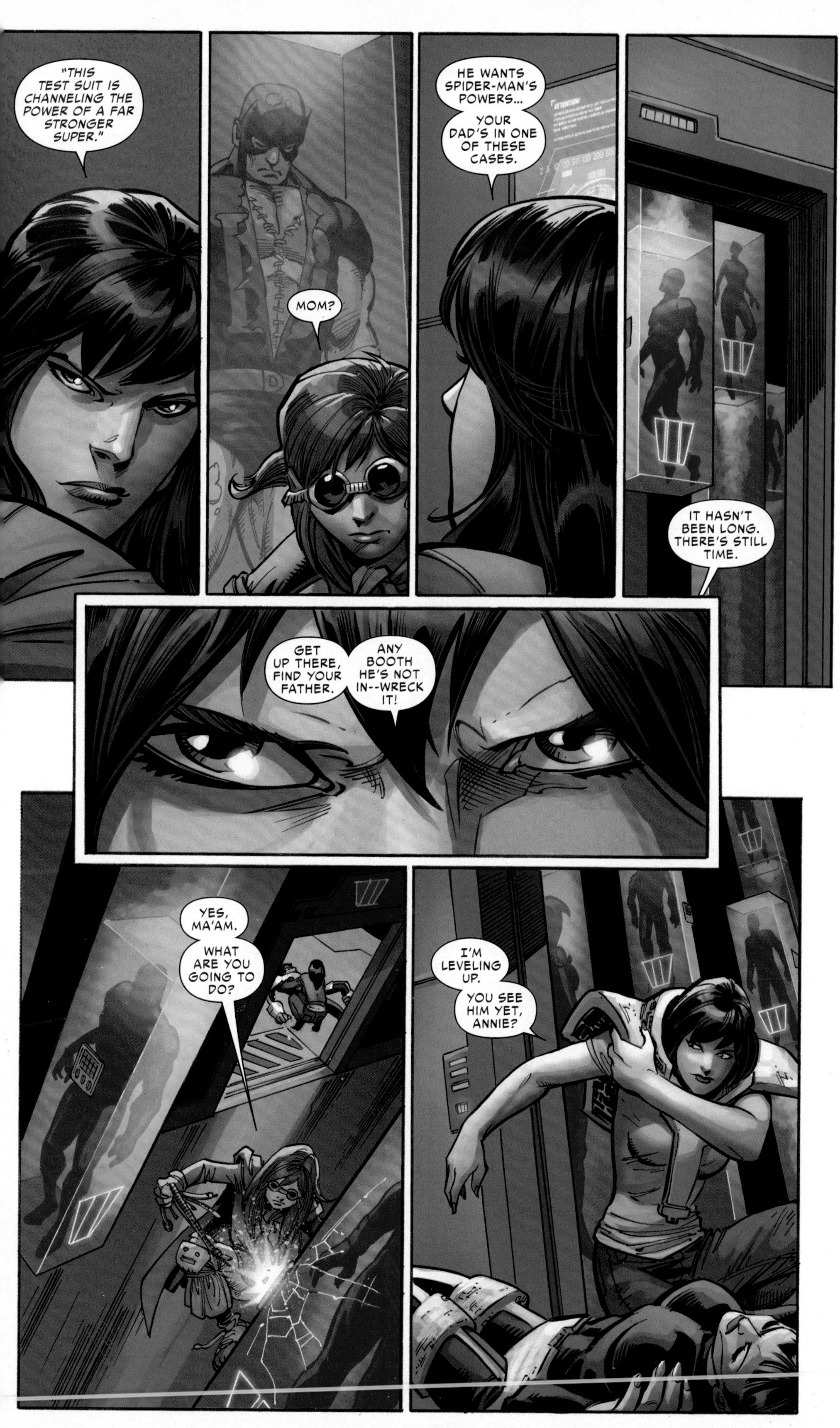
"THIS TEST SUIT IS CHANNELING THE POWER OF A FAR STRONGER SUPER."
MOM?
HE WANTS SPIDER-MAN'S POWERS...
YOUR DAD'S IN ONE OF THESE CASES.
IT HASN'T BEEN LONG. THERE'S STILL TIME.
GET UP THERE, FIND YOUR FATHER.
ANY BOOTH HE'S NOT IN--WRECK IT!
YES, MA'AM.
WHAT ARE YOU GOING TO DO?
I'M LEVELING UP.
YOU SEE HIM YET, ANNIE?

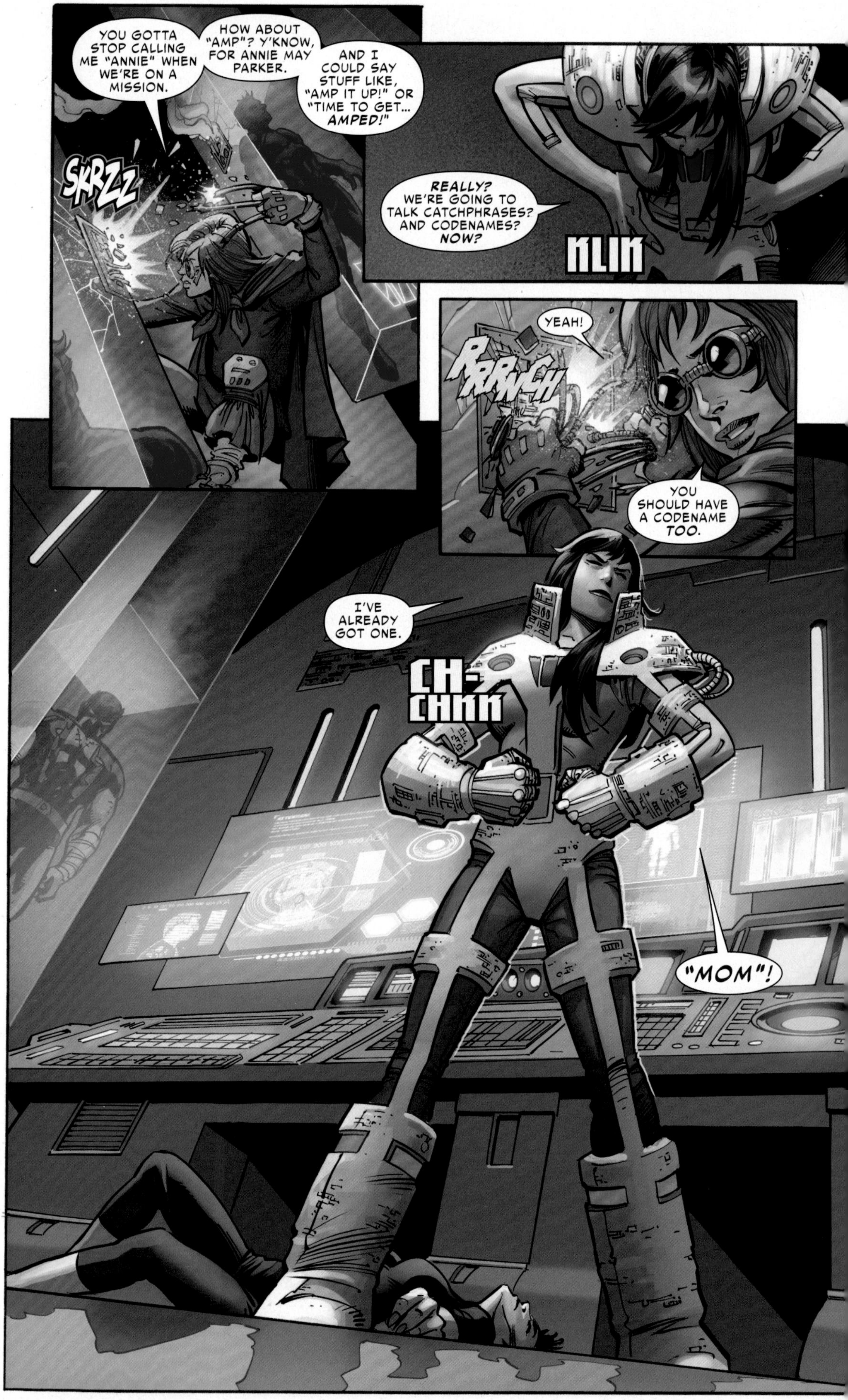
YOU GOTTA STOP CALLING ME "ANNIE" WHEN WE'RE ON A MISSION.
HOW ABOUT "AMP"? Y'KNOW, FOR ANNIE MAY PARKER.
AND I COULD SAY STUFF LIKE, "AMP IT UP!" OR "TIME TO GET... AMPED!"
SKRZZ
REALLY? WE'RE GOING TO TALK CATCHPHRASES? AND CODENAMES? NOW?
KLIK
YEAH!
RRRNCH
YOU SHOULD HAVE A CODENAME TOO.
I'VE ALREADY GOT ONE.
CH-CHKK
"MOM"!

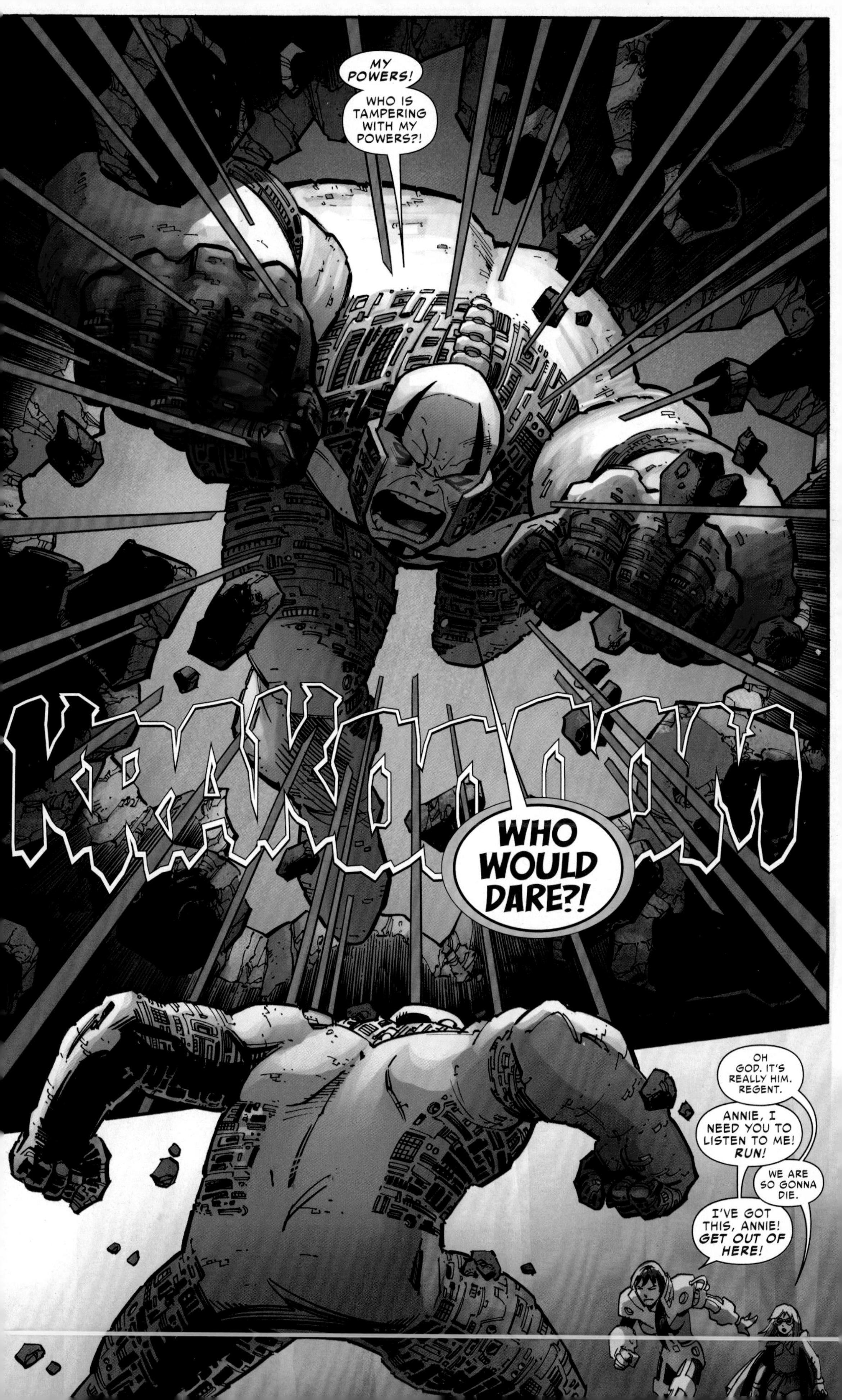
MY POWERS!
WHO IS TAMPERING WITH MY POWERS?!
KRAKOOOOM
WHO WOULD DARE?!
OH GOD. IT'S REALLY HIM. REGENT.
ANNIE, I NEED YOU TO LISTEN TO ME! RUN!
WE ARE SO GONNA DIE.
I'VE GOT THIS, ANNIE! GET OUT OF HERE!

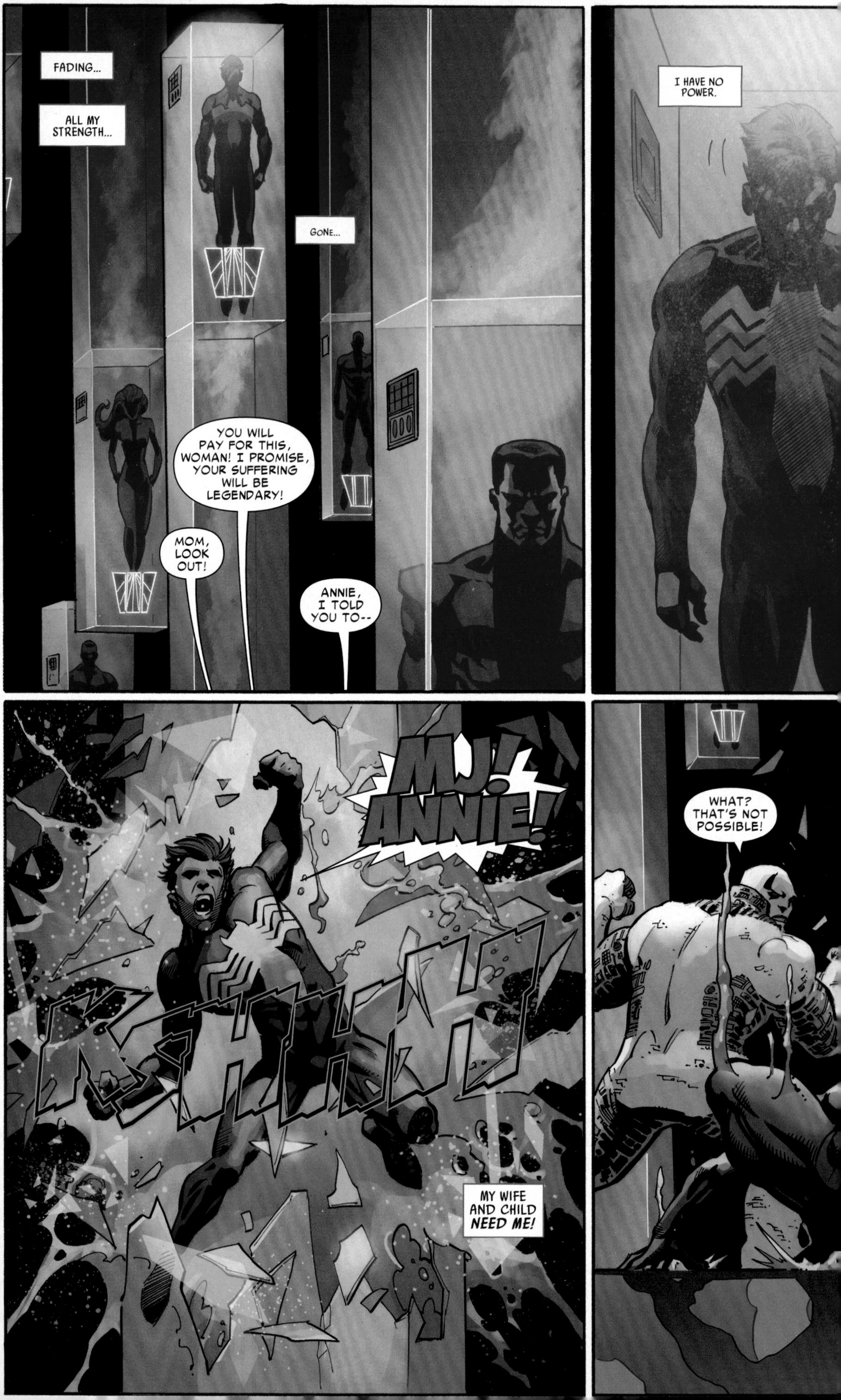
FADING...
ALL MY STRENGTH...
GONE...
YOU WILL PAY FOR THIS, WOMAN! I PROMISE, YOUR SUFFERING WILL BE LEGENDARY!
MOM, LOOK OUT!
ANNIE, I TOLD YOU TO--
I HAVE NO POWER.
MJ! ANNIE!
KRUNCH
MY WIFE AND CHILD NEED ME!
WHAT? THAT'S NOT POSSIBLE!

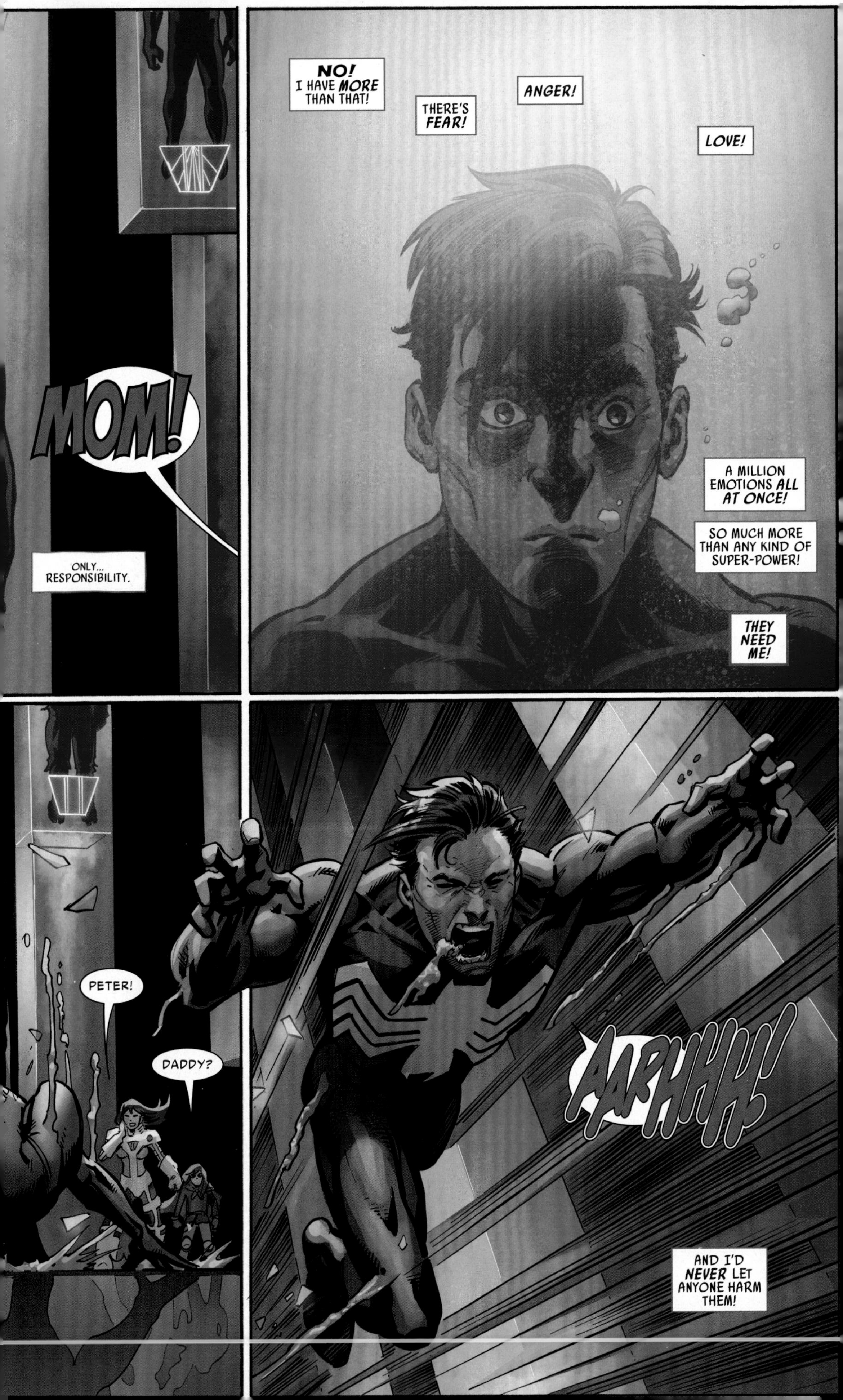
NO! I HAVE MORE THAN THAT!
THERE'S FEAR!
ANGER!
LOVE!
MOM!
ONLY... RESPONSIBILITY.
A MILLION EMOTIONS ALL AT ONCE!
SO MUCH MORE THAN ANY KIND OF SUPER-POWER!
THEY NEED ME!
PETER!
DADDY?
AARHHH!
AND I'D NEVER LET ANYONE HARM THEM!

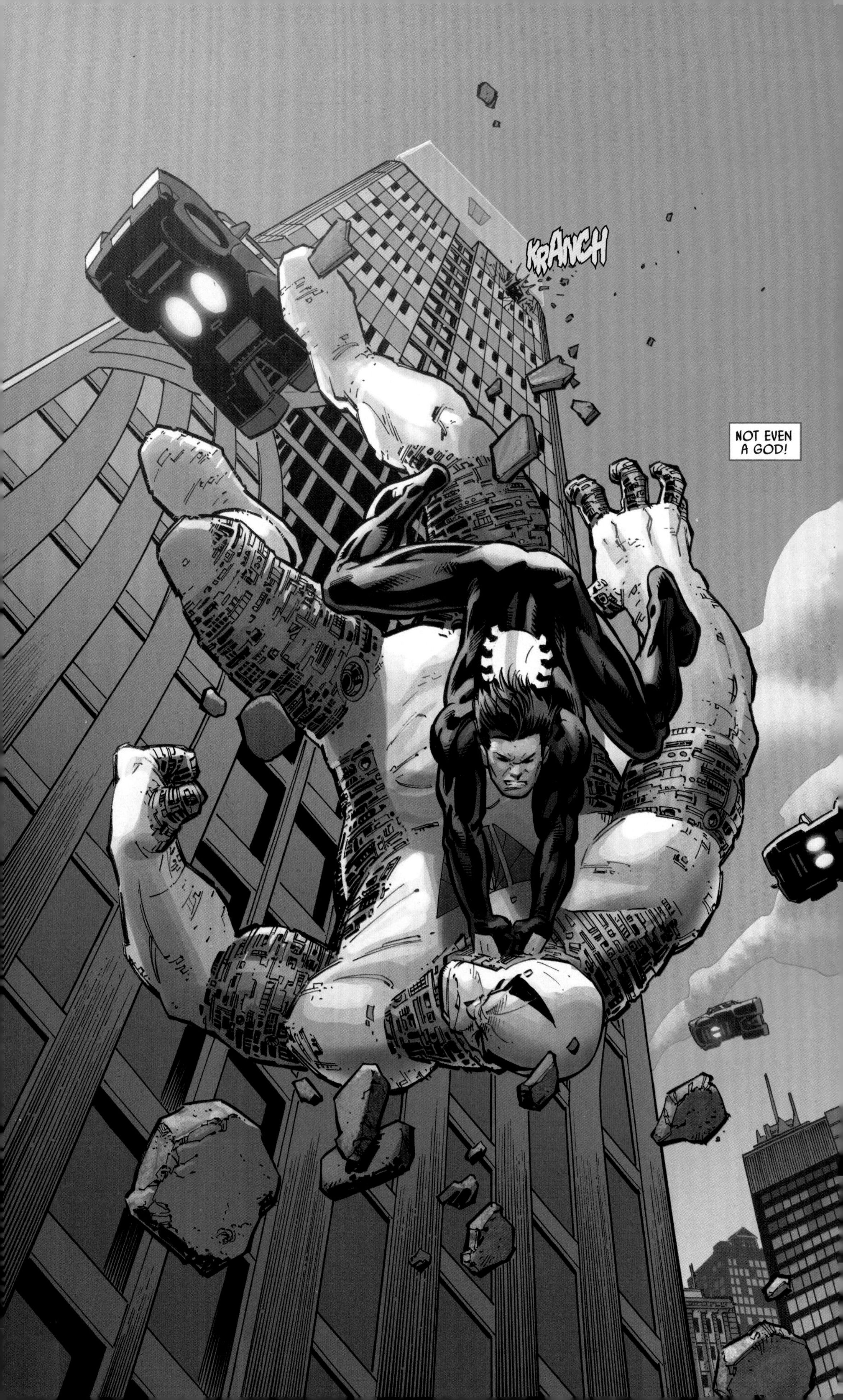
KRANCH
NOT EVEN A GOD!

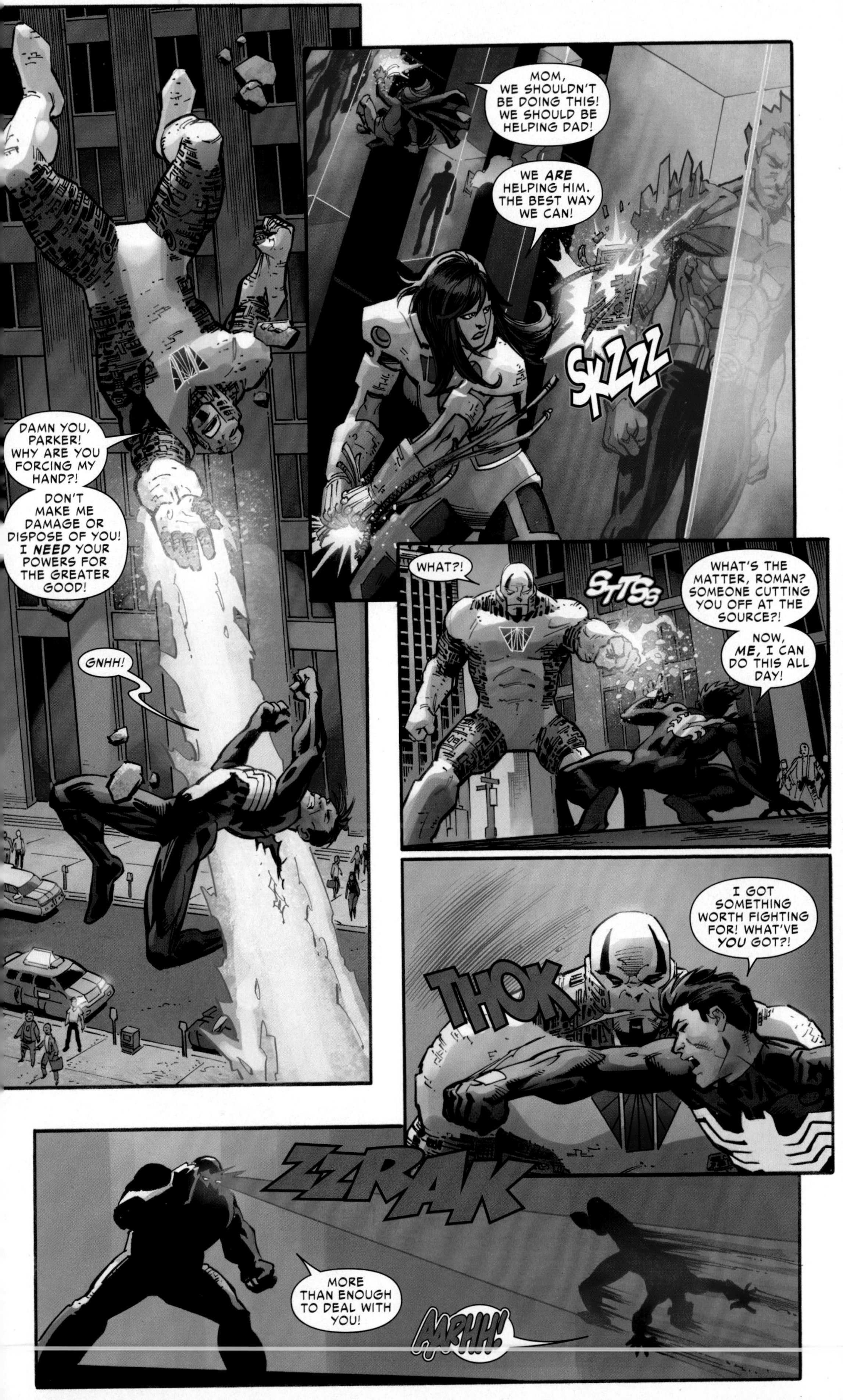
DAMN YOU, PARKER! WHY ARE YOU FORCING MY HAND?!
DON'T MAKE ME DAMAGE OR DISPOSE OF YOU! I NEED YOUR POWERS FOR THE GREATER GOOD!
GNHH!
MOM, WE SHOULDN'T BE DOING THIS! WE SHOULD BE HELPING DAD!
WE ARE HELPING HIM. THE BEST WAY WE CAN!
SKZZZ
WHAT?!
STTSS
WHAT'S THE MATTER, ROMAN? SOMEONE CUTTING YOU OFF AT THE SOURCE?!
NOW, ME, I CAN DO THIS ALL DAY!
I GOT SOMETHING WORTH FIGHTING FOR! WHAT'VE YOU GOT?!
THOK
ZZRAK
MORE THAN ENOUGH TO DEAL WITH YOU!
AARHH!

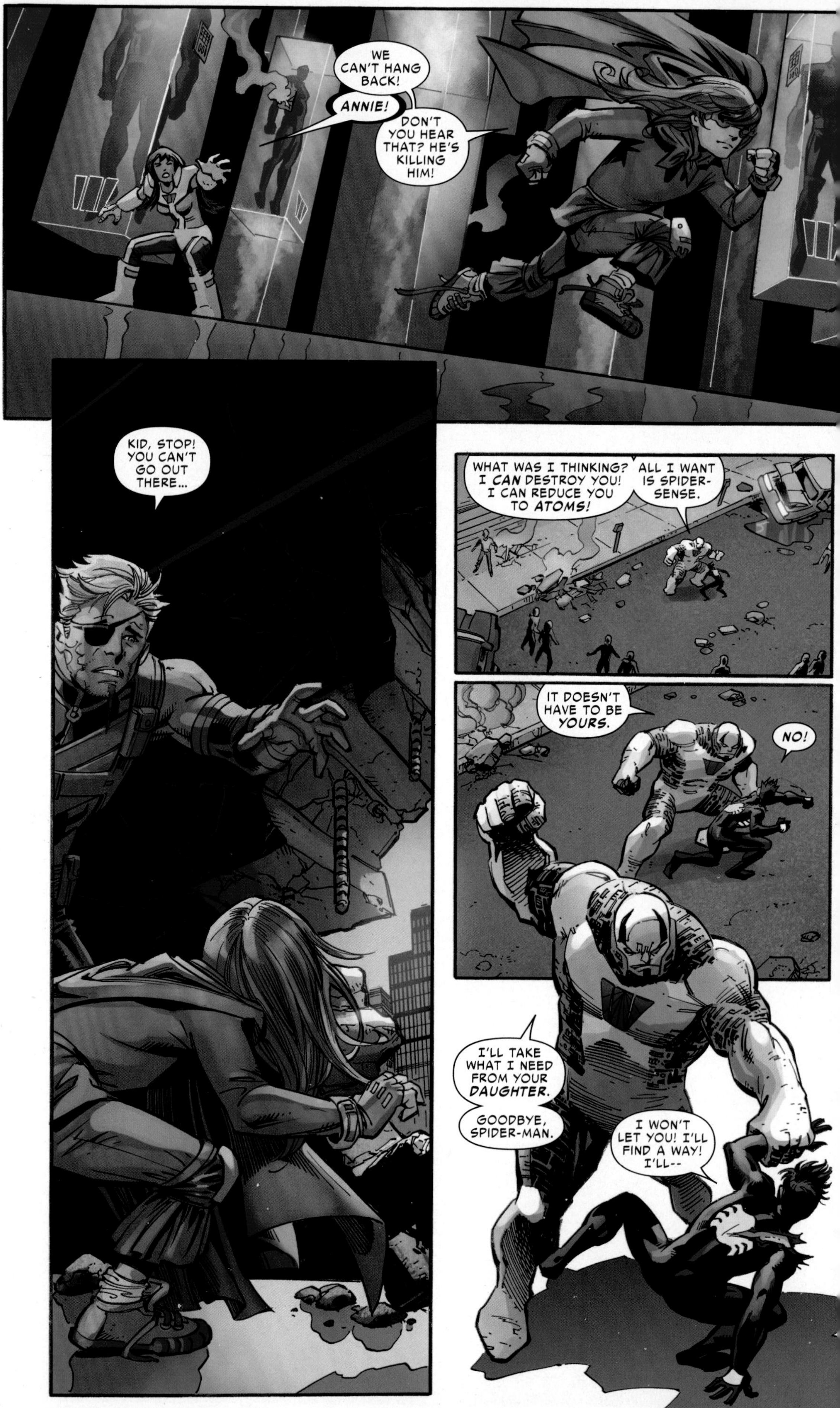
WE CAN'T HANG BACK!
ANNIE!
DON'T YOU HEAR THAT? HE'S KILLING HIM!
KID, STOP! YOU CAN'T GO OUT THERE...
WHAT WAS I THINKING? I CAN DESTROY YOU! I CAN REDUCE YOU TO ATOMS!
ALL I WANT IS SPIDER-SENSE.
IT DOESN'T HAVE TO BE YOURS.
NO!
I'LL TAKE WHAT I NEED FROM YOUR DAUGHTER.
GOODBYE, SPIDER-MAN.
I WON'T LET YOU! I'LL FIND A WAY! I'LL--

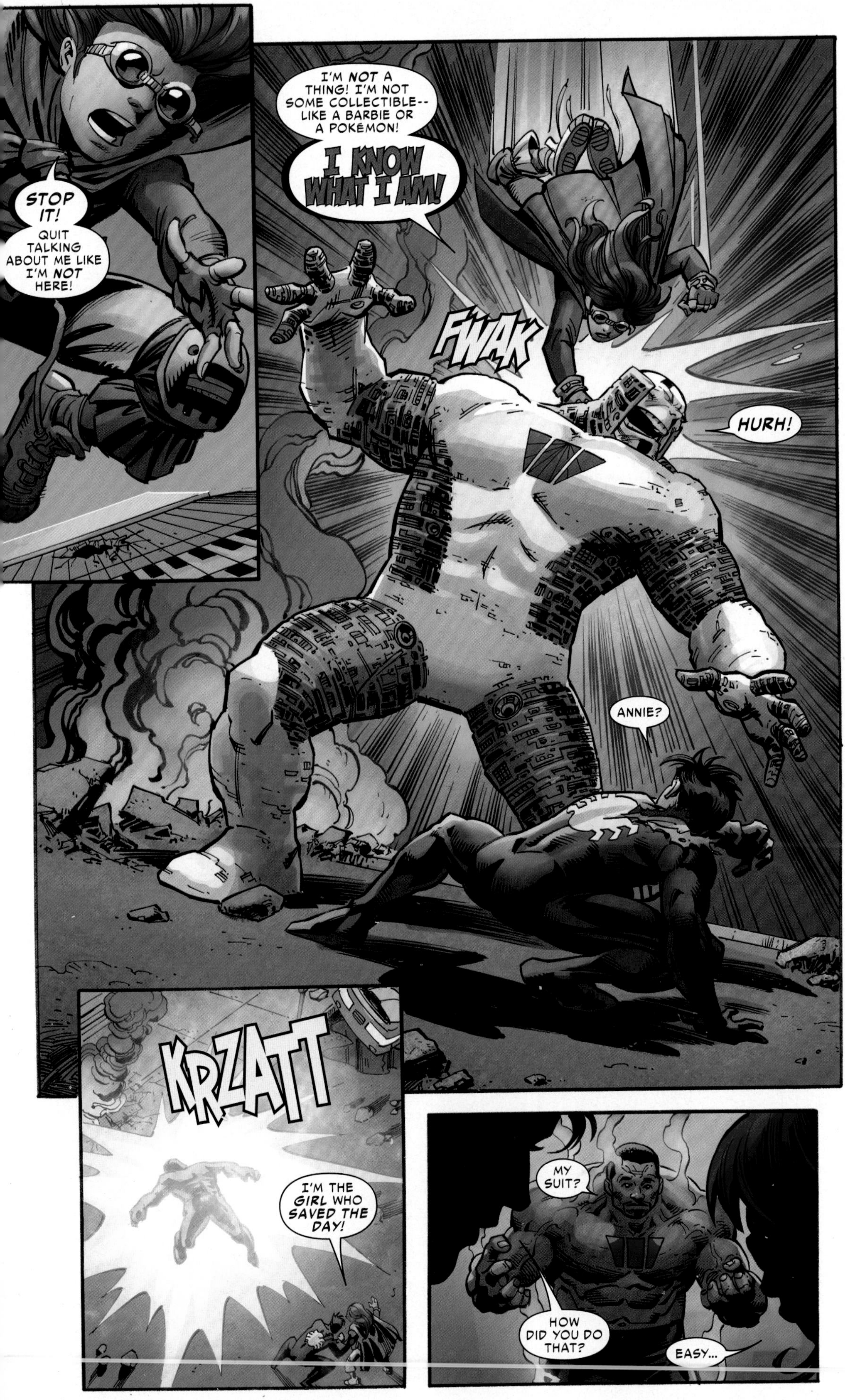
STOP IT! QUIT TALKING ABOUT ME LIKE I'M NOT HERE!
I'M NOT A THING! I'M NOT SOME COLLECTIBLE-- LIKE A BARBIE OR A POKÉMON!
I KNOW WHAT I AM!
FWAK
HURH!
ANNIE?
KRZATT
I'M THE GIRL WHO SAVED THE DAY!
MY SUIT?
HOW DID YOU DO THAT?
EASY...

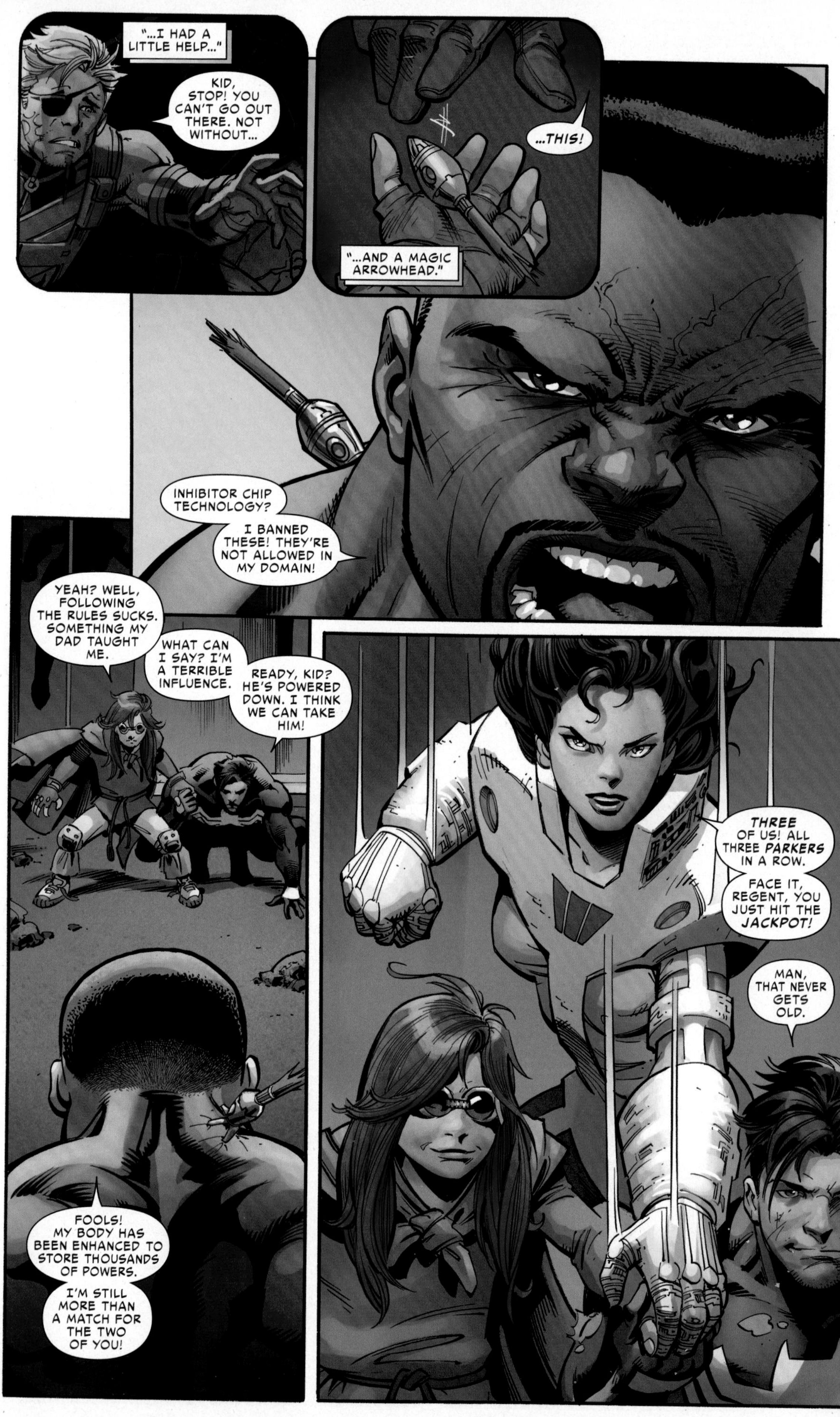

"...I HAD A LITTLE HELP..."
KID, STOP! YOU CAN'T GO OUT THERE. NOT WITHOUT...
...THIS!
"...AND A MAGIC ARROWHEAD."
INHIBITOR CHIP TECHNOLOGY?
I BANNED THESE! THEY'RE NOT ALLOWED IN MY DOMAIN!
YEAH? WELL, FOLLOWING THE RULES SUCKS. SOMETHING MY DAD TAUGHT ME.
WHAT CAN I SAY? I'M A TERRIBLE INFLUENCE.
READY, KID? HE'S POWERED DOWN. I THINK WE CAN TAKE HIM!
FOOLS! MY BODY HAS BEEN ENHANCED TO STORE THOUSANDS OF POWERS.
I'M STILL MORE THAN A MATCH FOR THE TWO OF YOU!
THREE OF US! ALL THREE PARKERS IN A ROW.
FACE IT, REGENT, YOU JUST HIT THE JACKPOT!
MAN, THAT NEVER GETS OLD.

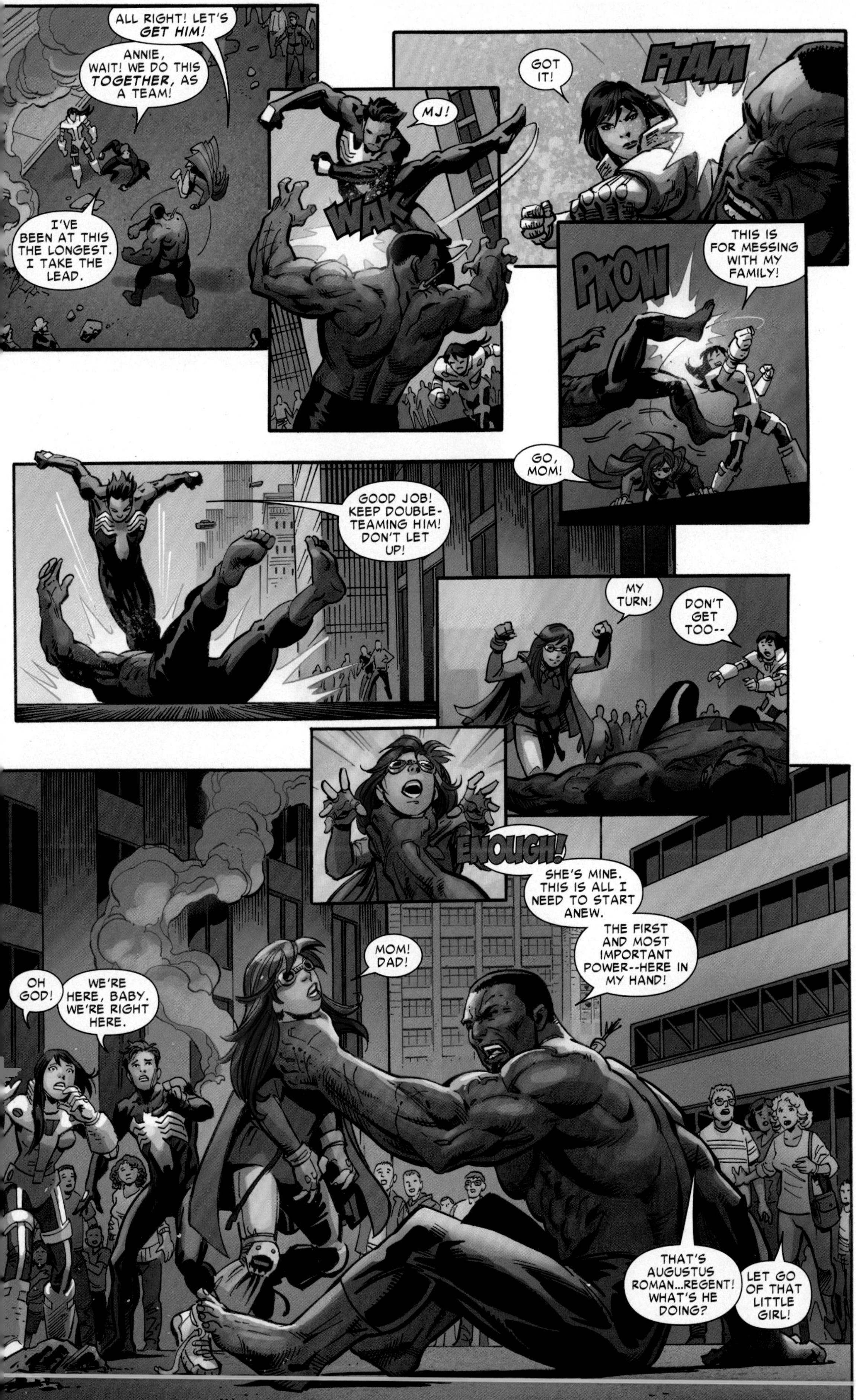
ALL RIGHT! LET'S GET HIM!
ANNIE, WAIT! WE DO THIS TOGETHER, AS A TEAM!
I'VE BEEN AT THIS THE LONGEST. I TAKE THE LEAD.
MJ!
WAK
GOT IT!
FTAM
THIS IS FOR MESSING WITH MY FAMILY!
PKOW
GO, MOM!
GOOD JOB! KEEP DOUBLE-TEAMING HIM! DON'T LET UP!
MY TURN!
DON'T GET TOO--
ENOUGH!
SHE'S MINE. THIS IS ALL I NEED TO START ANEW.
THE FIRST AND MOST IMPORTANT POWER--HERE IN MY HAND!
MOM! DAD!
OH GOD!
WE'RE HERE, BABY. WE'RE RIGHT HERE.
THAT'S AUGUSTUS ROMAN...REGENT! WHAT'S HE DOING?
LET GO OF THAT LITTLE GIRL!

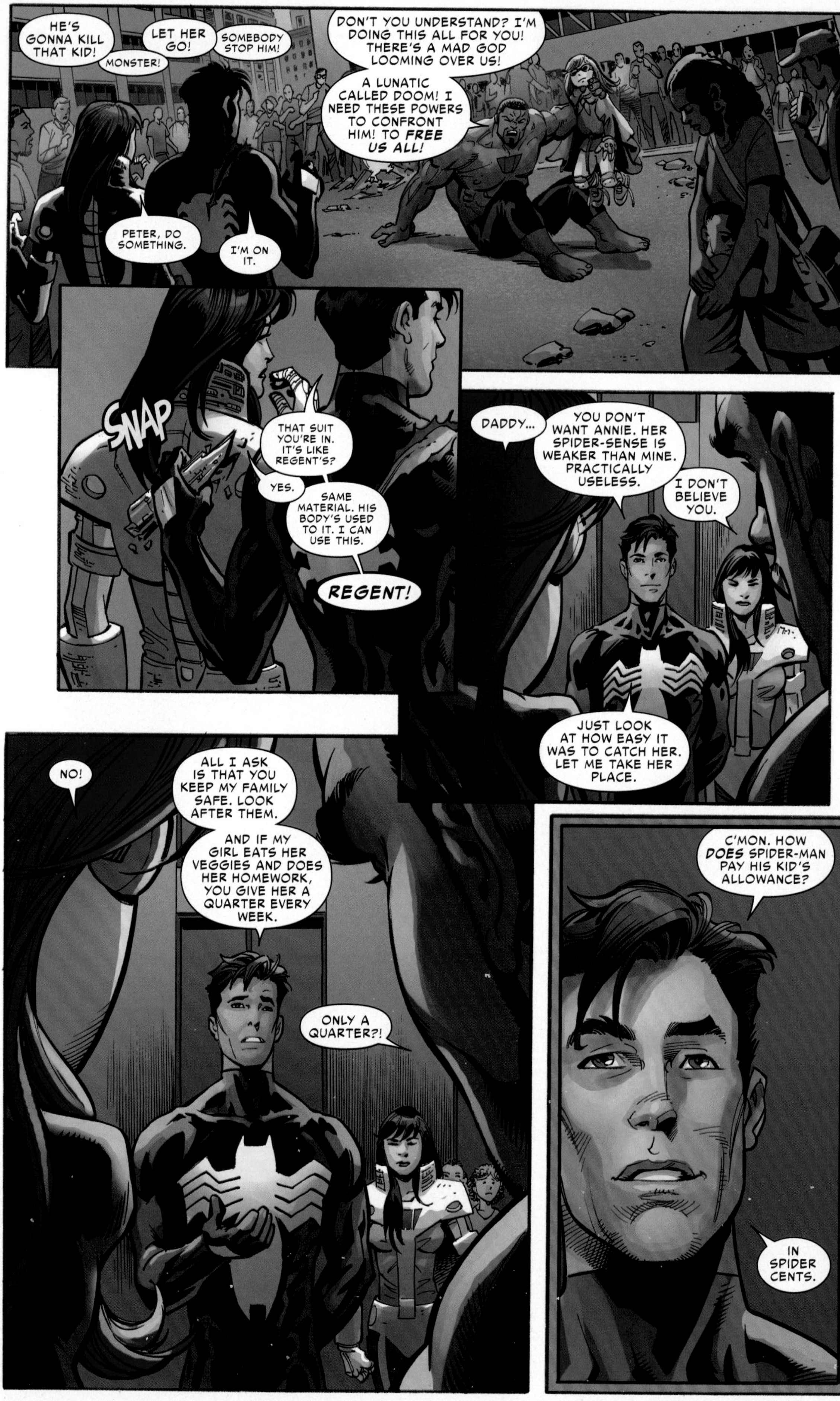

HE'S GONNA KILL THAT KID!
MONSTER!
LET HER GO!
SOMEBODY STOP HIM!
DON'T YOU UNDERSTAND? I'M DOING THIS ALL FOR YOU! THERE'S A MAD GOD LOOMING OVER US!
A LUNATIC CALLED DOOM! I NEED THESE POWERS TO CONFRONT HIM! TO FREE US ALL!
PETER, DO SOMETHING.
I'M ON IT.
SNAP
THAT SUIT YOU'RE IN. IT'S LIKE REGENT'S?
YES.
SAME MATERIAL. HIS BODY'S USED TO IT. I CAN USE THIS.
REGENT!
DADDY...
YOU DON'T WANT ANNIE. HER SPIDER-SENSE IS WEAKER THAN MINE. PRACTICALLY USELESS.
I DON'T BELIEVE YOU.
JUST LOOK AT HOW EASY IT WAS TO CATCH HER. LET ME TAKE HER PLACE.
NO!
ALL I ASK IS THAT YOU KEEP MY FAMILY SAFE. LOOK AFTER THEM.
AND IF MY GIRL EATS HER VEGGIES AND DOES HER HOMEWORK, YOU GIVE HER A QUARTER EVERY WEEK.
ONLY A QUARTER?!
C'MON. HOW DOES SPIDER-MAN PAY HIS KID'S ALLOWANCE?
IN SPIDER CENTS.

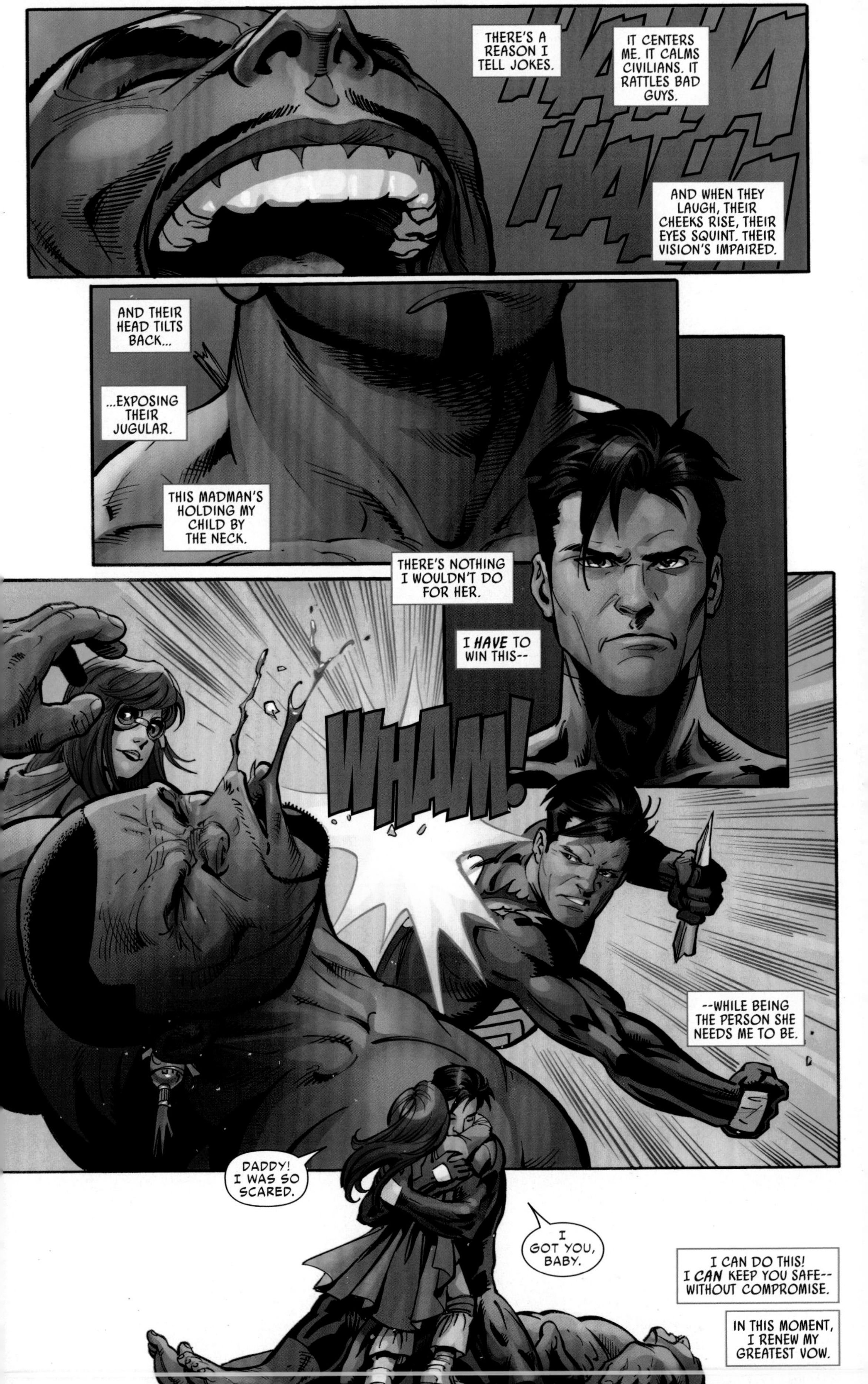
THERE'S A REASON I TELL JOKES.
IT CENTERS ME. IT CALMS CIVILIANS. IT RATTLES BAD GUYS.
HAHA HAHA
AND WHEN THEY LAUGH, THEIR CHEEKS RISE, THEIR EYES SQUINT. THEIR VISION'S IMPAIRED.
AND THEIR HEAD TILTS BACK...
...EXPOSING THEIR JUGULAR.
THIS MADMAN'S HOLDING MY CHILD BY THE NECK.
THERE'S NOTHING I WOULDN'T DO FOR HER.
I *HAVE* TO WIN THIS--
WHAM!
--WHILE BEING THE PERSON SHE NEEDS ME TO BE.
DADDY! I WAS SO SCARED.
I GOT YOU, BABY.
I CAN DO THIS! I ***CAN*** KEEP YOU SAFE-- WITHOUT COMPROMISE.
IN THIS MOMENT, I RENEW MY GREATEST VOW.

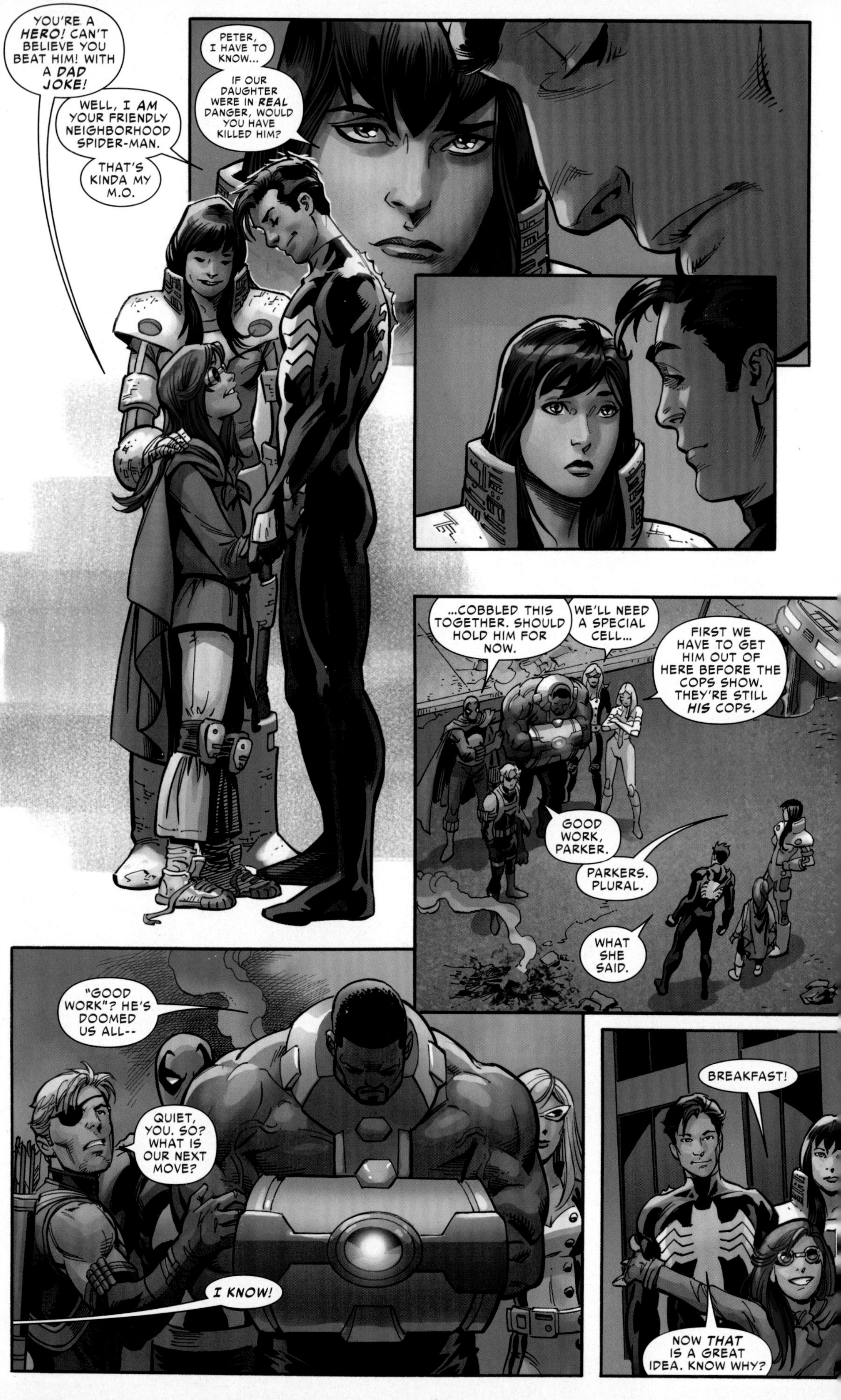
YOU'RE A HERO! CAN'T BELIEVE YOU BEAT HIM! WITH A DAD JOKE!
WELL, I AM YOUR FRIENDLY NEIGHBORHOOD SPIDER-MAN.
THAT'S KINDA MY M.O.
PETER, I HAVE TO KNOW...
IF OUR DAUGHTER WERE IN REAL DANGER, WOULD YOU HAVE KILLED HIM?
...COBBLED THIS TOGETHER. SHOULD HOLD HIM FOR NOW.
WE'LL NEED A SPECIAL CELL...
FIRST WE HAVE TO GET HIM OUT OF HERE BEFORE THE COPS SHOW. THEY'RE STILL HIS COPS.
GOOD WORK, PARKER.
PARKERS. PLURAL.
WHAT SHE SAID.
"GOOD WORK"? HE'S DOOMED US ALL--
QUIET, YOU. SO? WHAT IS OUR NEXT MOVE?
I KNOW!
BREAKFAST!
NOW THAT IS A GREAT IDEA. KNOW WHY?

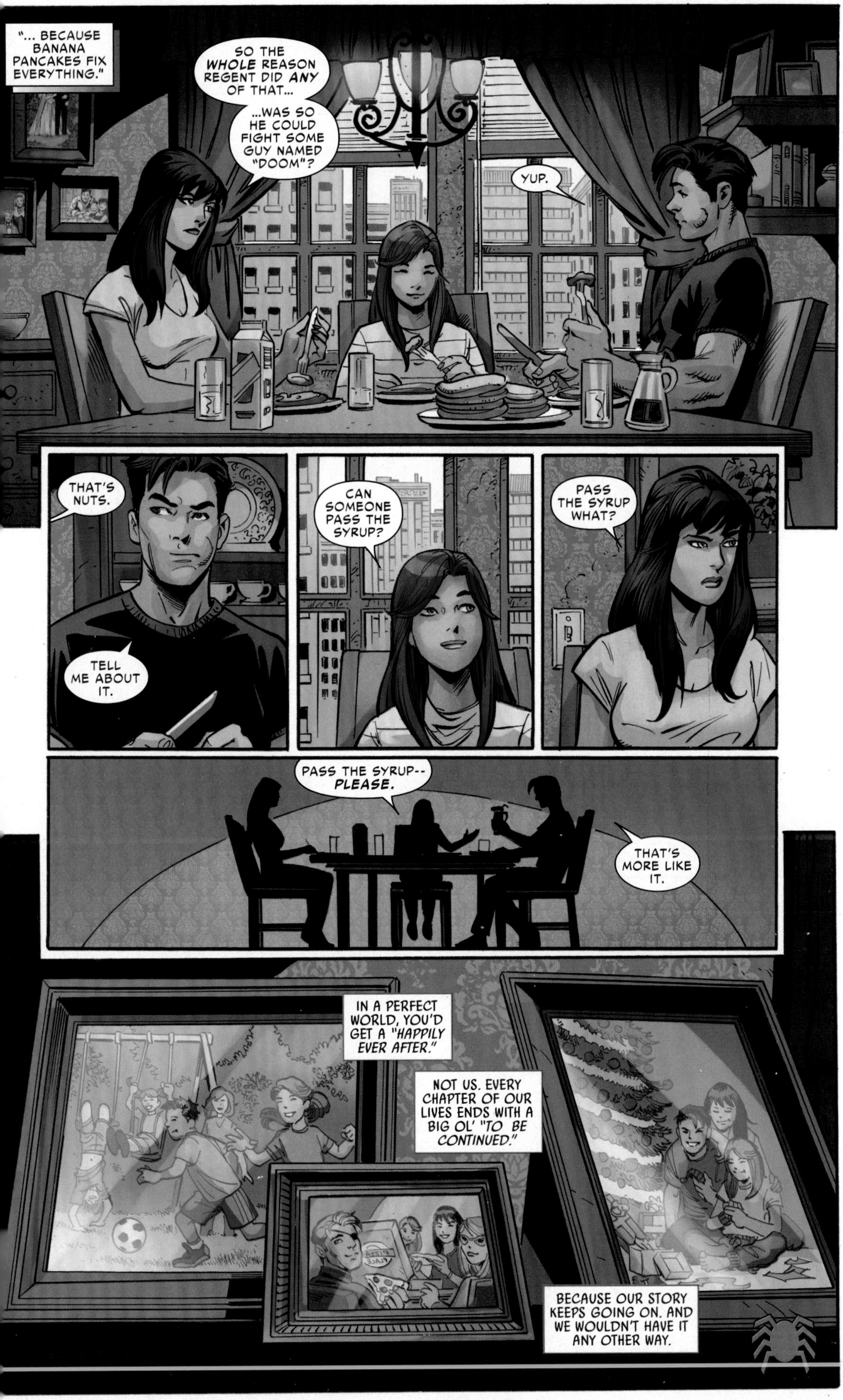
"... BECAUSE BANANA PANCAKES FIX EVERYTHING."
SO THE WHOLE REASON REGENT DID ANY OF THAT...
...WAS SO HE COULD FIGHT SOME GUY NAMED "DOOM"?
YUP.
THAT'S NUTS.
TELL ME ABOUT IT.
CAN SOMEONE PASS THE SYRUP?
PASS THE SYRUP WHAT?
PASS THE SYRUP-- PLEASE.
THAT'S MORE LIKE IT.
IN A PERFECT WORLD, YOU'D GET A "HAPPILY EVER AFTER."
NOT US. EVERY CHAPTER OF OUR LIVES ENDS WITH A BIG OL' "TO BE CONTINUED."
BECAUSE OUR STORY KEEPS GOING ON. AND WE WOULDN'T HAVE IT ANY OTHER WAY.

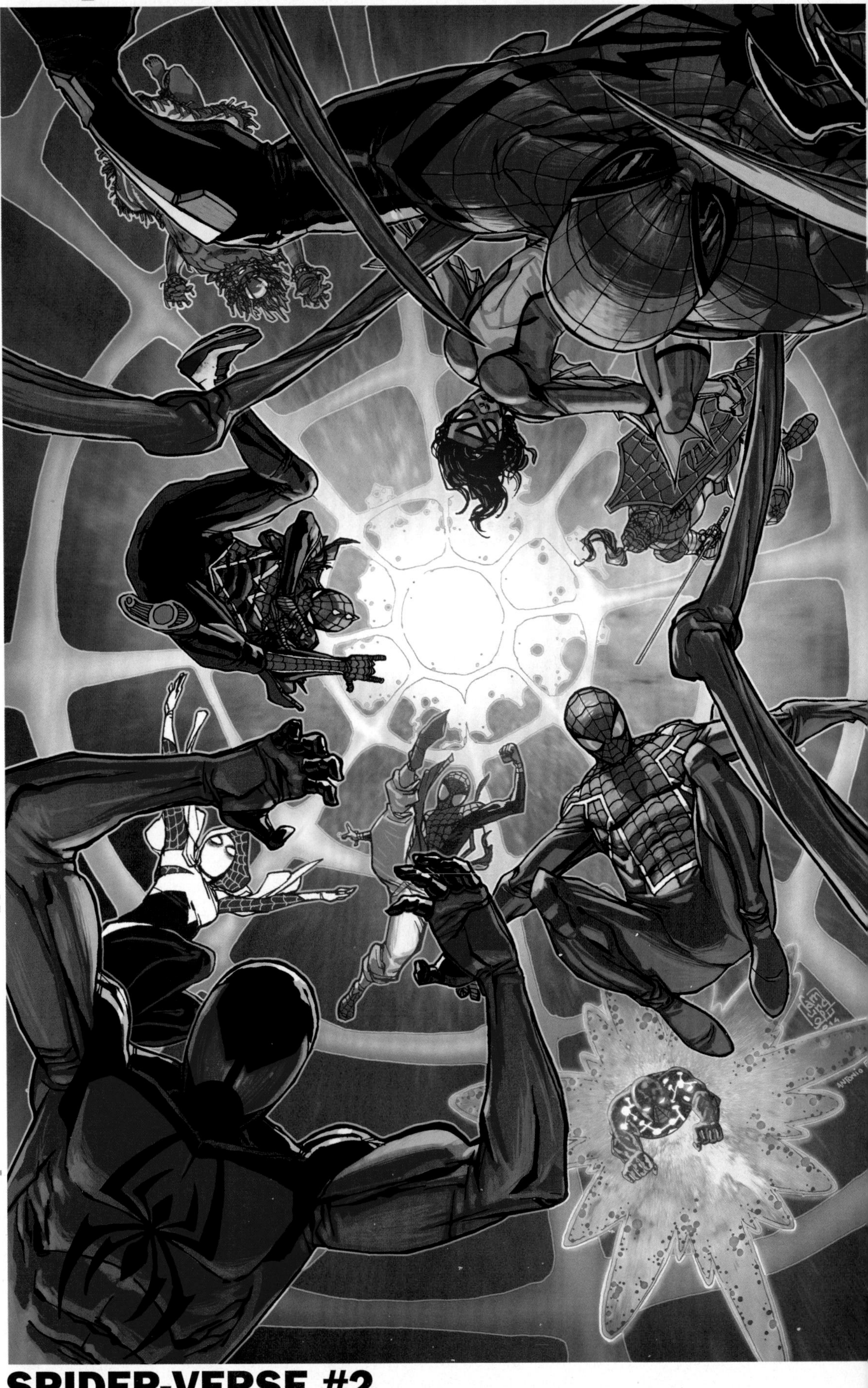

SPIDER-VERSE #2
"IT'S THE LITTLE THINGS"

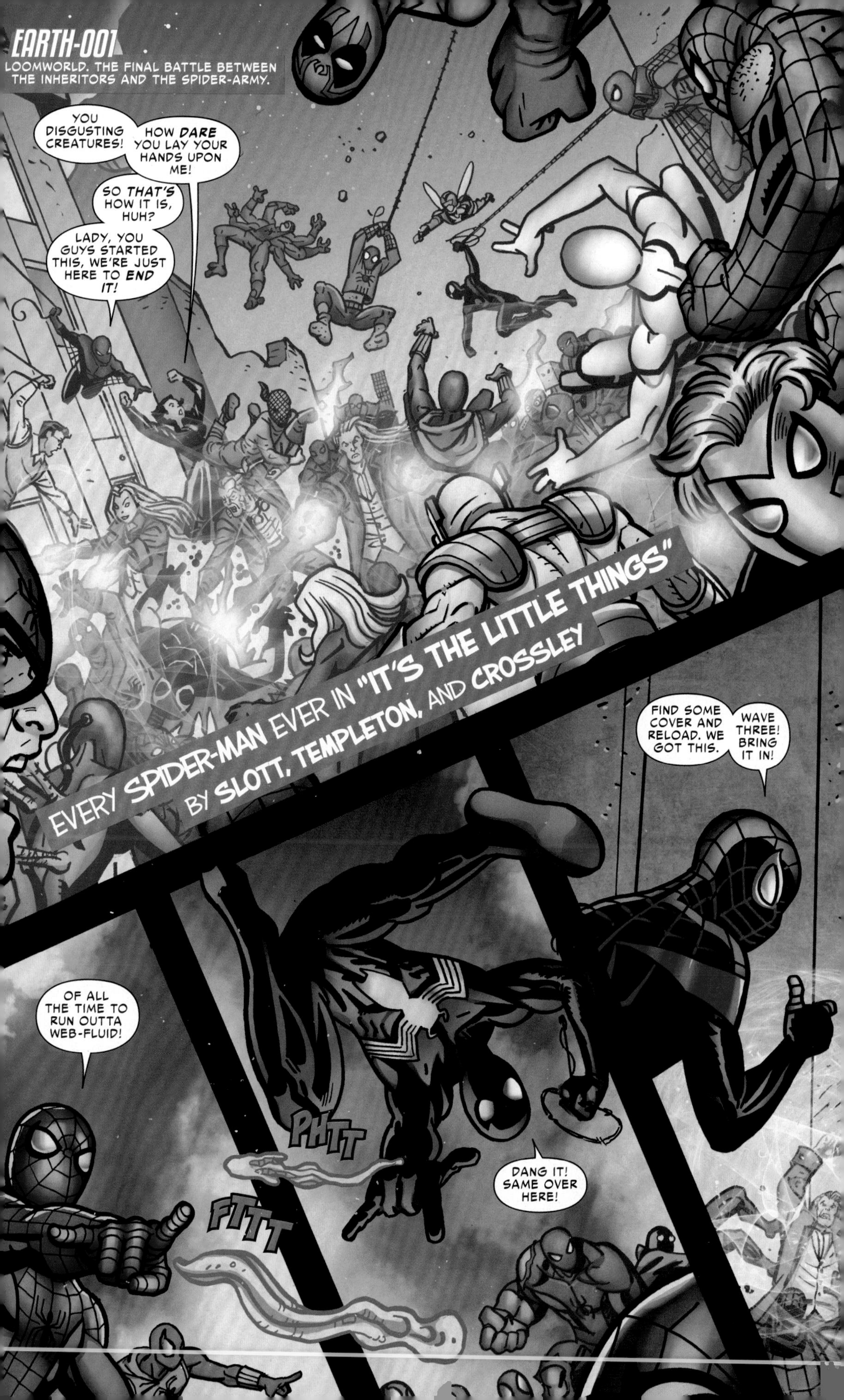
EARTH-001
LOOMWORLD. THE FINAL BATTLE BETWEEN THE INHERITORS AND THE SPIDER-ARMY.
YOU DISGUSTING CREATURES!
HOW DARE YOU LAY YOUR HANDS UPON ME!
SO THAT'S HOW IT IS, HUH?
LADY, YOU GUYS STARTED THIS, WE'RE JUST HERE TO END IT!
EVERY SPIDER-MAN EVER IN "IT'S THE LITTLE THINGS"
BY SLOTT, TEMPLETON, AND CROSSLEY
FIND SOME COVER AND RELOAD. WE GOT THIS.
WAVE THREE! BRING IT IN!
OF ALL THE TIME TO RUN OUTTA WEB-FLUID!
PHTT
FTTT
DANG IT! SAME OVER HERE!

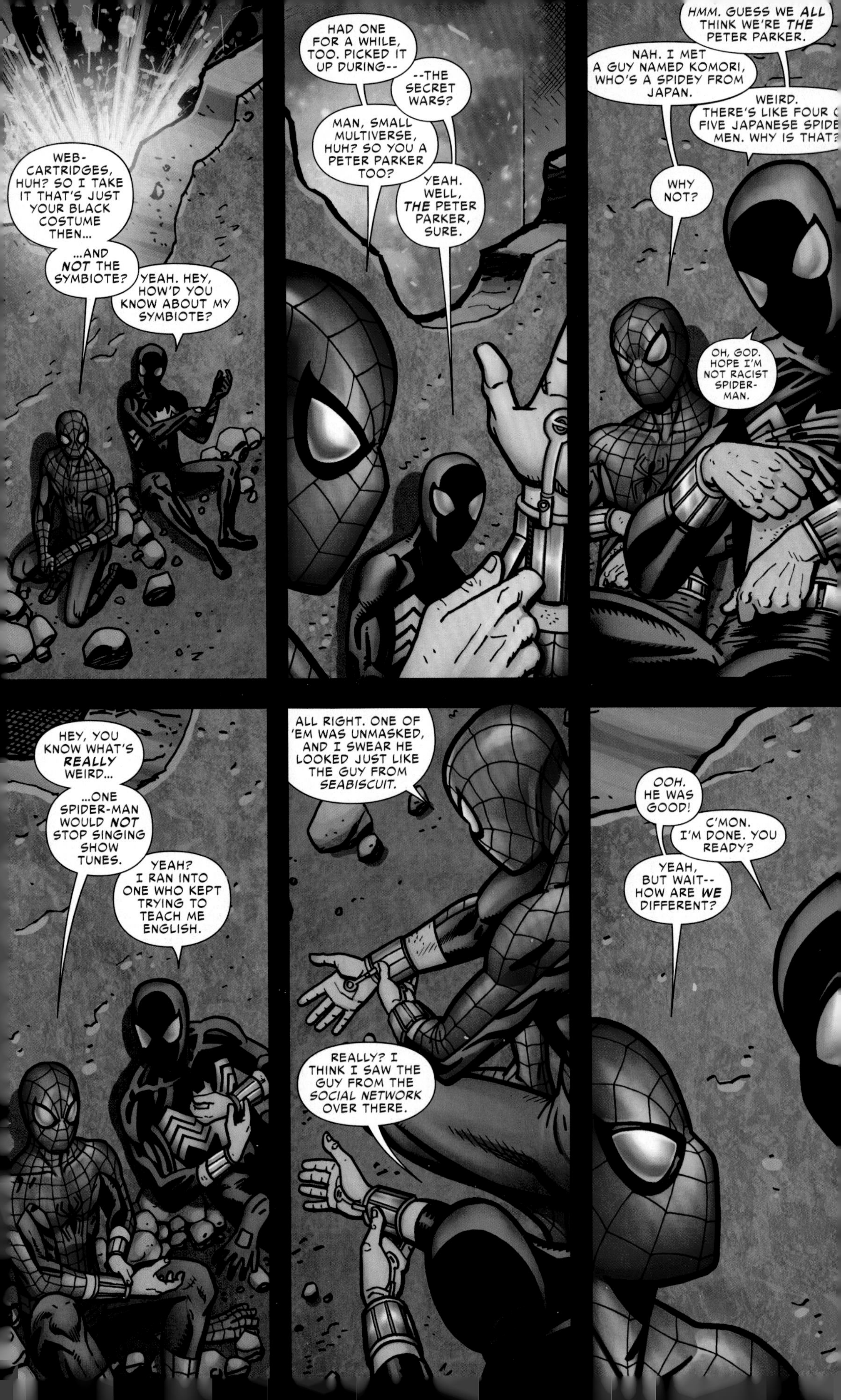
WEB-CARTRIDGES, HUH? SO I TAKE IT THAT'S JUST YOUR BLACK COSTUME THEN...
...AND *NOT* THE SYMBIOTE?
YEAH. HEY, HOW'D YOU KNOW ABOUT MY SYMBIOTE?
HAD ONE FOR A WHILE, TOO. PICKED IT UP DURING--
--THE SECRET WARS?
MAN, SMALL MULTIVERSE, HUH? SO YOU A PETER PARKER TOO?
YEAH. WELL, *THE* PETER PARKER, SURE.
HMM. GUESS WE *ALL* THINK WE'RE *THE* PETER PARKER.
NAH. I MET A GUY NAMED KOMORI, WHO'S A SPIDEY FROM JAPAN.
WEIRD. THERE'S LIKE FOUR
FIVE JAPANESE SPIDE
MEN. WHY IS THAT?
WHY NOT?
OH, GOD. HOPE I'M NOT RACIST SPIDER-MAN.
HEY, YOU KNOW WHAT'S *REALLY* WEIRD...
...ONE SPIDER-MAN WOULD *NOT* STOP SINGING SHOW TUNES.
YEAH? I RAN INTO ONE WHO KEPT TRYING TO TEACH ME ENGLISH.
ALL RIGHT. ONE OF 'EM WAS UNMASKED, AND I SWEAR HE LOOKED JUST LIKE THE GUY FROM *SEABISCUIT.*
REALLY? I THINK I SAW THE GUY FROM THE *SOCIAL NETWORK* OVER THERE.
OOH. HE WAS GOOD!
C'MON. I'M DONE. YOU READY?
YEAH, BUT WAIT-- HOW ARE *WE* DIFFERENT?

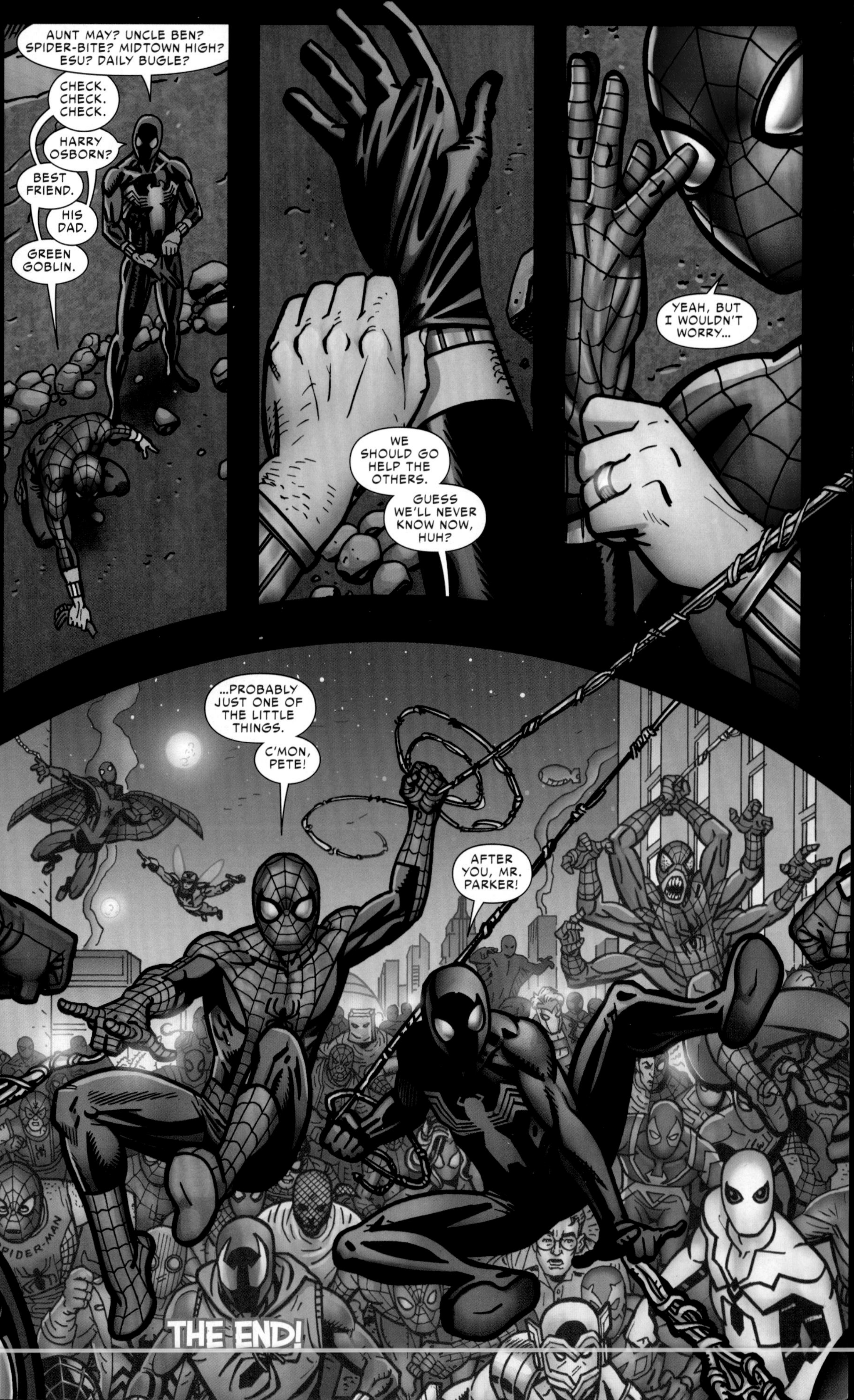
AUNT MAY? UNCLE BEN? SPIDER-BITE? MIDTOWN HIGH? ESU? DAILY BUGLE?
CHECK. CHECK. CHECK.
HARRY OSBORN?
BEST FRIEND.
HIS DAD.
GREEN GOBLIN.
WE SHOULD GO HELP THE OTHERS.
GUESS WE'LL NEVER KNOW NOW, HUH?
YEAH, BUT I WOULDN'T WORRY...
...PROBABLY JUST ONE OF THE LITTLE THINGS.
C'MON, PETE!
AFTER YOU, MR. PARKER!
THE END!

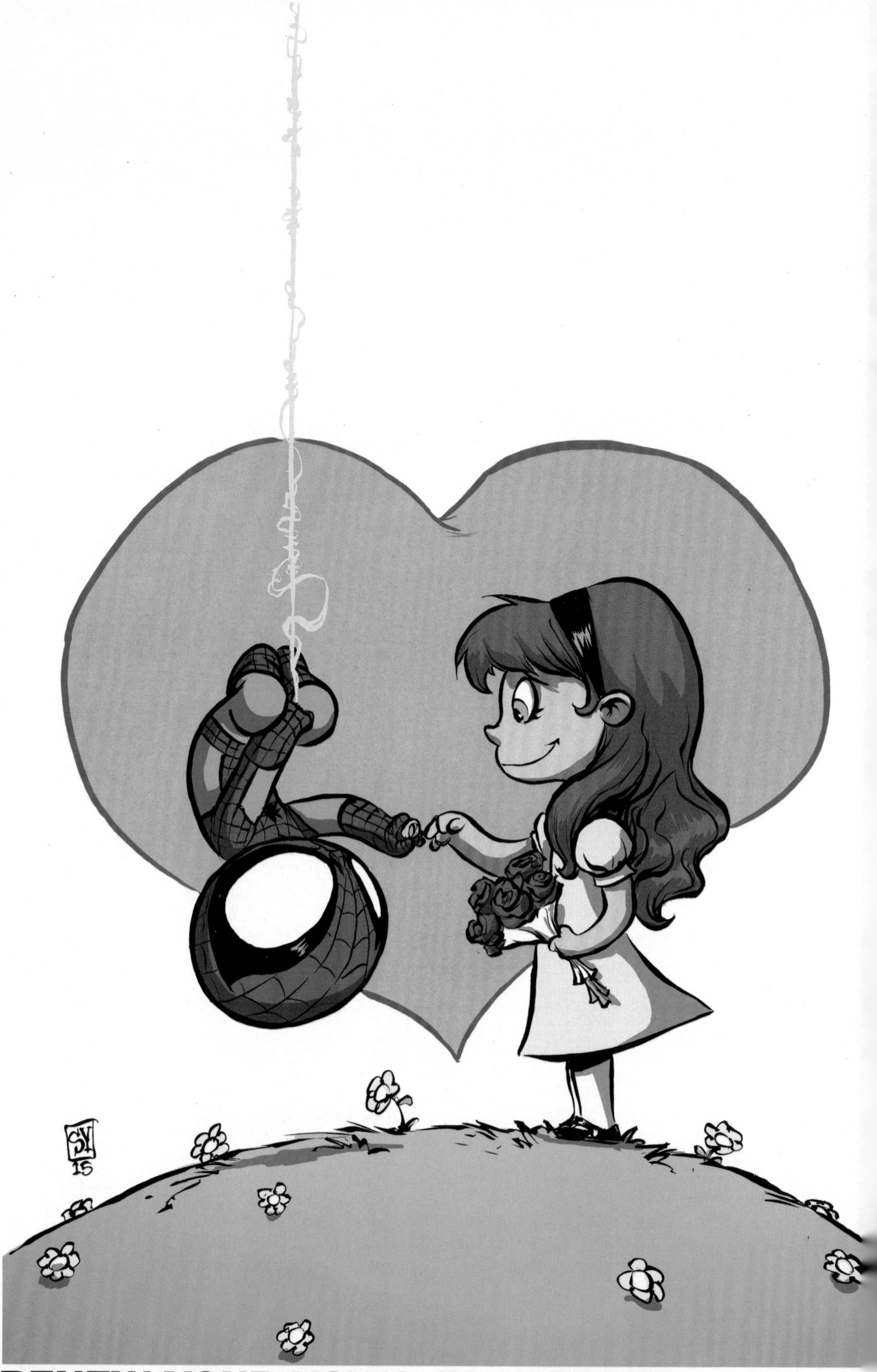

RENEW YOUR VOWS #1 VARIANT
BY SKOTTIE YOUNG

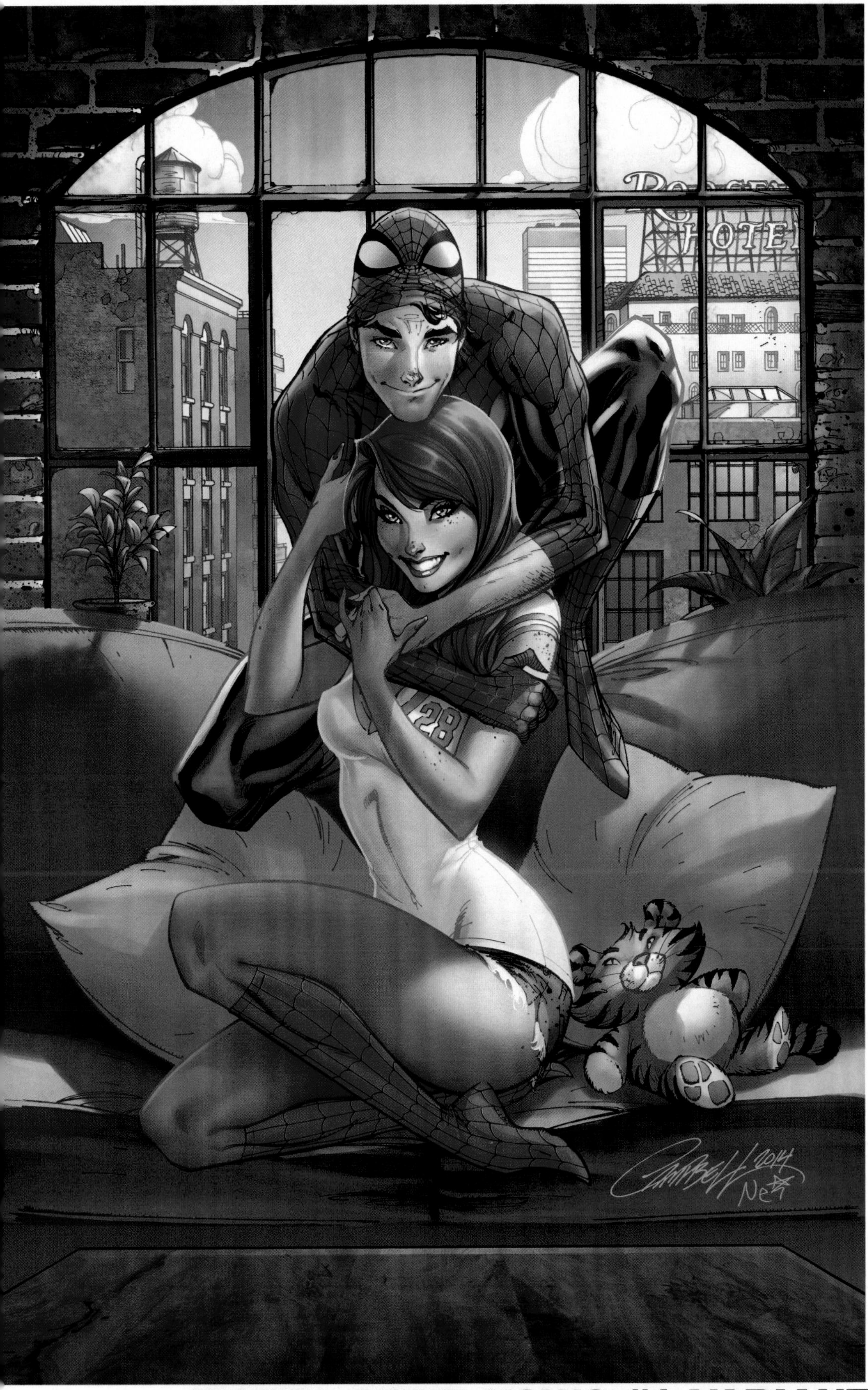

HOTEL
28

RENEW YOUR VOWS #1 VARIANT

BY J. SCOTT CAMPBELL & NEI RUFFINO

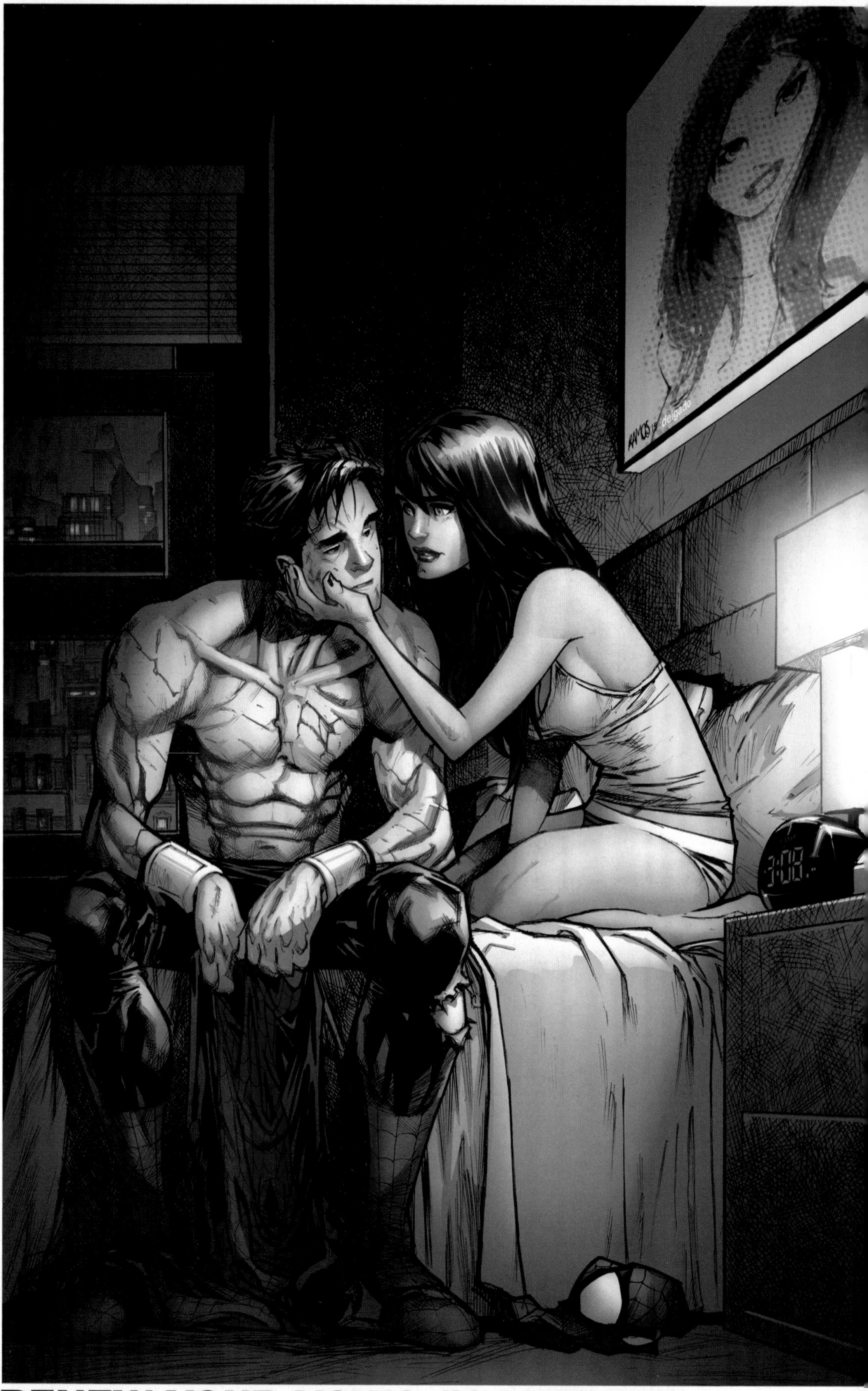

RENEW YOUR VOWS #1 VARIANT

BY HUMBERTO RAMOS & EDGAR DELGADO

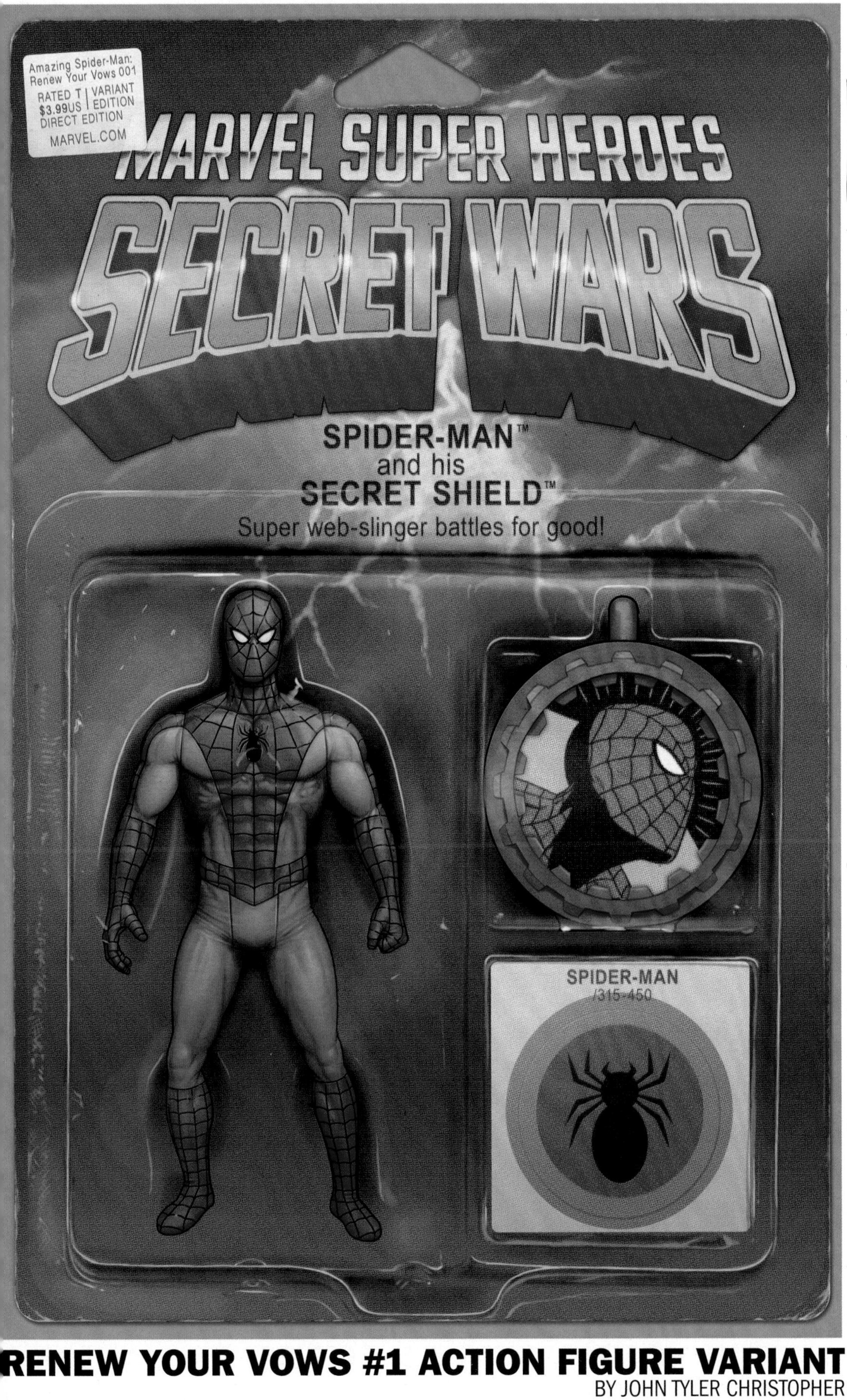
Amazing Spider-Man: Renew Your Vows 001
RATED T
VARIANT EDITION
$3.99US
DIRECT EDITION
MARVEL.COM
MARVEL SUPER HEROES
SECRET WARS
SPIDER-MAN™
and his
SECRET SHIELD™
Super web-slinger battles for good!
SPIDER-MAN
/315-450

RENEW YOUR VOWS #1 ACTION FIGURE VARIANT

BY JOHN TYLER CHRISTOPHER

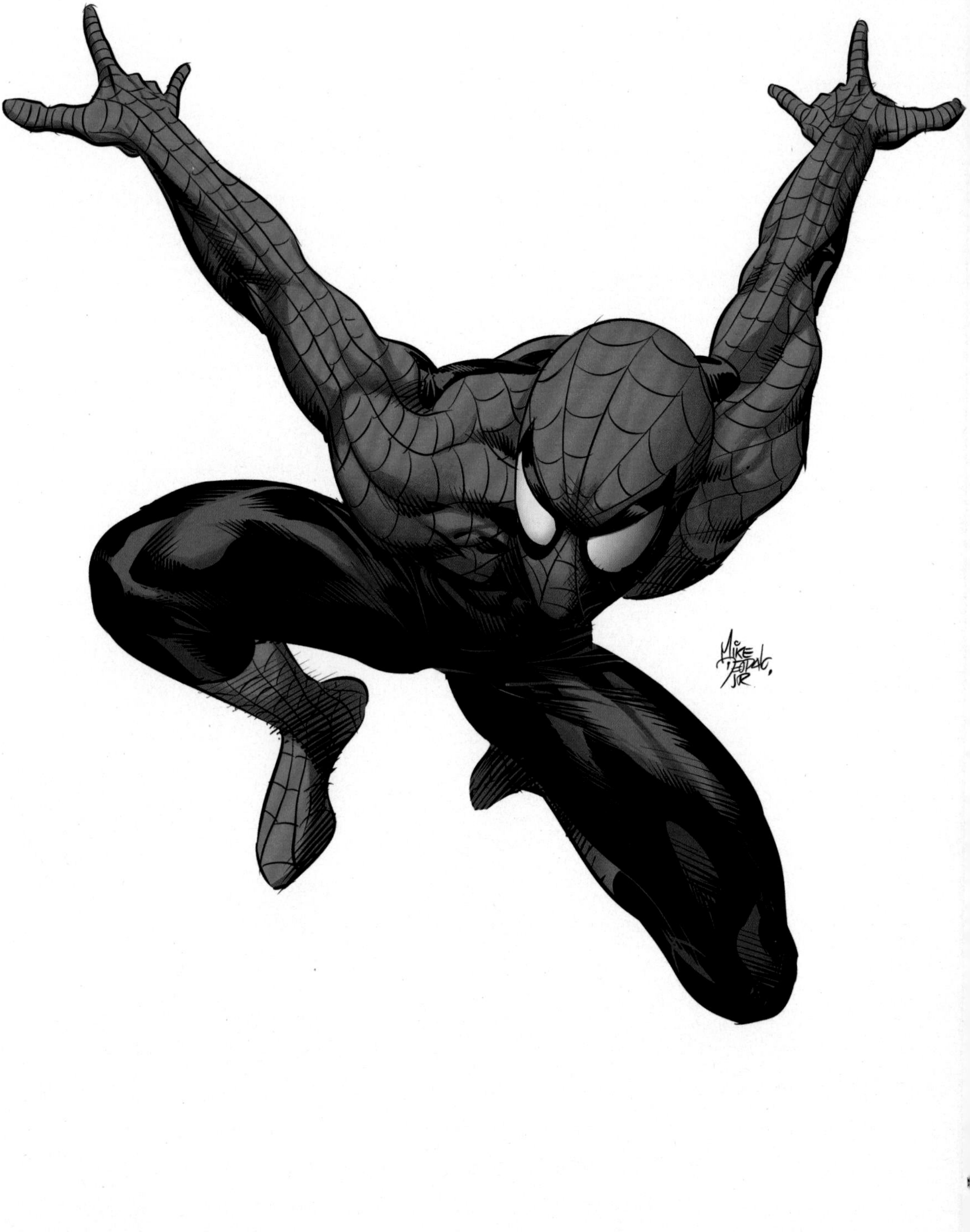

RENEW YOUR VOWS #1 ANT-SIZED VARIANT
BY MIKE DEODATO & FRANK MARTIN

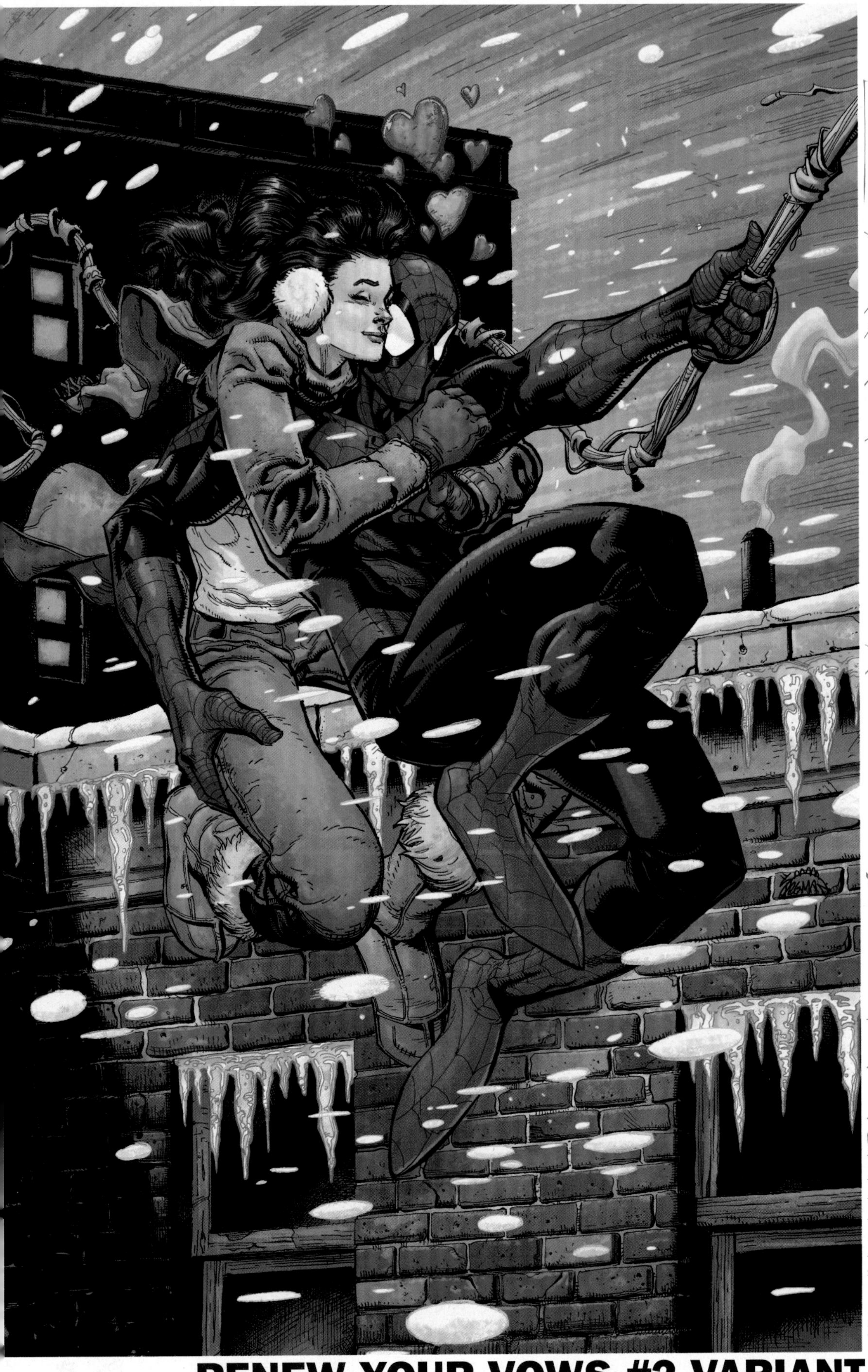

RENEW YOUR VOWS #2 VARIANT
BY RYAN STEGMAN & DAVE STEWART

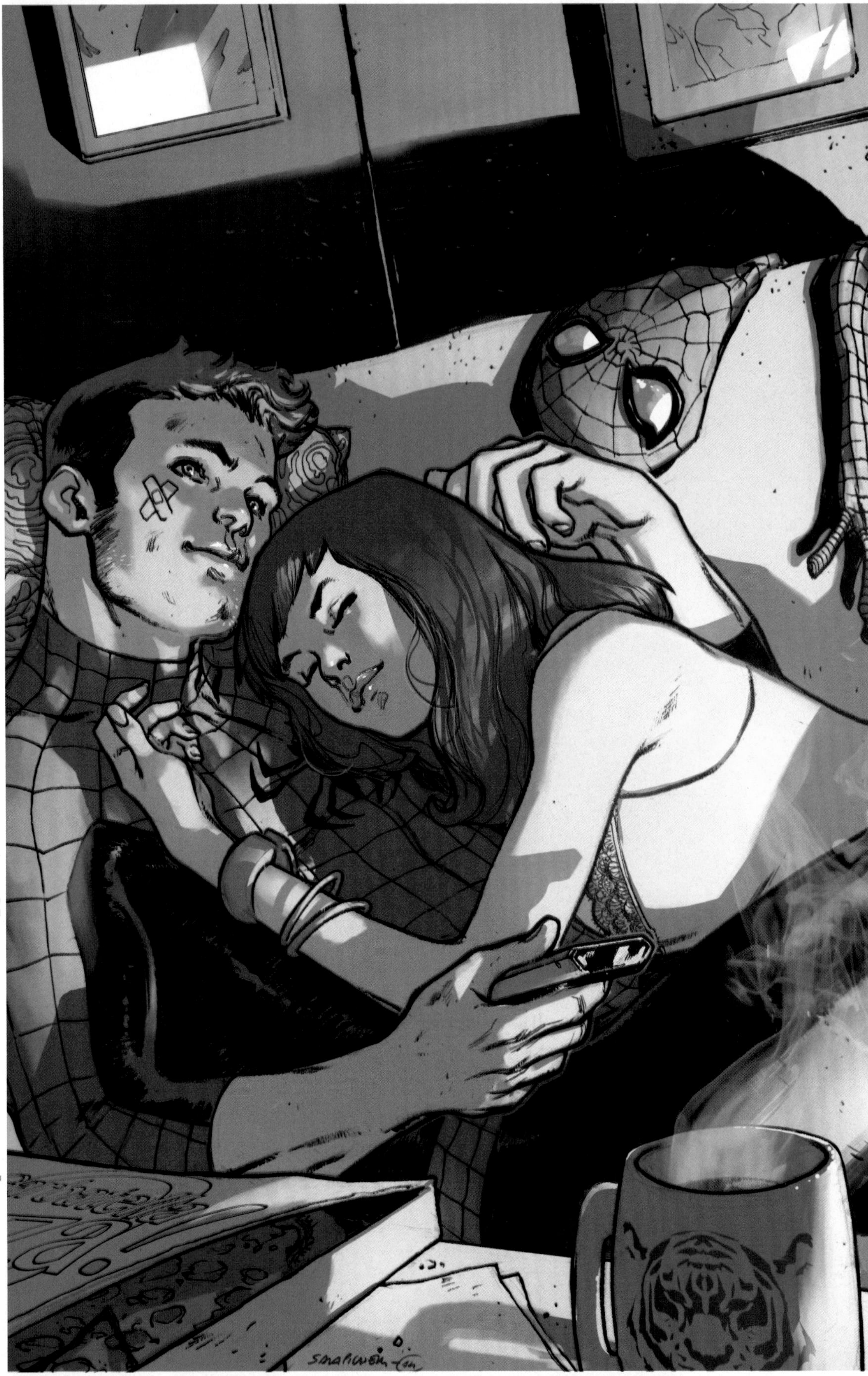

RENEW YOUR VOWS #3 VARIANT
BY SARA PICHELLI

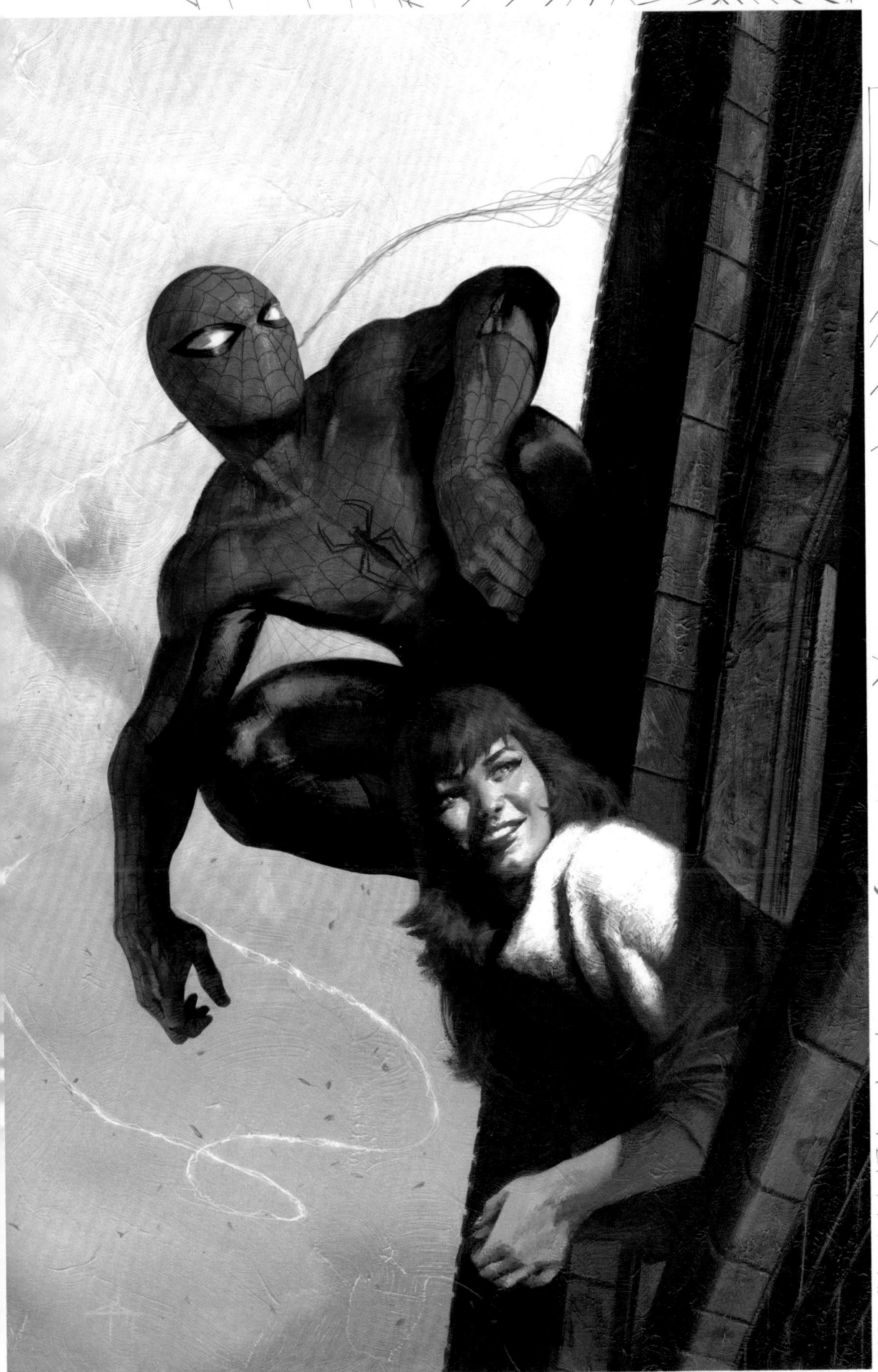

RENEW YOUR VOWS #4 VARIANT
BY GABRIELE DELL'OTTO

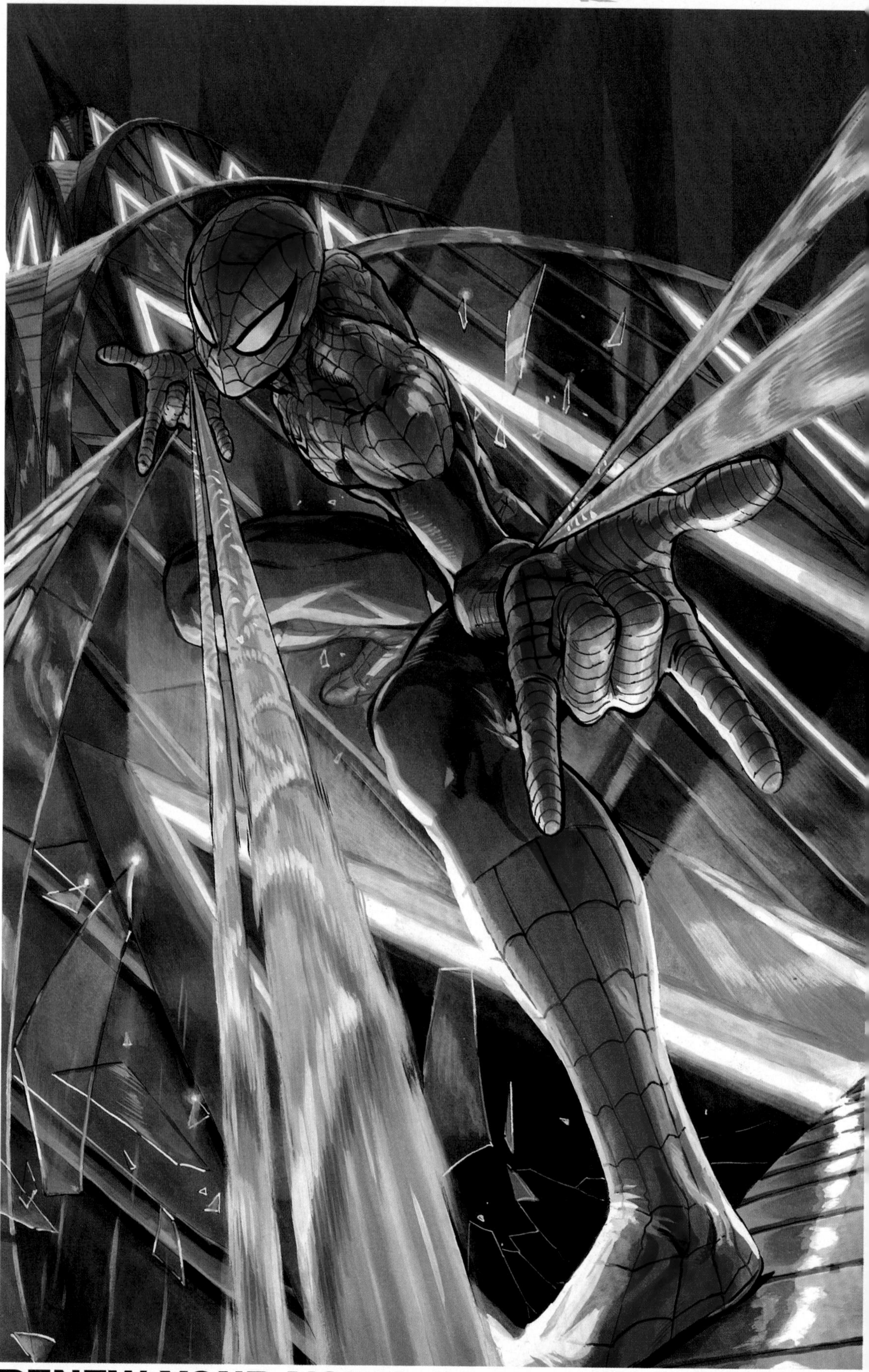

RENEW YOUR VOWS #4 MANGA VARIANT
BY YUSUKE MURATA

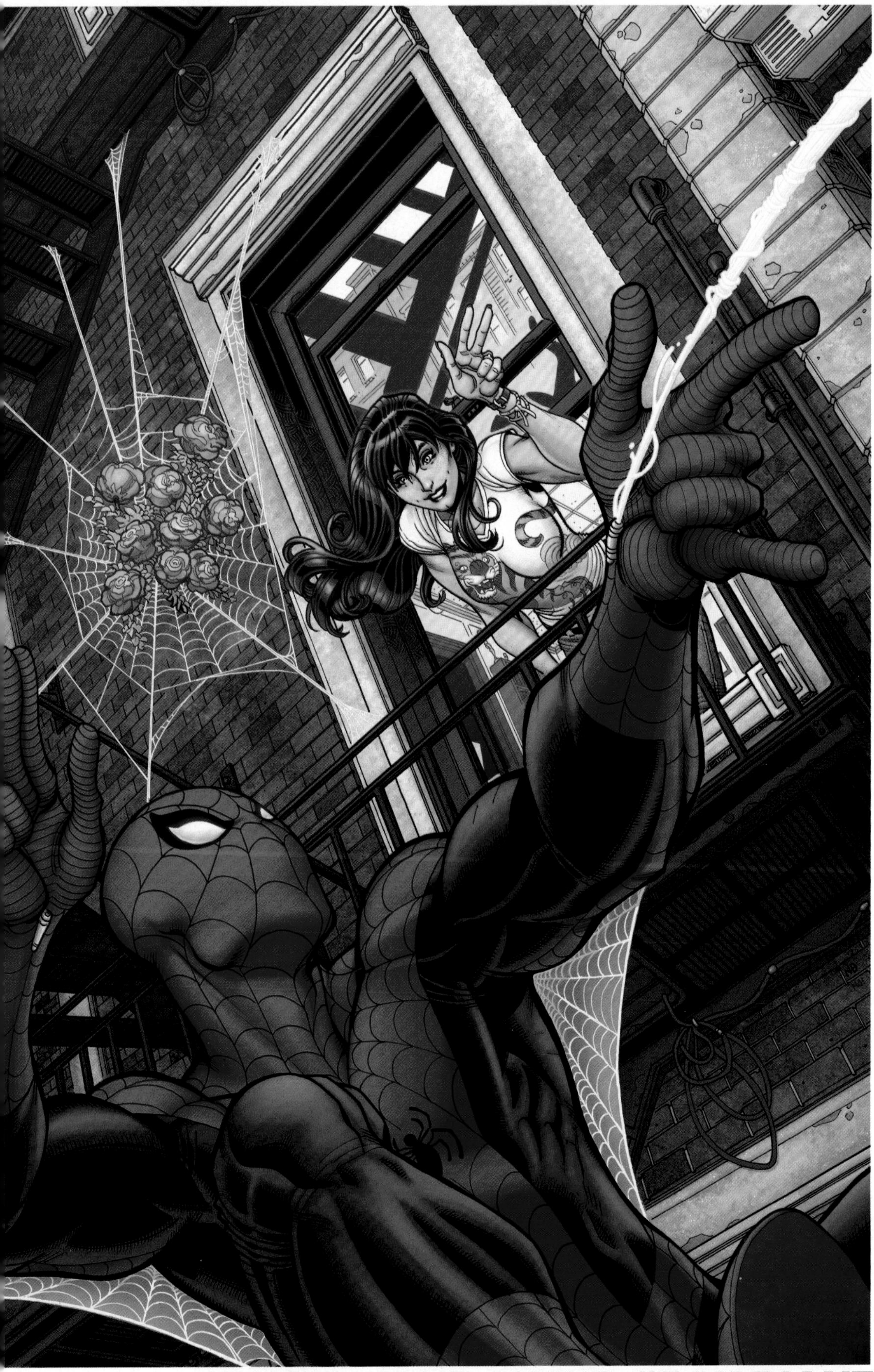

RENEW YOUR VOWS #5 VARIANT
BY NICK BRADSHAW & MORRY HOLLOWELL

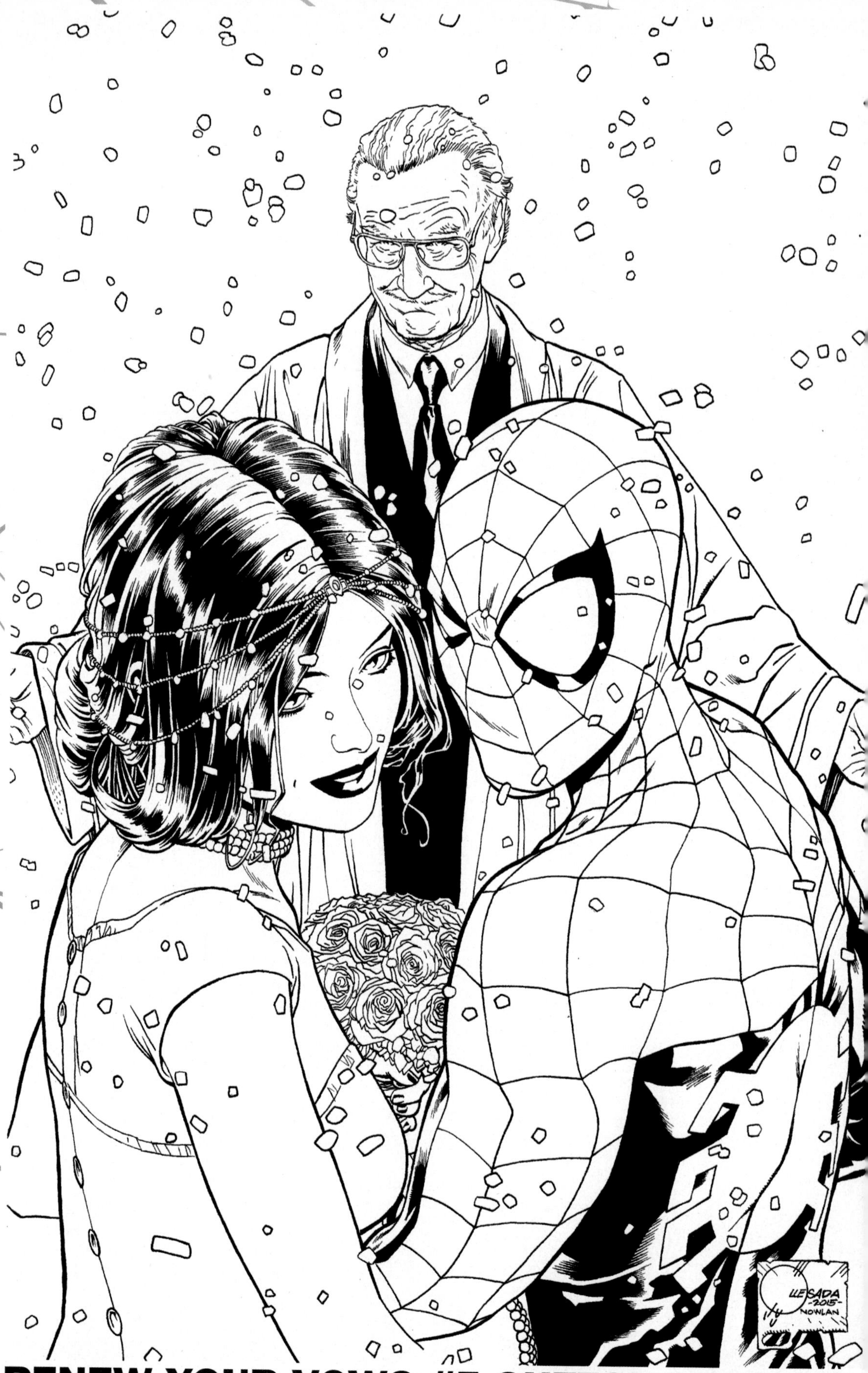
-2015-
NOWLAN

RENEW YOUR VOWS #5 SKETCH VARIANT

BY JOE QUESADA & KEVIN NOWLAN

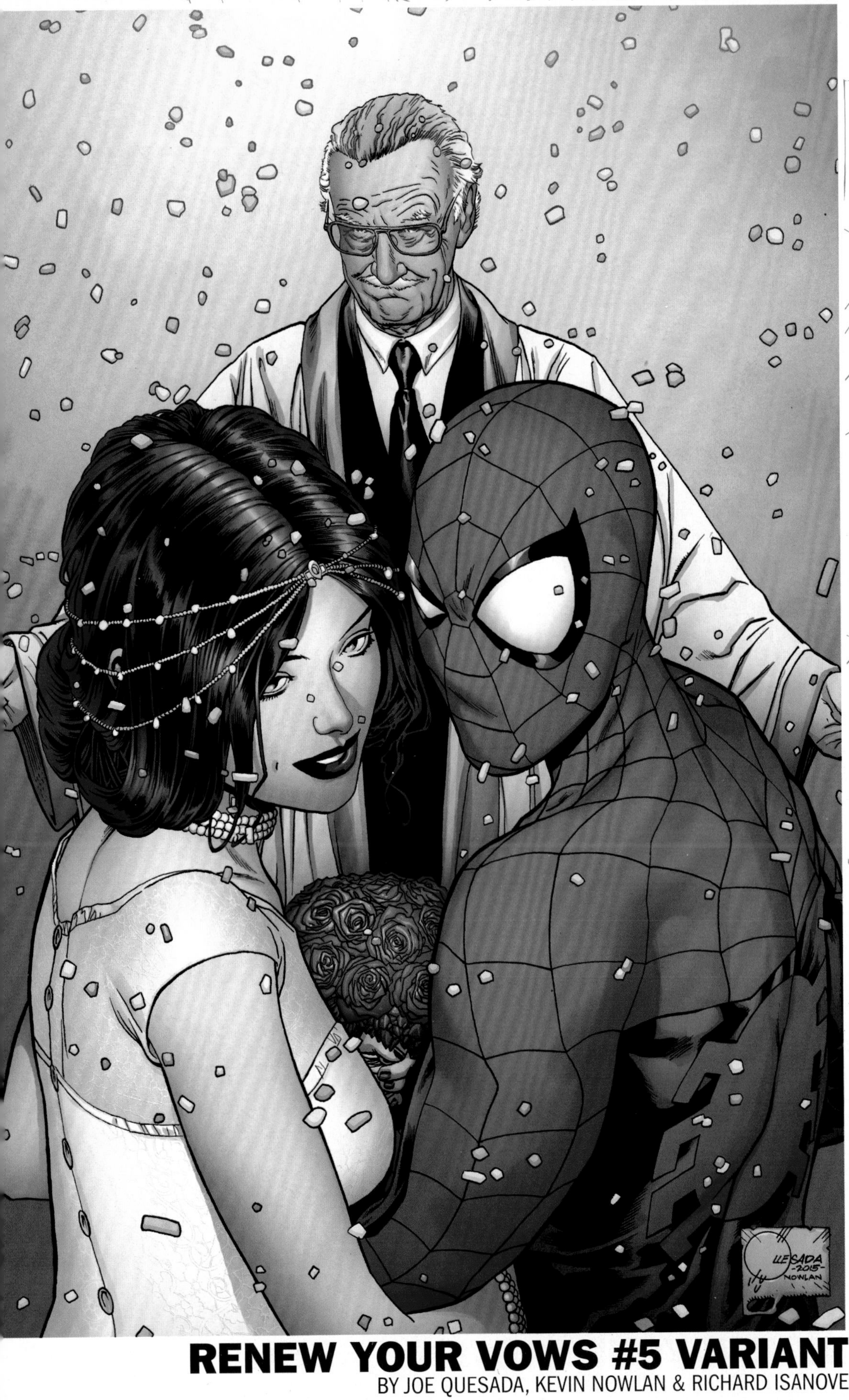
-2015-
NOWLAN

RENEW YOUR VOWS #5 VARIANT

BY JOE QUESADA, KEVIN NOWLAN & RICHARD ISANOVE

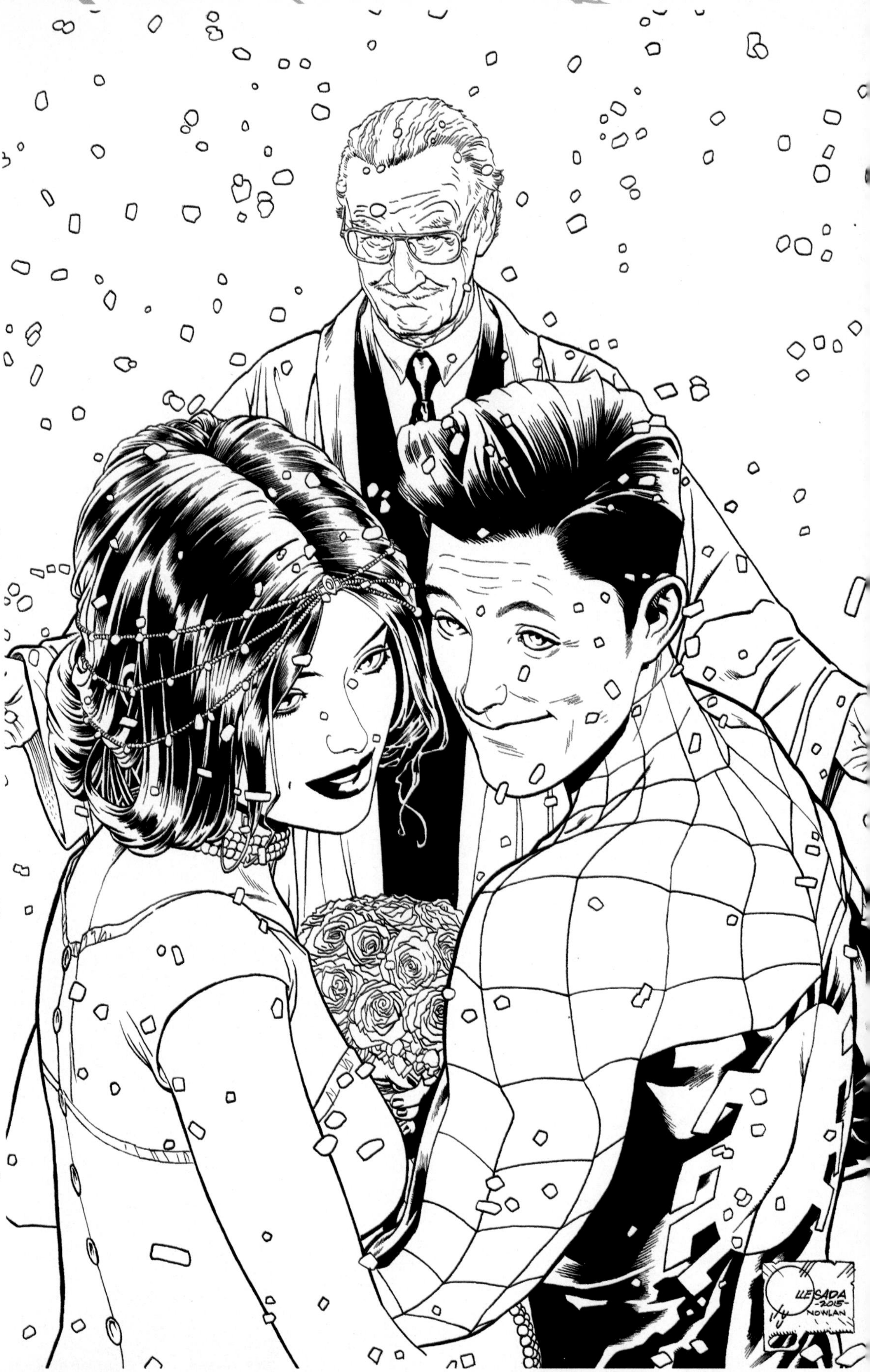
QUESADA
-2015-
NOWLAN

RENEW YOUR VOWS #5 SKETCH VARIANT

BY JOE QUESADA & KEVIN NOWLAN

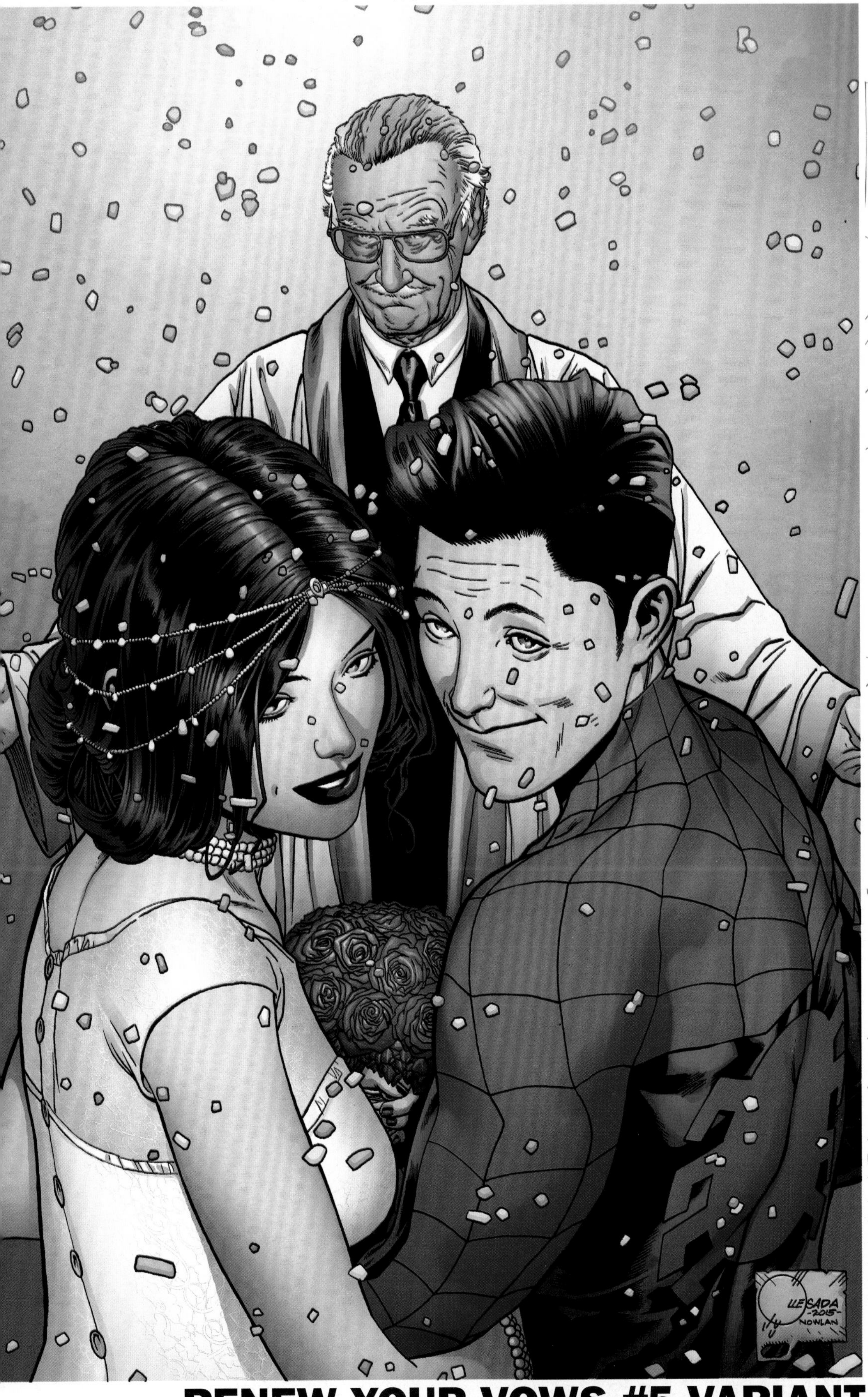
QUESADA
-2015-
NOWLAN

RENEW YOUR VOWS #5 VARIANT

BY JOE QUESADA, KEVIN NOWLAN & RICHARD ISANOVE

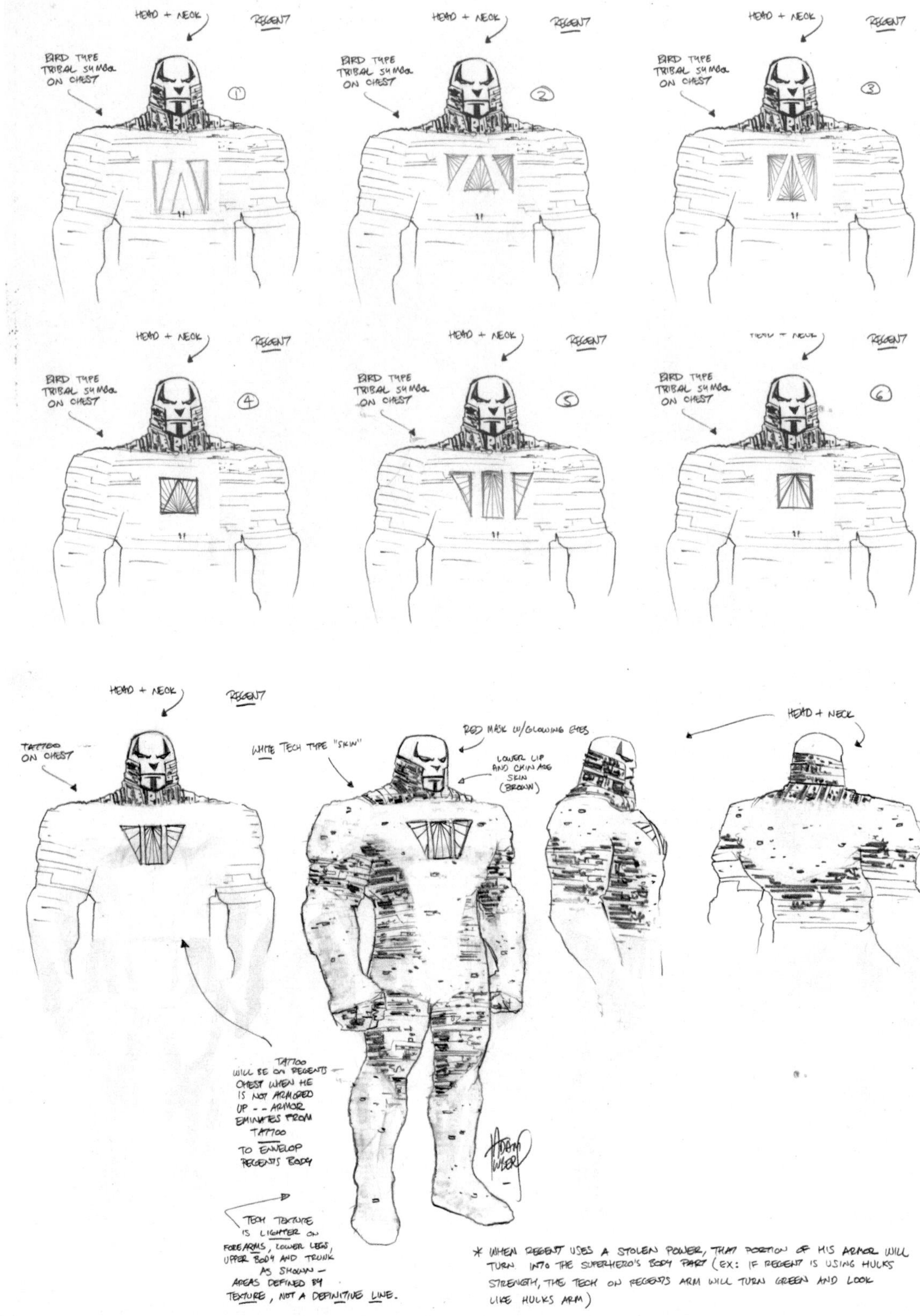
HEAD + NECK
REGENT
BIRD TYPE TRIBAL SYMBOL ON CHEST
1
2
3
4
5
6
TATTOO ON CHEST
WHITE TECH TYPE "SKIN"
RED MASK W/GLOWING EYES
LOWER LIP AND CHIN ARE SKIN (BROWN)
TATTOO WILL BE ON REGENTS CHEST WHEN HE IS NOT ARMORED UP -- ARMOR EMINATES FROM TATTOO TO ENVELOP REGENTS BODY
TECH TEXTURE IS LIGHTER ON FOREARMS, LOWER LEGS, UPPER BODY AND TRUNK AS SHOWN — AREAS DEFINED BY TEXTURE, NOT A DEFINITIVE LINE.
* WHEN REGENT USES A STOLEN POWER, THAT PORTION OF HIS ARMOR WILL TURN INTO THE SUPERHERO'S BODY PART (EX: IF REGENT IS USING HULKS STRENGTH, THE TECH ON REGENTS ARM WILL TURN GREEN AND LOOK LIKE HULKS ARM)

REGENT DESIGNS

BY ADAM KUBERT

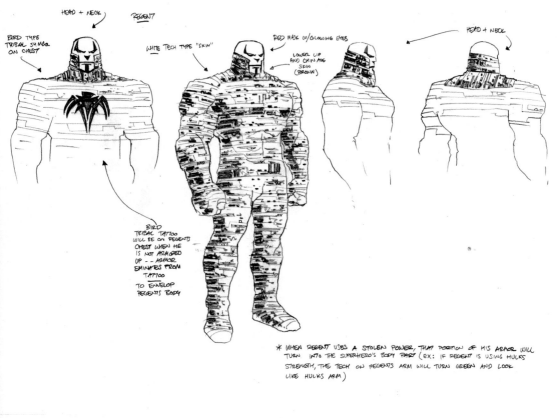

BIRD TYPE TRIBAL SYMBOL ON CHEST

HEAD + NECK

REGENT

WHITE TECH TYPE "SKIN"

RED MASK W/GLOWING EYES

LOWER LIP AND CHIN ARE SKIN (BROWN)

HEAD + NECK

BIRD TRIBAL TATTOO WILL BE ON REGENTS CHEST WHEN HE IS NOT ARMORED UP — ARMOR EMINATES FROM TATTOO TO ENVELOP REGENTS BODY

* WHEN REGENT USES A STOLEN POWER, THAT PORTION OF HIS ARMOR WILL TURN INTO THE SUPERHERO'S BODY PART (EX: IF REGENT IS USING HULKS STRENGTH, THE TECH ON REGENTS ARM WILL TURN GREEN AND LOOK LIKE HULKS ARM)

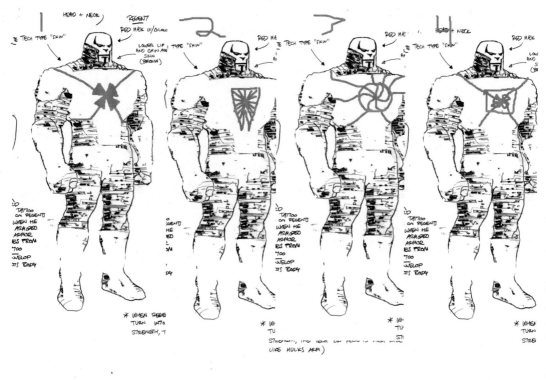

HEAD + NECK

REGENT
RED MASK W/GLOW

TE TECH TYPE "SKIN"

LOWER LIP AND CHIN ARE SKIN (BROWN)

TYPE "SKIN"

RED MA

TE TECH TYPE "SKIN"

RED MA

TE TECH TYPE "SKIN"

HEAD + NECK

RED MASK

LOW AND S (B

TATTOO ON REGENTS WHEN HE ARMORED ARMOR ES FROM 700 NVELOP TS BODY

* WHEN REGE TURN INTO STRENGTH, T

* WH TU STRENGTH, THE TECH ON REGENT WILL LIKE HULKS ARM)

* WH TU STI

* WHEN TURN STRE

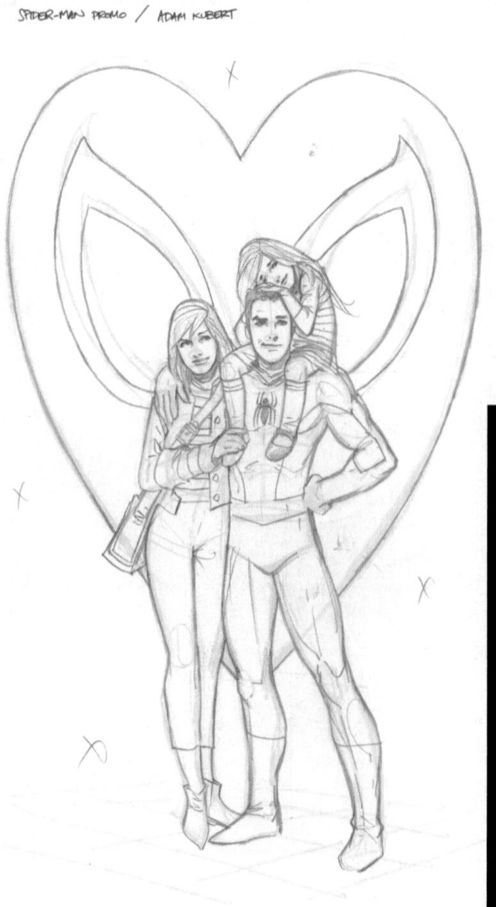
SPIDER-MAN PROMO / ADAM KUBERT

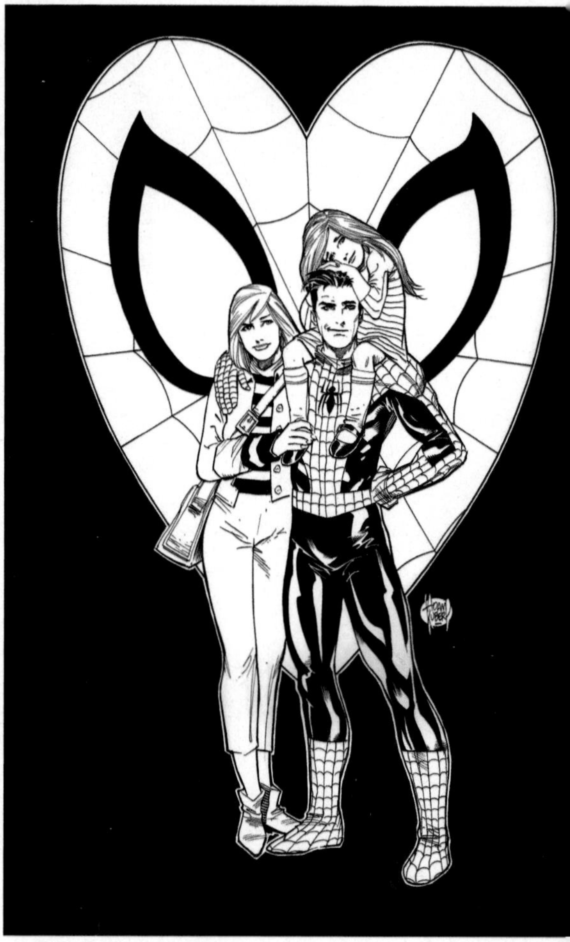

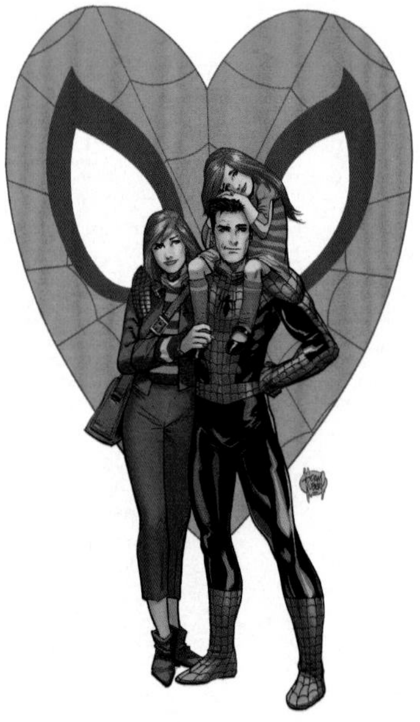

#1 COVER PROCESS
BY ADAM KUBERT & JUSTIN PONSOR

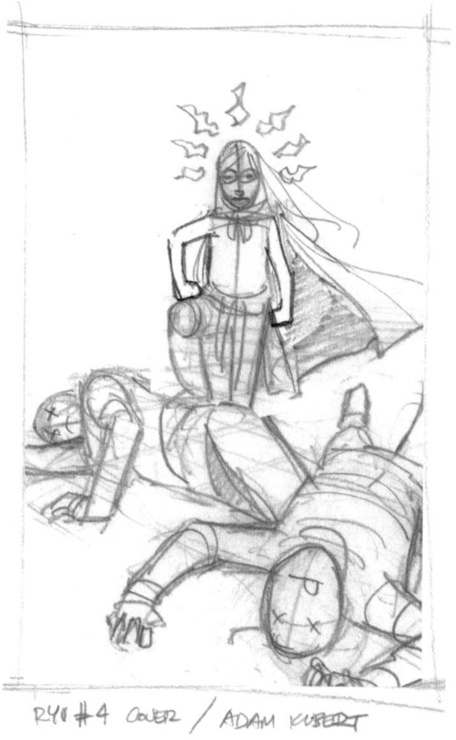
RYII #4 COVER / ADAM KUBERT

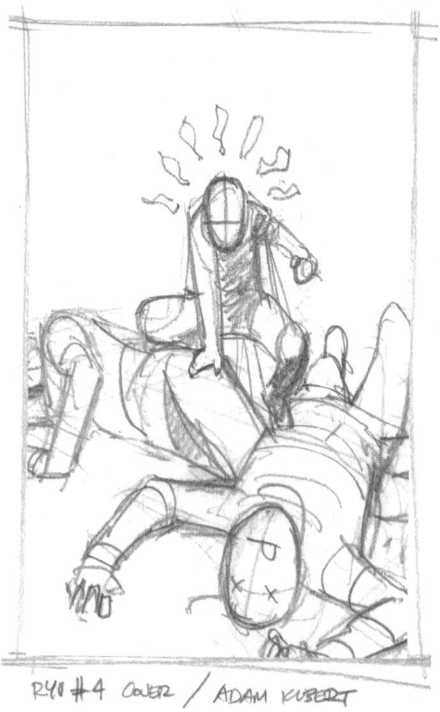
RYII #4 COVER / ADAM KUBERT

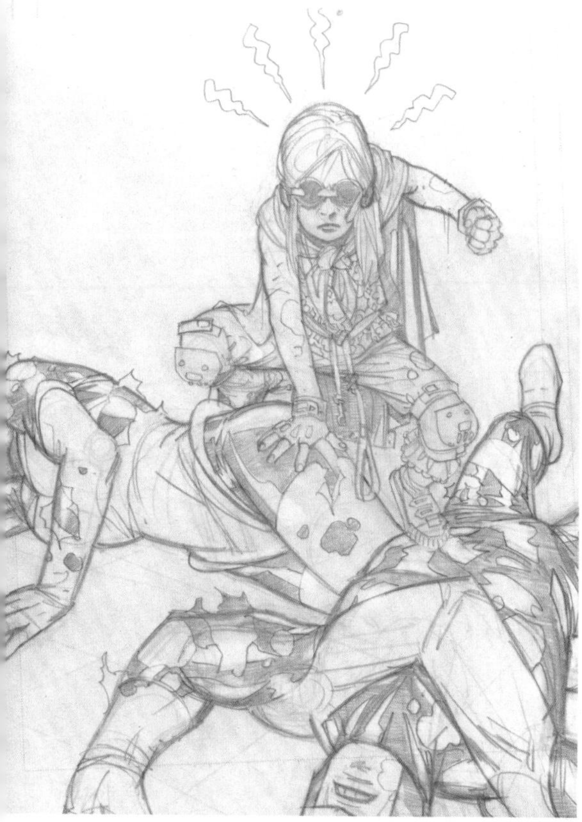

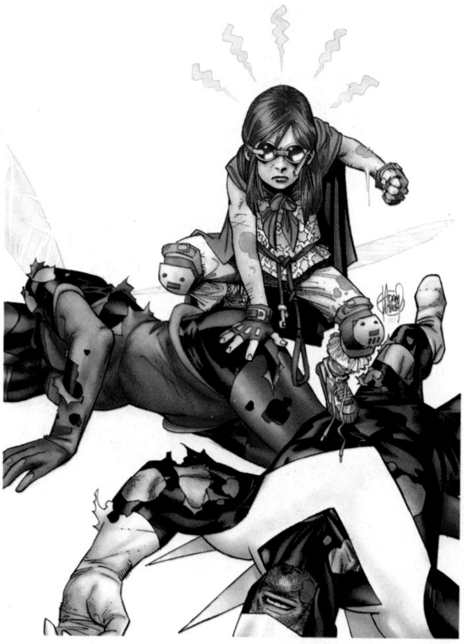

#4 COVER PROCESS
BY ADAM KUBERT & MORRY HOLLOWELL

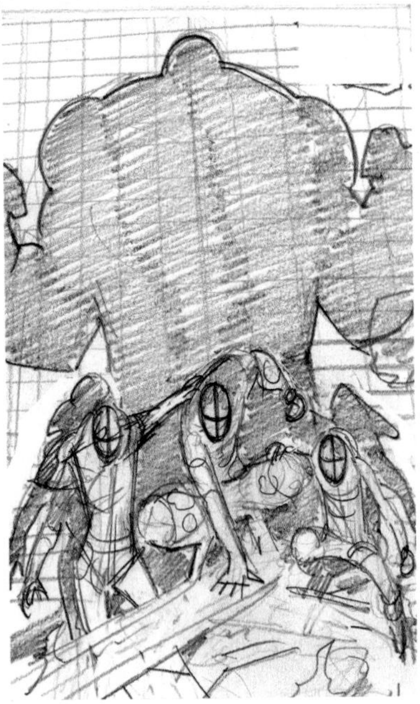

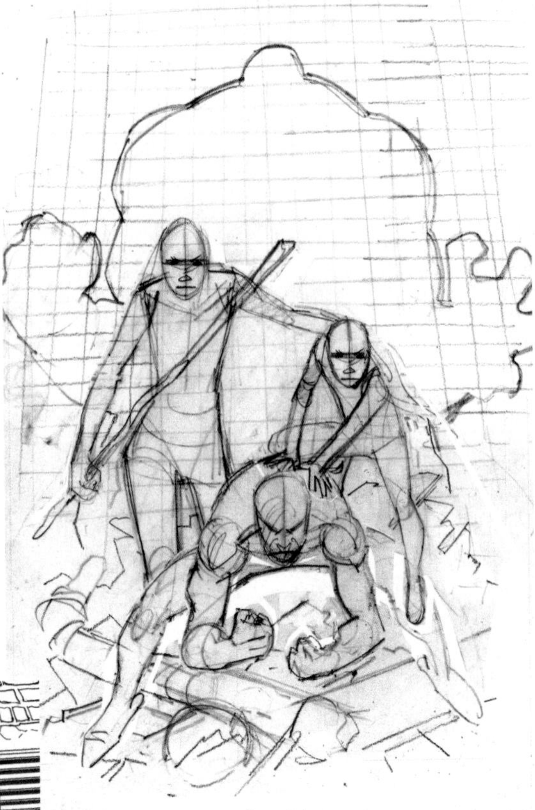

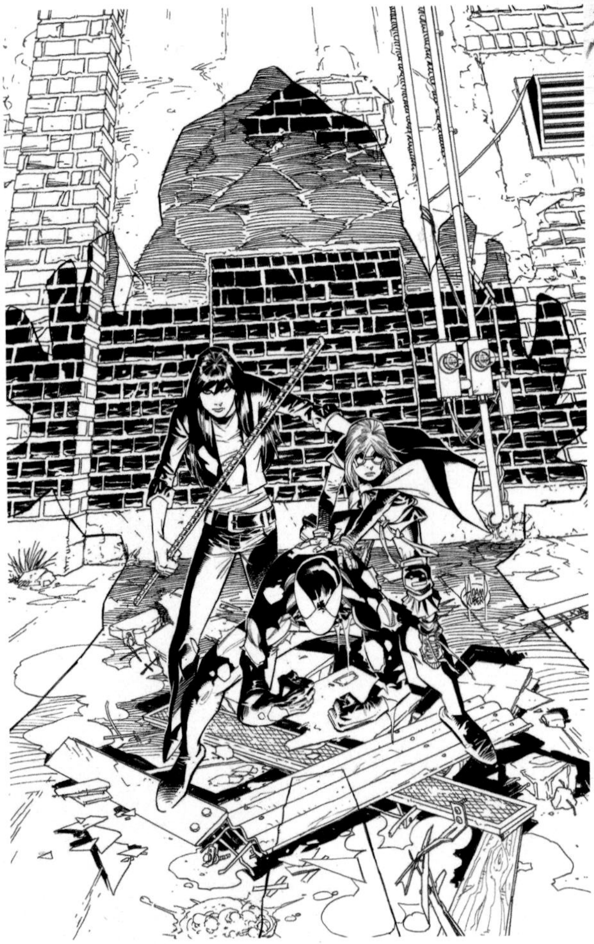

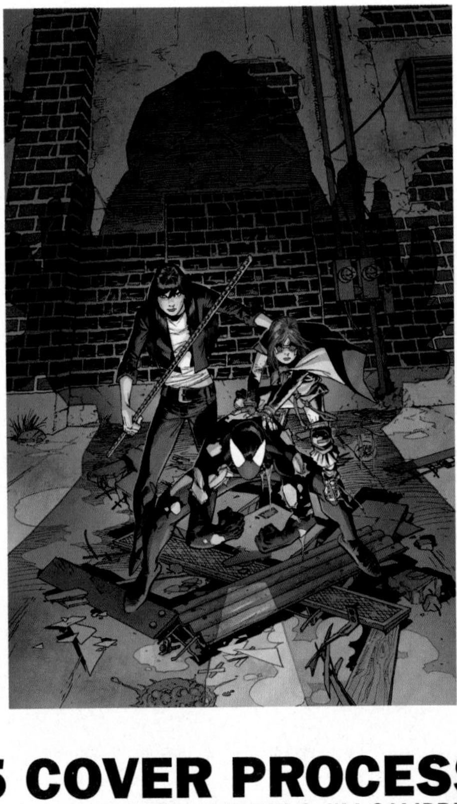

#5 COVER PROCESS

BY ADAM KUBERT & JIM CAMPBEL